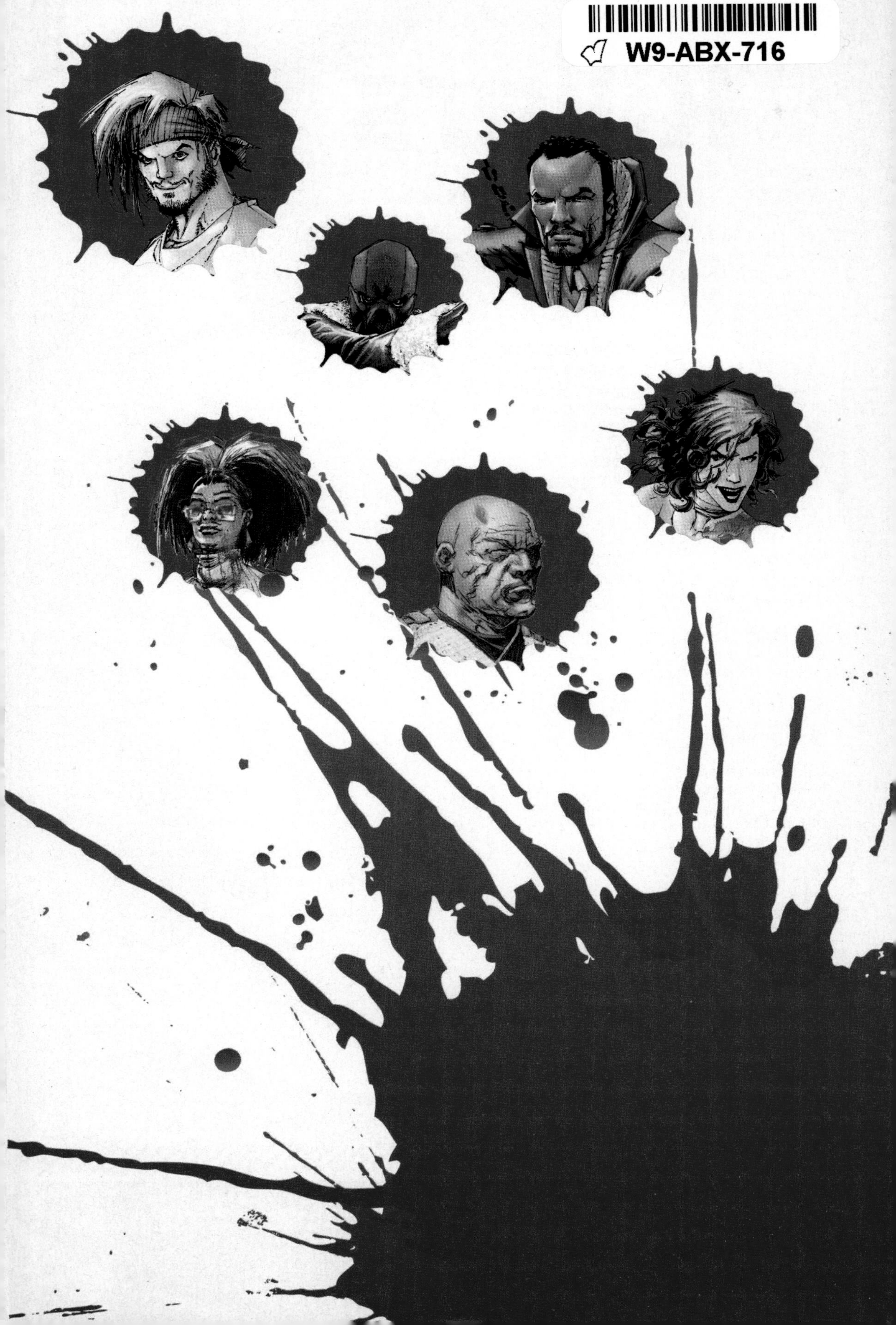

Ki-6 killers™

WRITER
B. CLAY MOORE

ARTIST
FERNANDO DAGNINO

COLOR ARTIST
JOSÉ VILLARRUBIA

LETTERER
JEFF POWELL

COVERS BY
JONBOY MEYERS

ASSISTANT EDITOR
DREW BAUMGARTNER

EDITORS
KARL BOLLERS
DAVID MENCHEL

GALLERY
ULISES ARREOLA
YANNICK CORBOZ
FERNANDO DAGNINO
ANDY FISH
VERONICA FISH
SANFORD GREENE
KEN LASHLEY
JASON MASTERS
KENNETH ROCAFORT
LARRY STROMAN
ROB STULL

COLLECTION BACK COVER ART
DAVID NAKAYAMA

COLLECTION COVER ART
CULLY HAMNER

COLLECTION FRONT ART
JONBOY MEYERS
TOMÁS GIORELLO
WHILCE PORTACIO

COLLECTION EDITOR
IVAN COHEN

COLLECTION DESIGNER
STEVE BLACKWELL

DAN MINTZ Chairman FRED PIERCE Publisher WALTER BLACK VP Operations MATTHEW KLEIN VP Sales & Marketing ROBERT MEYERS Senior Editorial Director
TRAVIS ESCARFULLERY Director of Design & Production PETER STERN Director of International Publishing & Merchandising LYSA HAWKINS, HEATHER ANTOS & GREG TUMBARELLO Editors
DAVID MENCHEL Associate Editor DREW BAUMGARTNER Assistant Editor JEFF WALKER Production & Design Manager GREGG KATZMAN Marketing Manager EMILY HECHT Digital Marketing Manager
JOHN PETRIE Senior Sales Manager KAT O'NEILL Sales & Live Events Manager CONNOR HILL Sales Operations Coordinator DANIELLE WARD Sales Manager

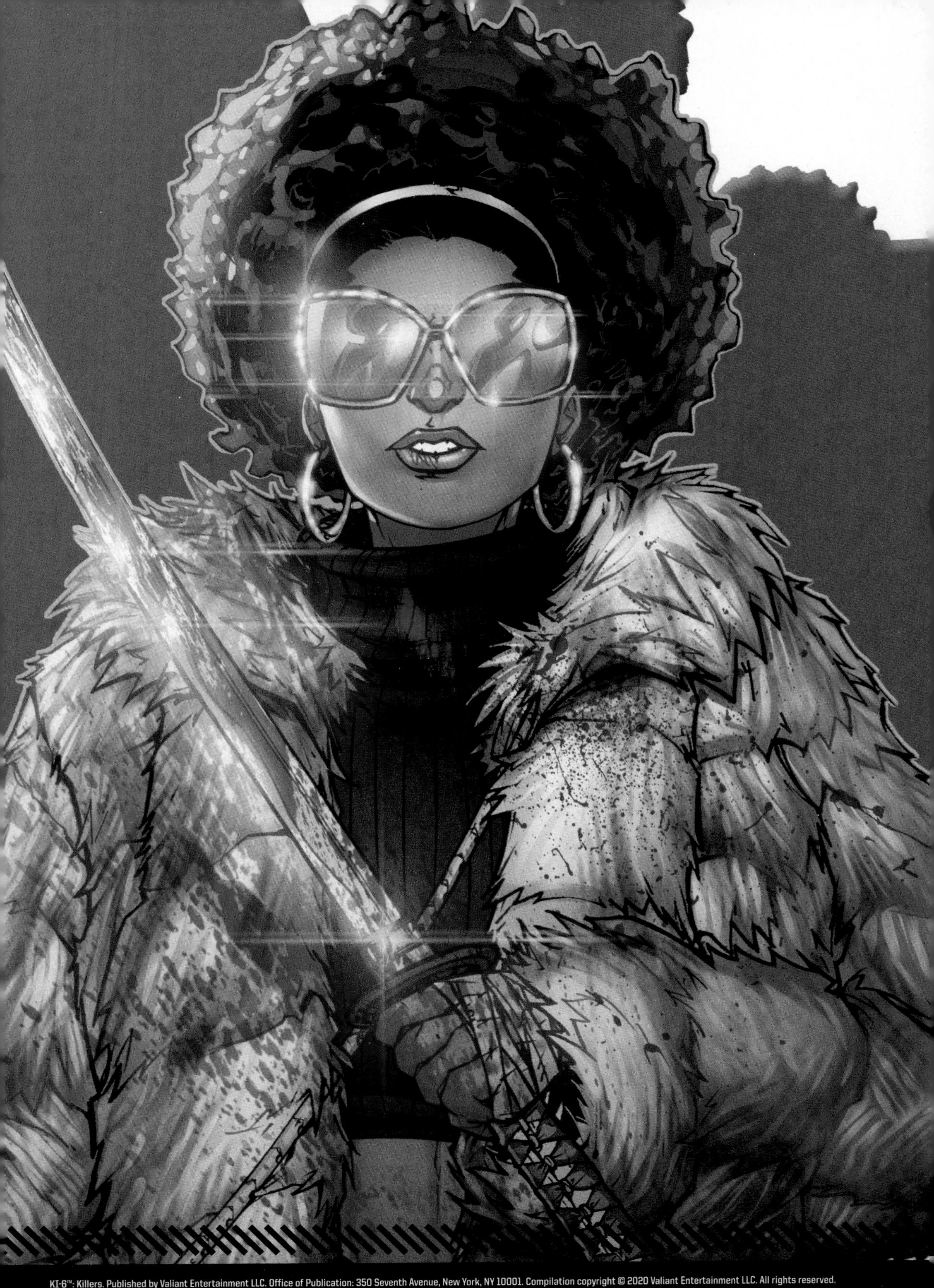

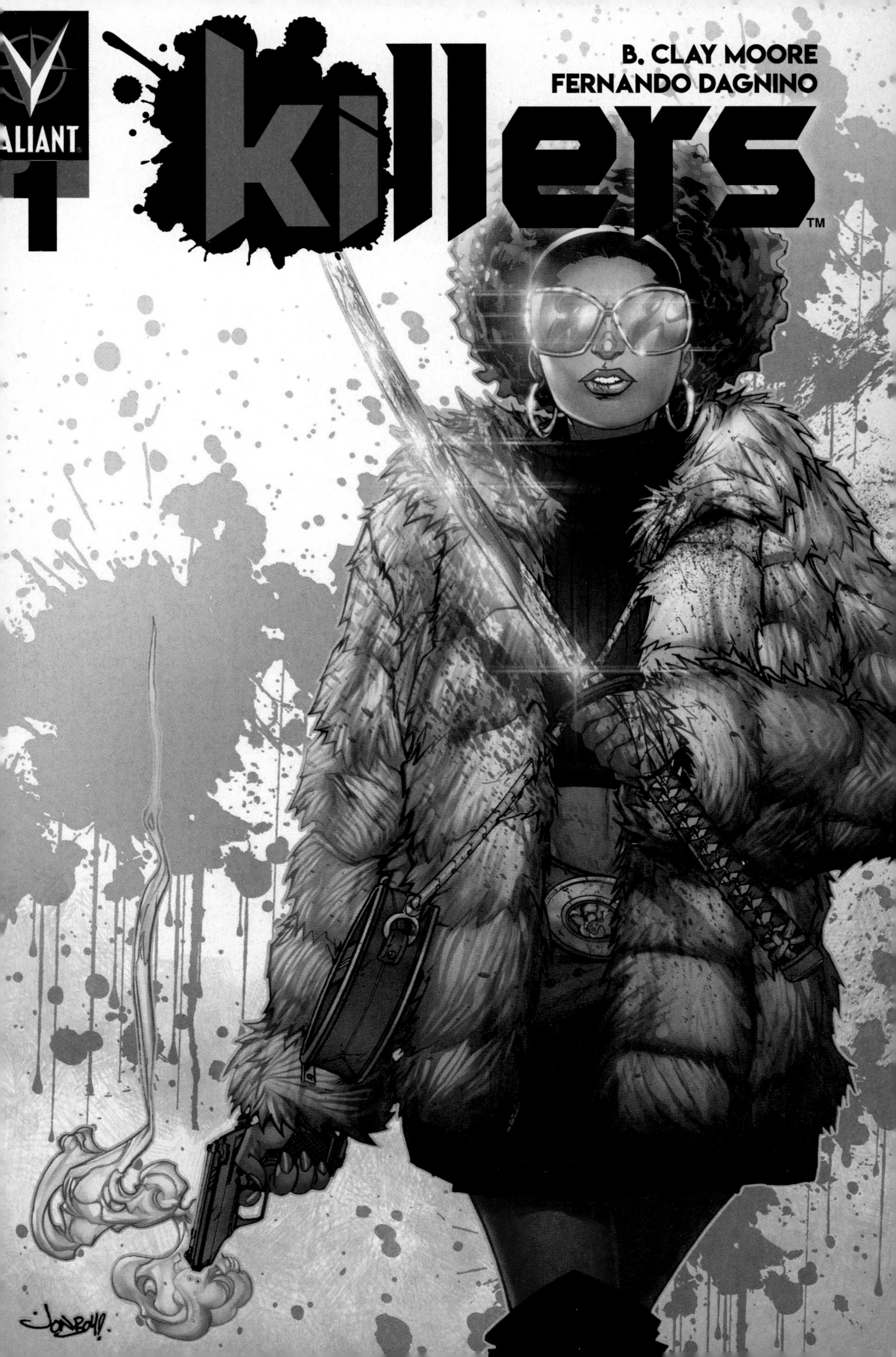
VALIANT
1
killers
B. CLAY MOORE
FERNANDO DAGNINO

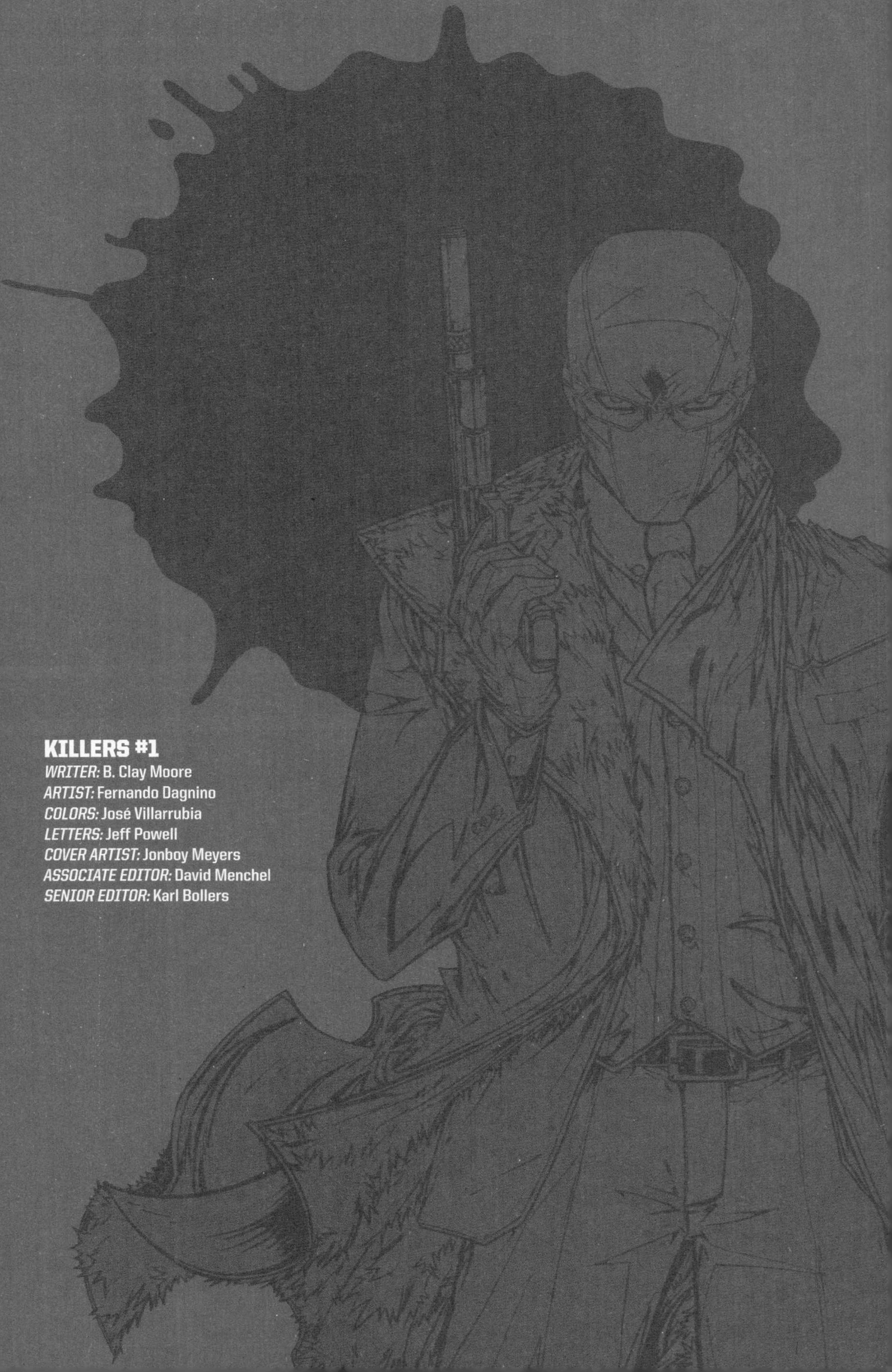

KILLERS #1

WRITER: B. Clay Moore
ARTIST: Fernando Dagnino
COLORS: José Villarrubia
LETTERS: Jeff Powell
COVER ARTIST: Jonboy Meyers
ASSOCIATE EDITOR: David Menchel
SENIOR EDITOR: Karl Bollers

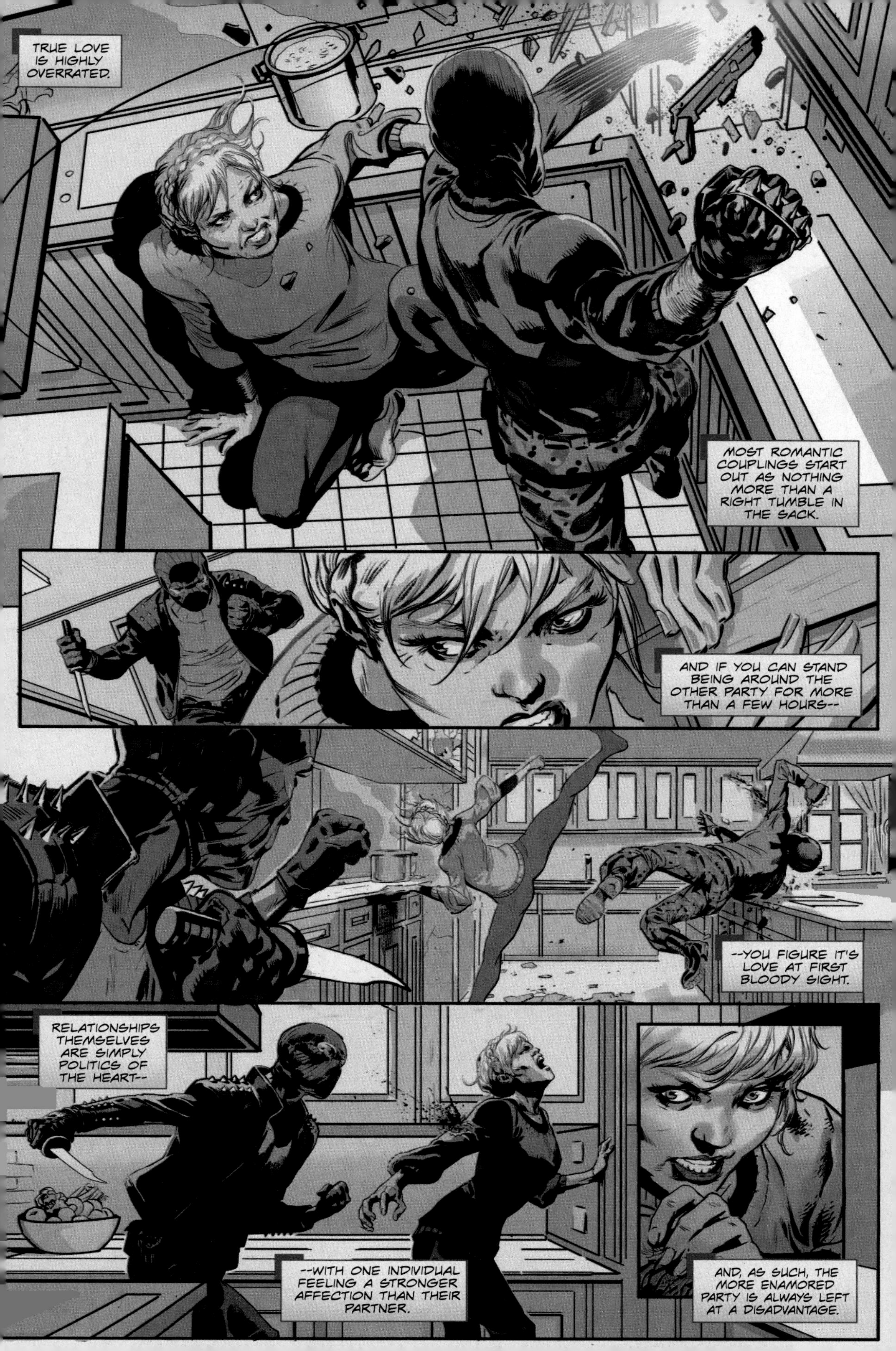
TRUE LOVE IS HIGHLY OVERRATED.
MOST ROMANTIC COUPLINGS START OUT AS NOTHING MORE THAN A RIGHT TUMBLE IN THE SACK.
AND IF YOU CAN STAND BEING AROUND THE OTHER PARTY FOR MORE THAN A FEW HOURS--
--YOU FIGURE IT'S LOVE AT FIRST BLOODY SIGHT.
RELATIONSHIPS THEMSELVES ARE SIMPLY POLITICS OF THE HEART--
--WITH ONE INDIVIDUAL FEELING A STRONGER AFFECTION THAN THEIR PARTNER.
AND, AS SUCH, THE MORE ENAMORED PARTY IS ALWAYS LEFT AT A DISADVANTAGE.

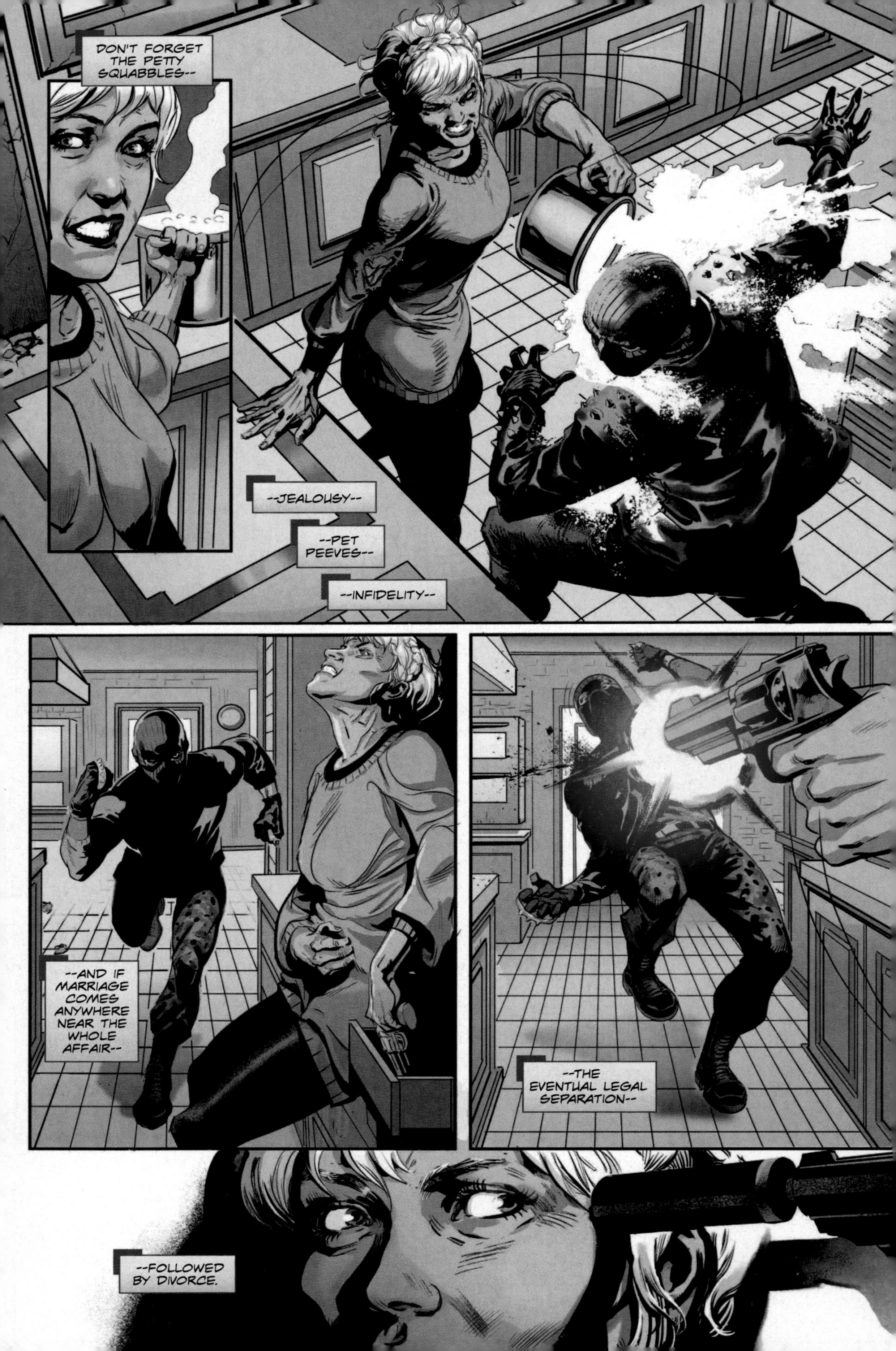
DON'T FORGET THE PETTY SQUABBLES--
--JEALOUSY--
--PET PEEVES--
--INFIDELITY--
--AND IF MARRIAGE COMES ANYWHERE NEAR THE WHOLE AFFAIR--
--THE EVENTUAL LEGAL SEPARATION--
--FOLLOWED BY DIVORCE.

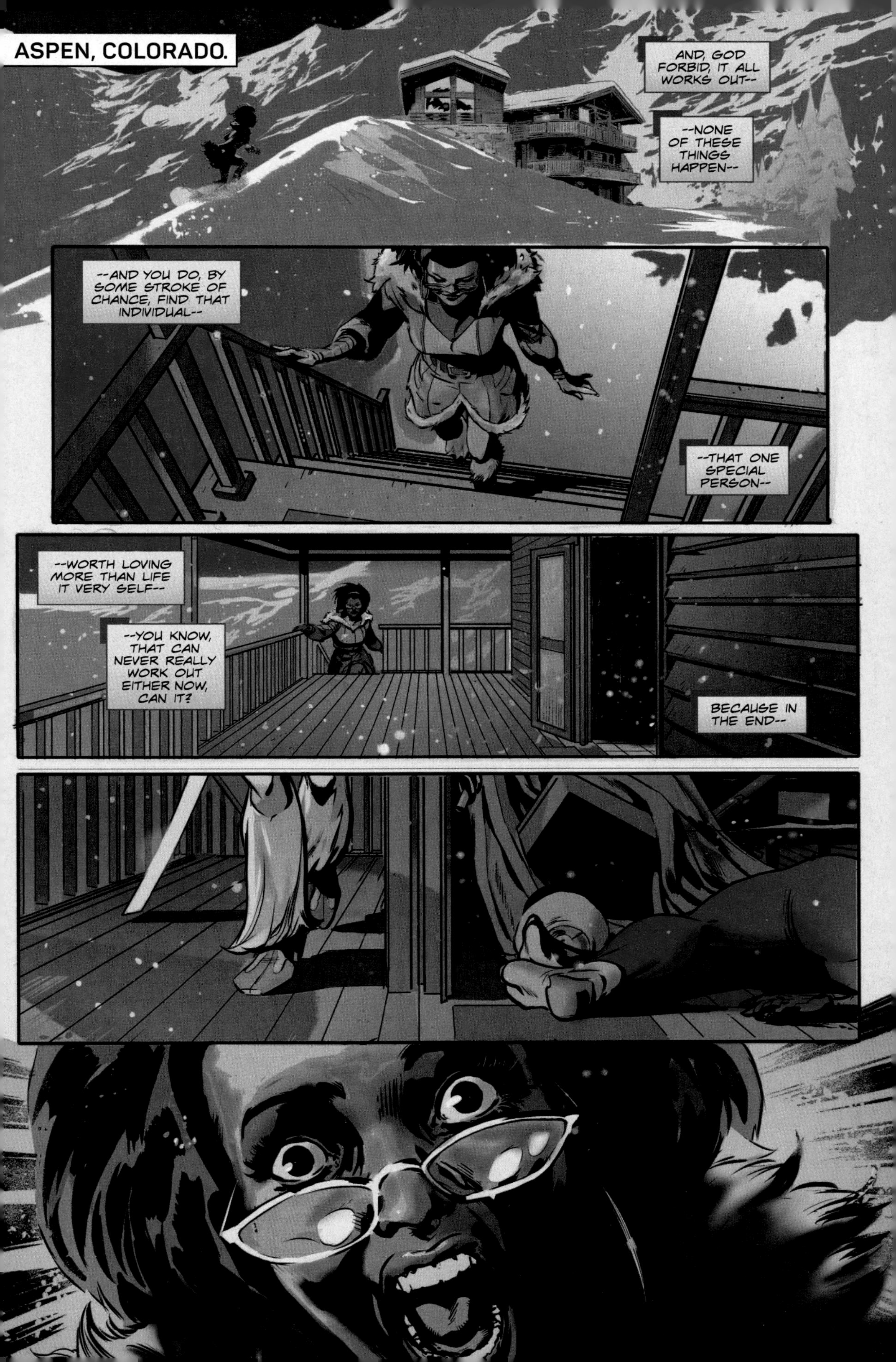
ASPEN, COLORADO.
AND, GOD FORBID, IT ALL WORKS OUT--
--NONE OF THESE THINGS HAPPEN--
--AND YOU DO, BY SOME STROKE OF CHANCE, FIND THAT INDIVIDUAL--
--THAT ONE SPECIAL PERSON--
--WORTH LOVING MORE THAN LIFE IT VERY SELF--
--YOU KNOW, THAT CAN NEVER REALLY WORK OUT EITHER NOW, CAN IT?
BECAUSE IN THE END--

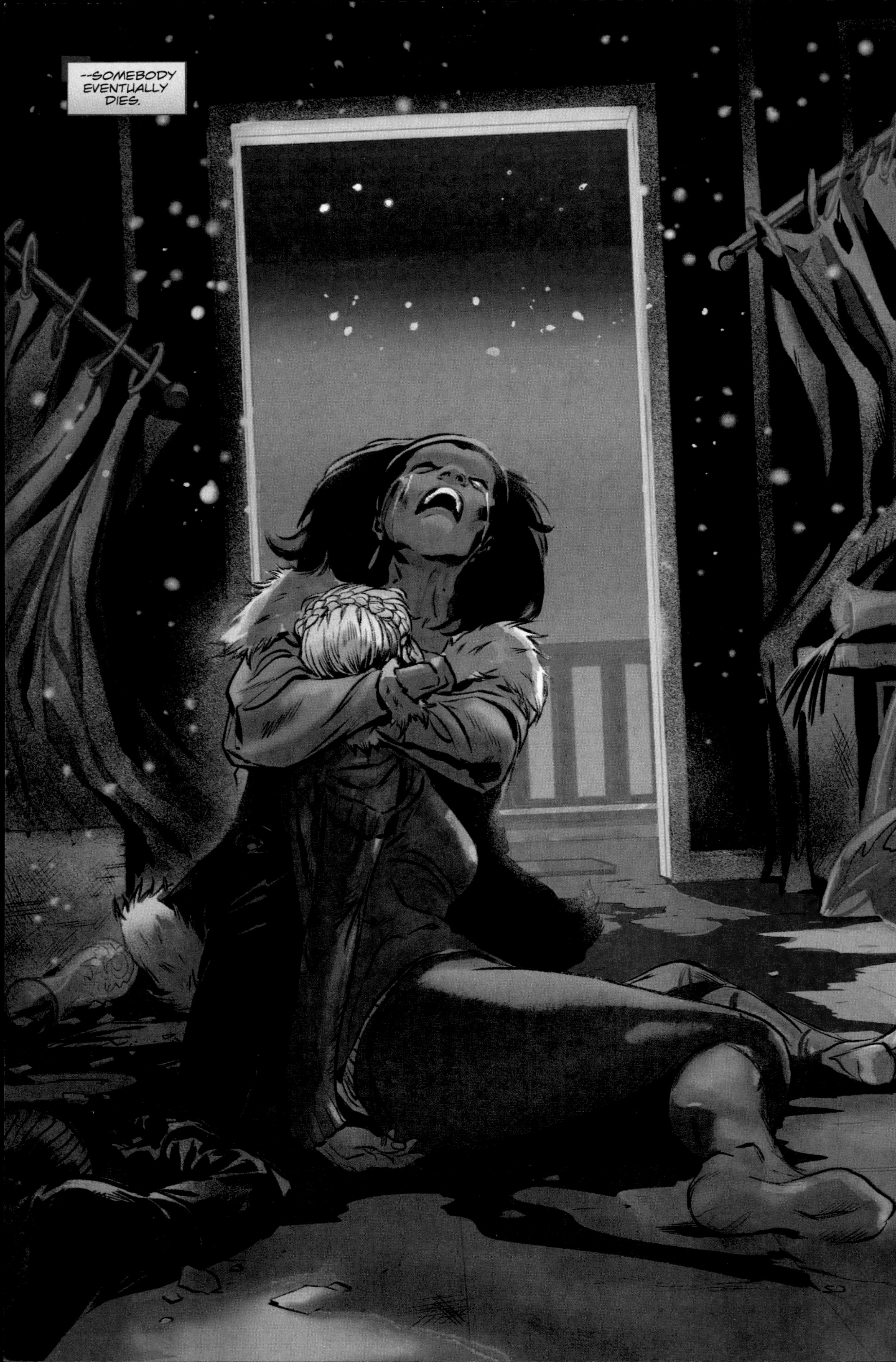
--SOMEBODY EVENTUALLY DIES.

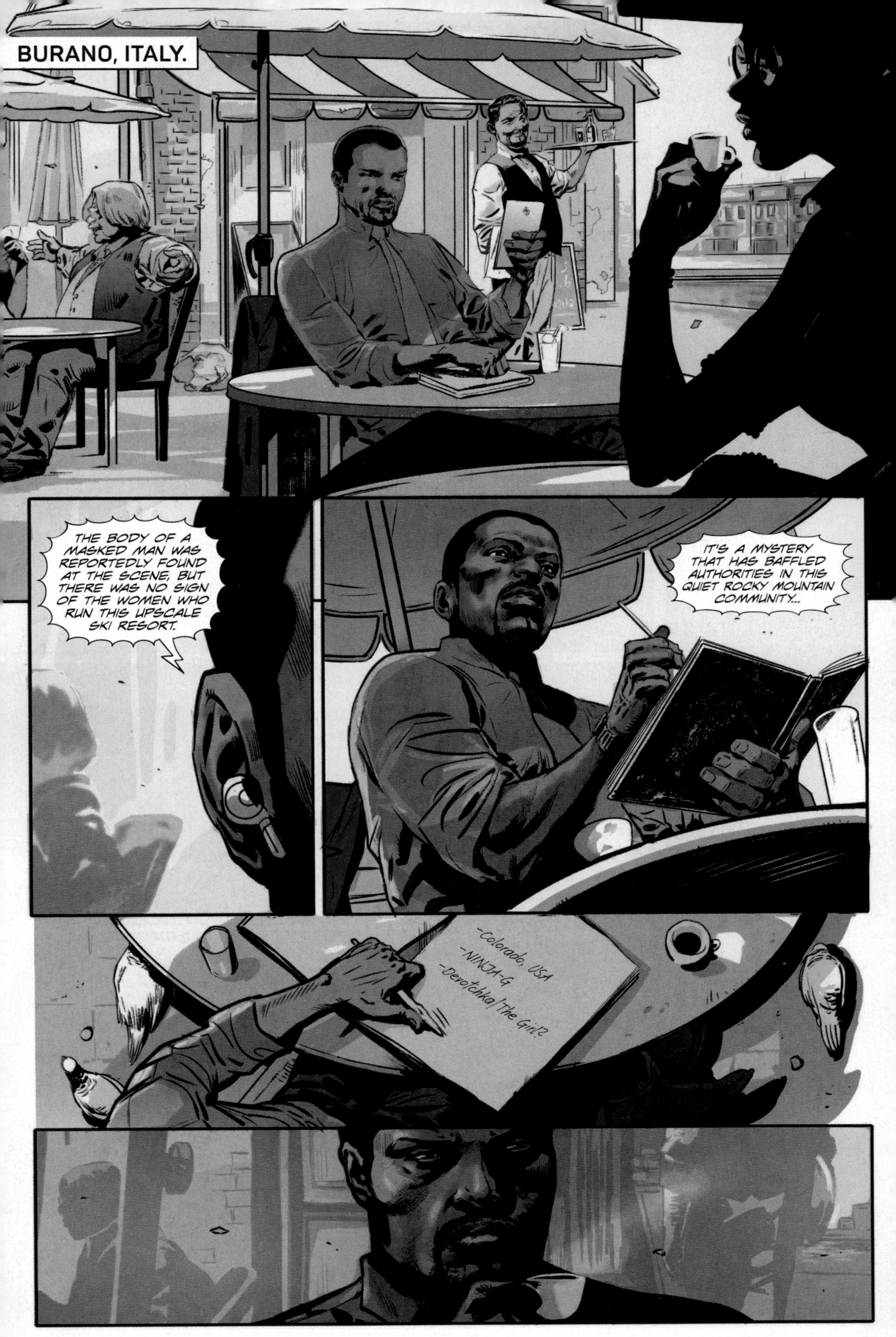
BURANO, ITALY.
THE BODY OF A MASKED MAN WAS REPORTEDLY FOUND AT THE SCENE, BUT THERE WAS NO SIGN OF THE WOMEN WHO RUN THIS UPSCALE SKI RESORT.
IT'S A MYSTERY THAT HAS BAFFLED AUTHORITIES IN THIS QUIET ROCKY MOUNTAIN COMMUNITY...
-Colorado, USA
-NINJA-G
-Devotchka/The Girl?

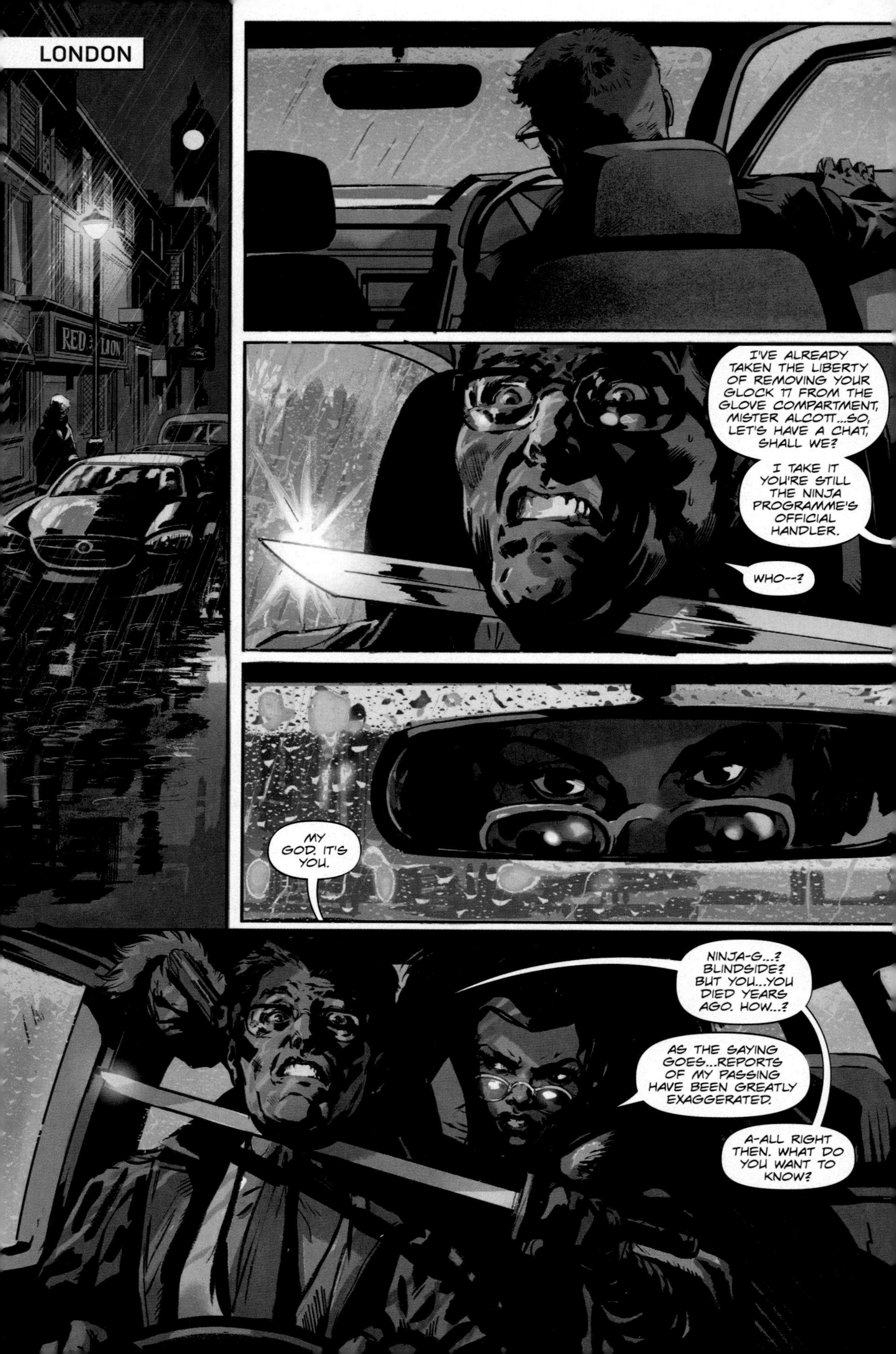
LONDON
RED LION
I'VE ALREADY TAKEN THE LIBERTY OF REMOVING YOUR GLOCK 17 FROM THE GLOVE COMPARTMENT, MISTER ALCOTT...SO, LET'S HAVE A CHAT, SHALL WE?
I TAKE IT YOU'RE STILL THE NINJA PROGRAMME'S OFFICIAL HANDLER.
WHO--?
MY GOD. IT'S YOU.
NINJA-G...? BLINDSIDE? BUT YOU...YOU DIED YEARS AGO. HOW...?
AS THE SAYING GOES...REPORTS OF MY PASSING HAVE BEEN GREATLY EXAGGERATED.
A-ALL RIGHT THEN. WHAT DO YOU WANT TO KNOW?

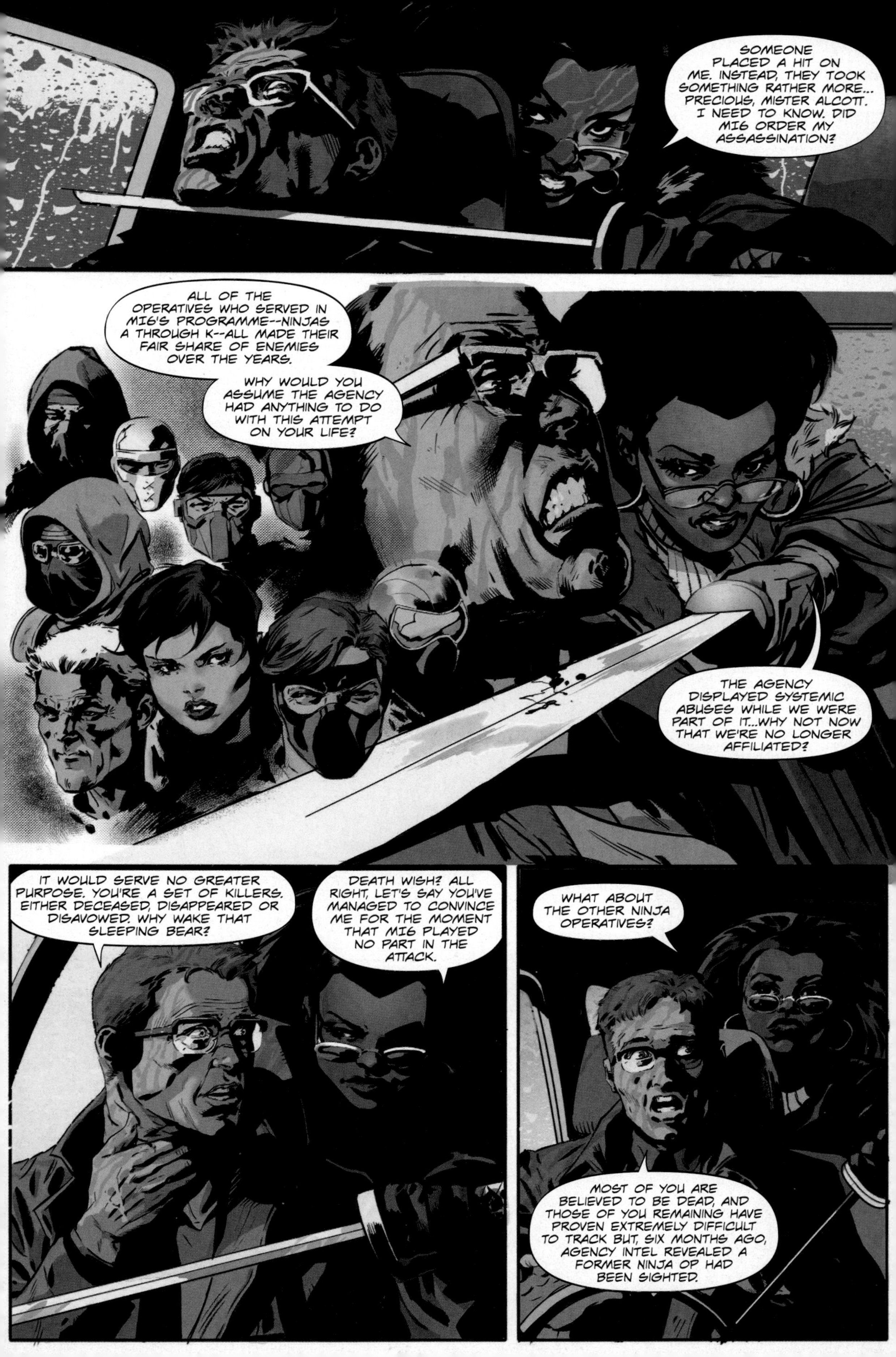
SOMEONE PLACED A HIT ON ME. INSTEAD, THEY TOOK SOMETHING RATHER MORE... PRECIOUS, MISTER ALCOTT. I NEED TO KNOW. DID MI6 ORDER MY ASSASSINATION?
ALL OF THE OPERATIVES WHO SERVED IN MI6'S PROGRAMME--NINJAS A THROUGH K--ALL MADE THEIR FAIR SHARE OF ENEMIES OVER THE YEARS.
WHY WOULD YOU ASSUME THE AGENCY HAD ANYTHING TO DO WITH THIS ATTEMPT ON YOUR LIFE?
THE AGENCY DISPLAYED SYSTEMIC ABUSES WHILE WE WERE PART OF IT...WHY NOT NOW THAT WE'RE NO LONGER AFFILIATED?
IT WOULD SERVE NO GREATER PURPOSE. YOU'RE A SET OF KILLERS. EITHER DECEASED, DISAPPEARED OR DISAVOWED. WHY WAKE THAT SLEEPING BEAR?
DEATH WISH? ALL RIGHT, LET'S SAY YOU'VE MANAGED TO CONVINCE ME FOR THE MOMENT THAT MI6 PLAYED NO PART IN THE ATTACK.
WHAT ABOUT THE OTHER NINJA OPERATIVES?
MOST OF YOU ARE BELIEVED TO BE DEAD, AND THOSE OF YOU REMAINING HAVE PROVEN EXTREMELY DIFFICULT TO TRACK BUT, SIX MONTHS AGO, AGENCY INTEL REVEALED A FORMER NINJA OP HAD BEEN SIGHTED.

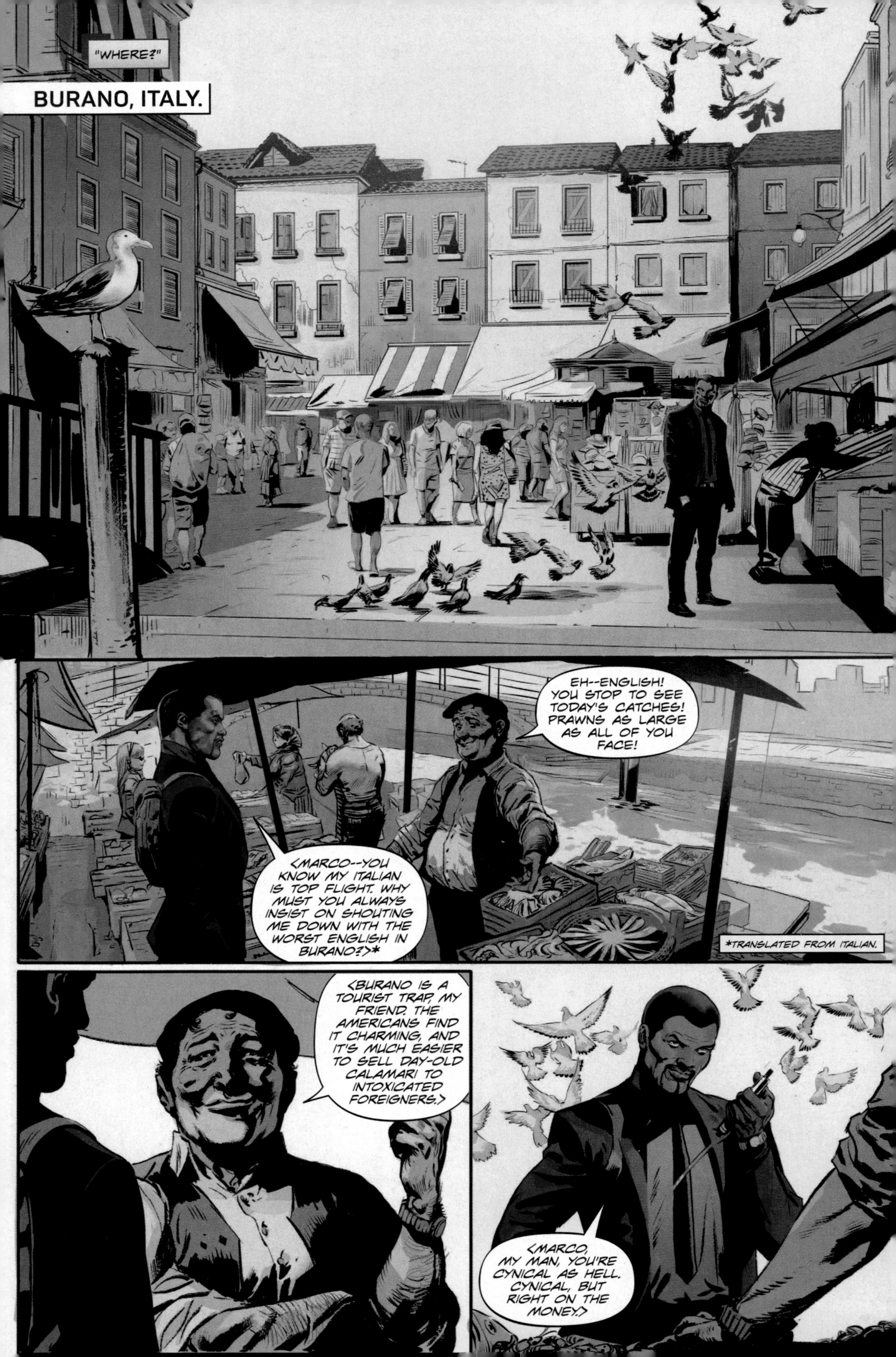
"WHERE?"
BURANO, ITALY.
EH--ENGLISH! YOU STOP TO SEE TODAY'S CATCHES! PRAWNS AS LARGE AS ALL OF YOU FACE!
<MARCO--YOU KNOW MY ITALIAN IS TOP FLIGHT. WHY MUST YOU ALWAYS INSIST ON SHOUTING ME DOWN WITH THE WORST ENGLISH IN BURANO?>*
*TRANSLATED FROM ITALIAN.
<BURANO IS A TOURIST TRAP, MY FRIEND. THE AMERICANS FIND IT CHARMING, AND IT'S MUCH EASIER TO SELL DAY-OLD CALAMARI TO INTOXICATED FOREIGNERS.>
<MARCO, MY MAN, YOU'RE CYNICAL AS HELL. CYNICAL, BUT RIGHT ON THE MONEY.>

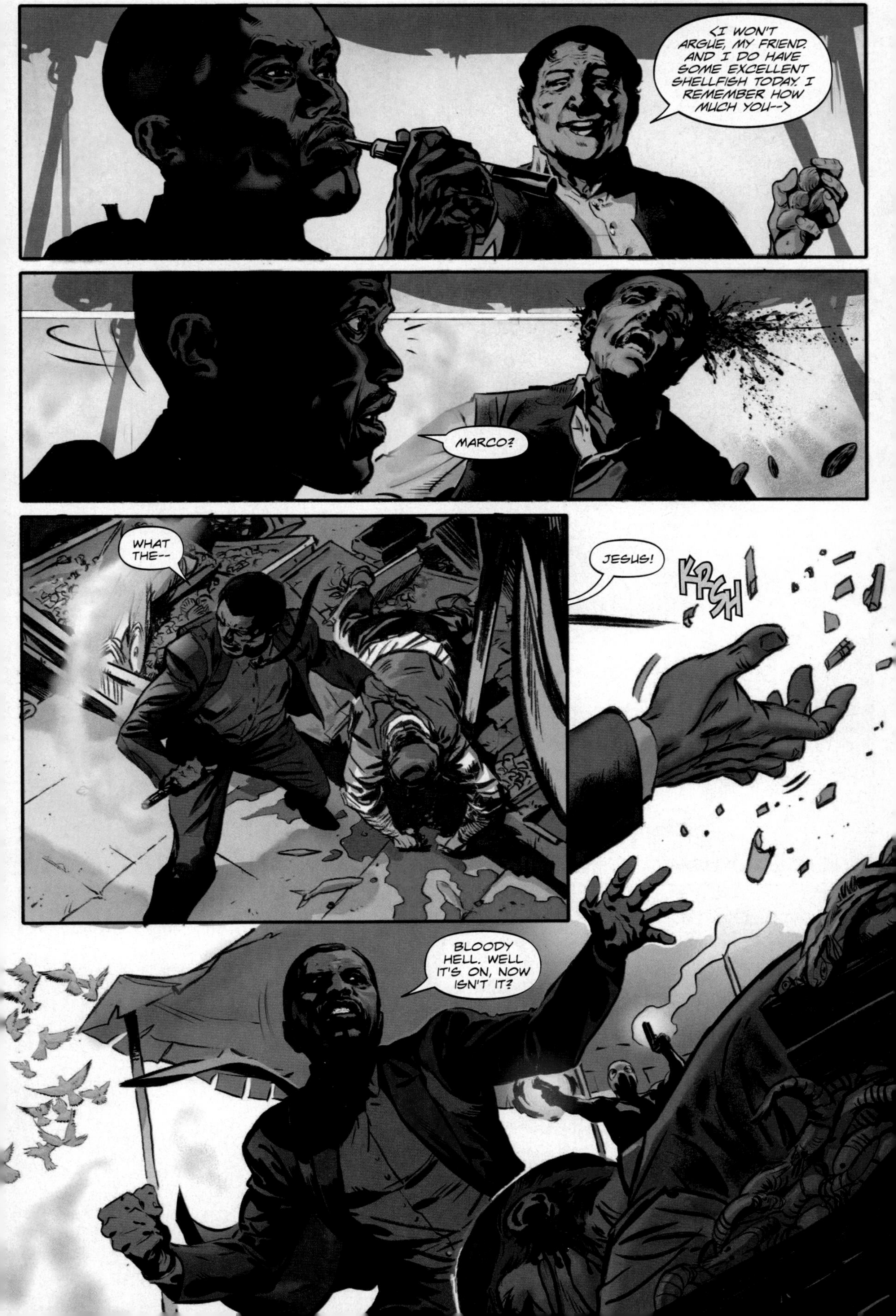
<I WON'T ARGUE, MY FRIEND. AND I DO HAVE SOME EXCELLENT SHELLFISH TODAY. I REMEMBER HOW MUCH YOU-->
MARCO?
WHAT THE--
JESUS!
KRSH
BLOODY HELL. WELL IT'S ON, NOW ISN'T IT?

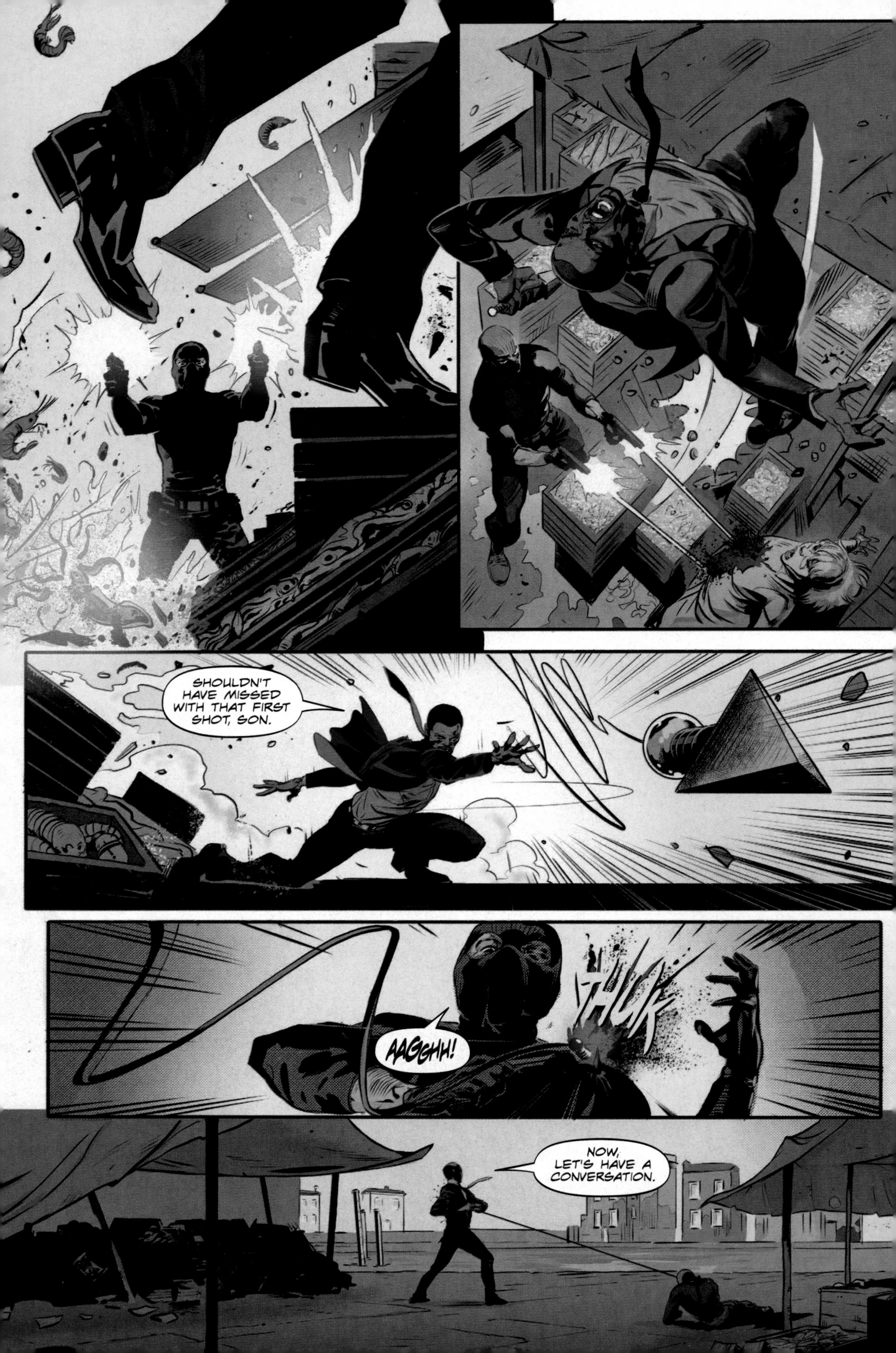
SHOULDN'T HAVE MISSED WITH THAT FIRST SHOT, SON.
AAGGHH!
THUK
NOW, LET'S HAVE A CONVERSATION.

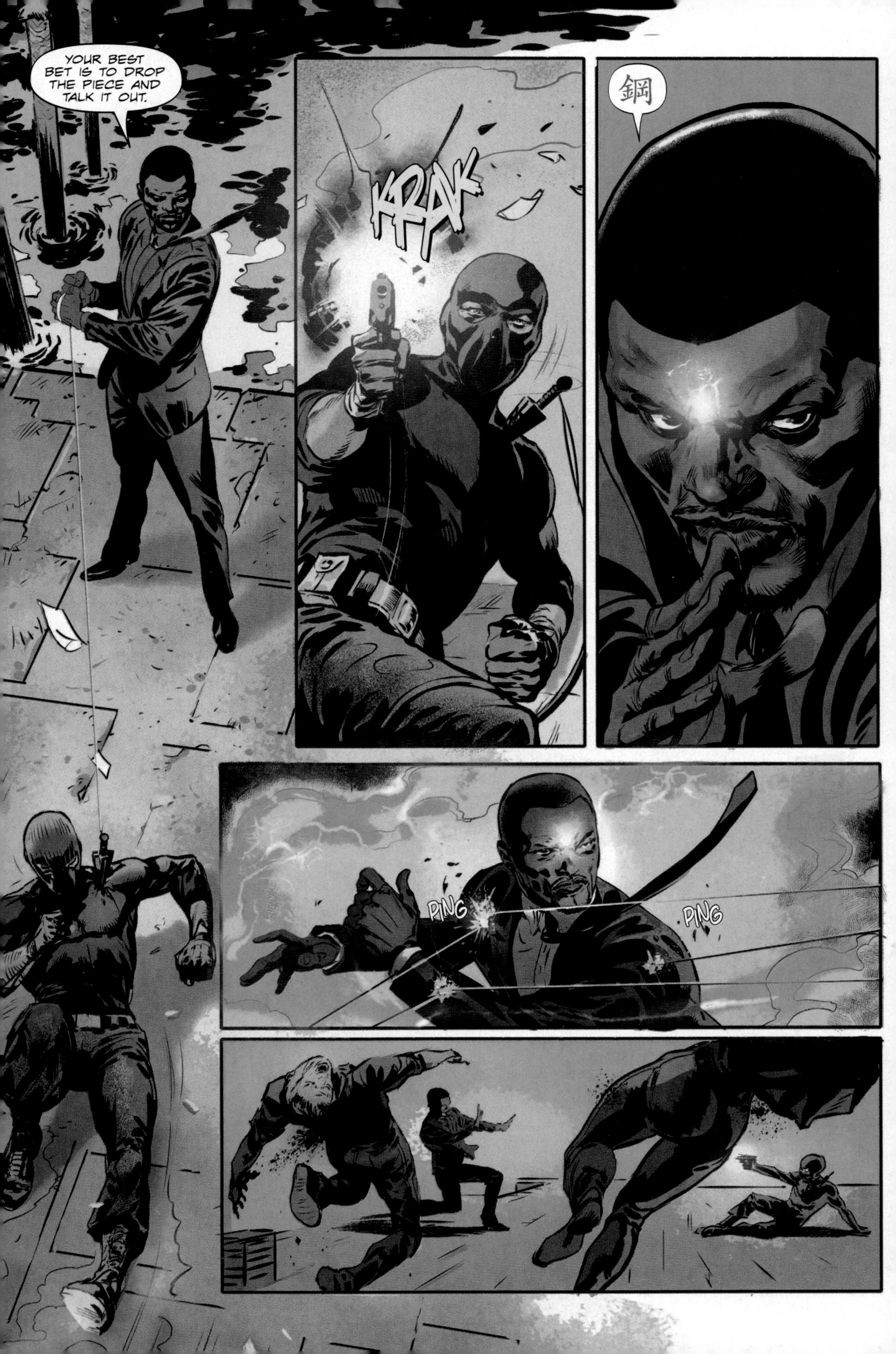
YOUR BEST BET IS TO DROP THE PIECE AND TALK IT OUT.
KRAK
鋼
PING
PING

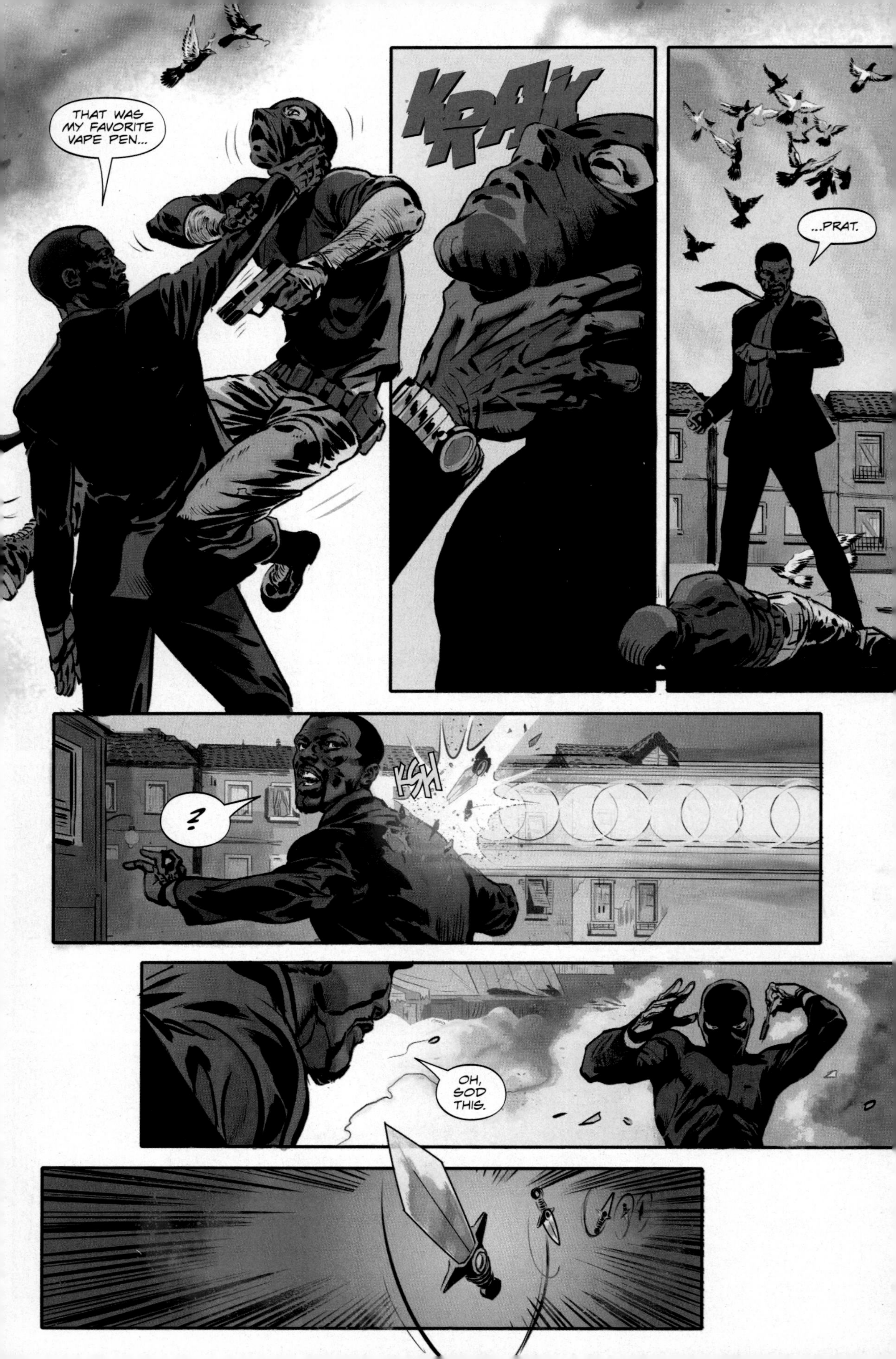
THAT WAS MY FAVORITE VAPE PEN...
KRAK
...PRAT.
KSH
?
OH, SOD THIS.

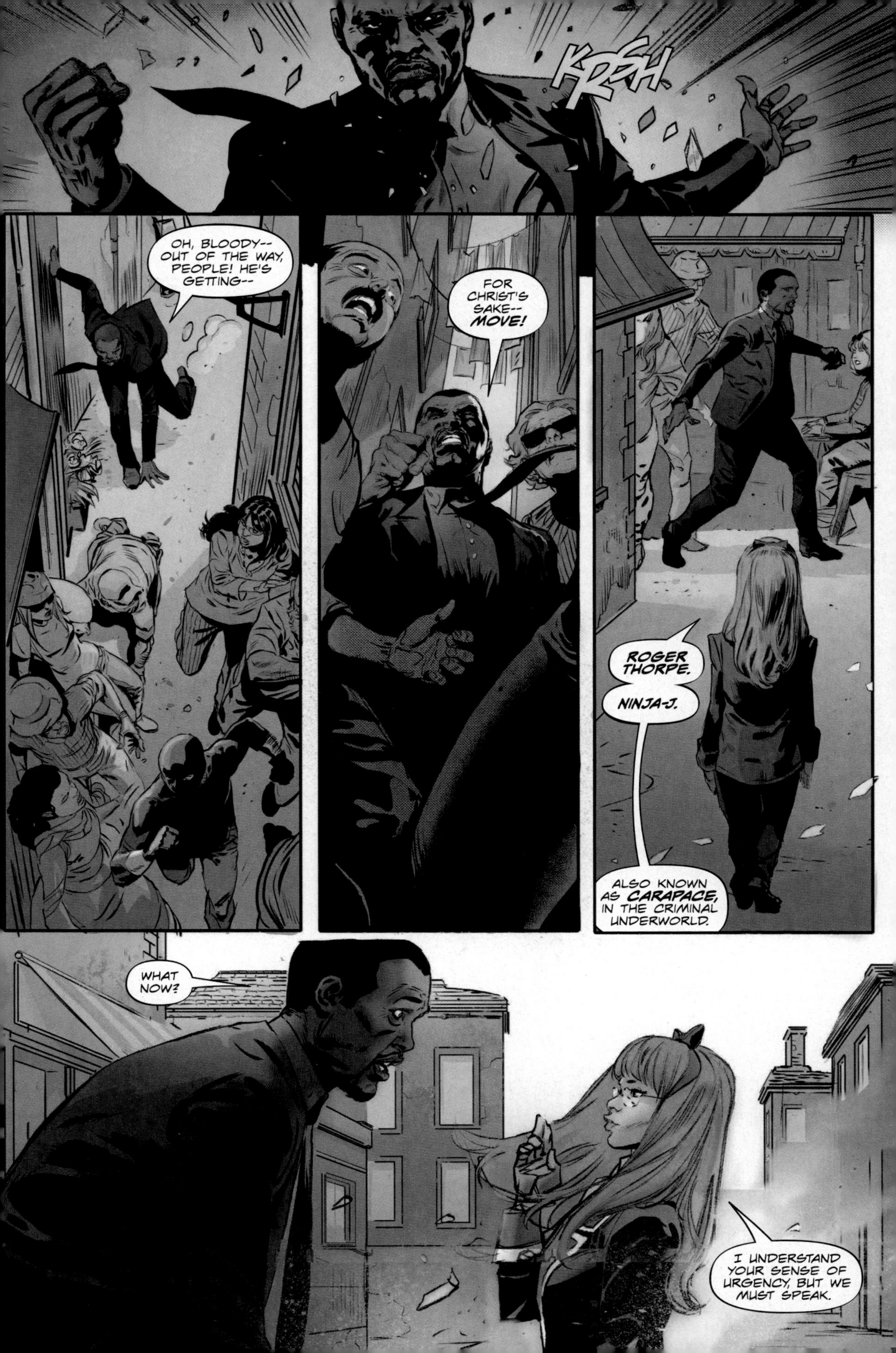
KRSH
OH, BLOODY-- OUT OF THE WAY, PEOPLE! HE'S GETTING--
FOR CHRIST'S SAKE-- MOVE!
ROGER THORPE.
NINJA-J.
ALSO KNOWN AS CARAPACE, IN THE CRIMINAL UNDERWORLD.
WHAT NOW?
I UNDERSTAND YOUR SENSE OF URGENCY, BUT WE MUST SPEAK.

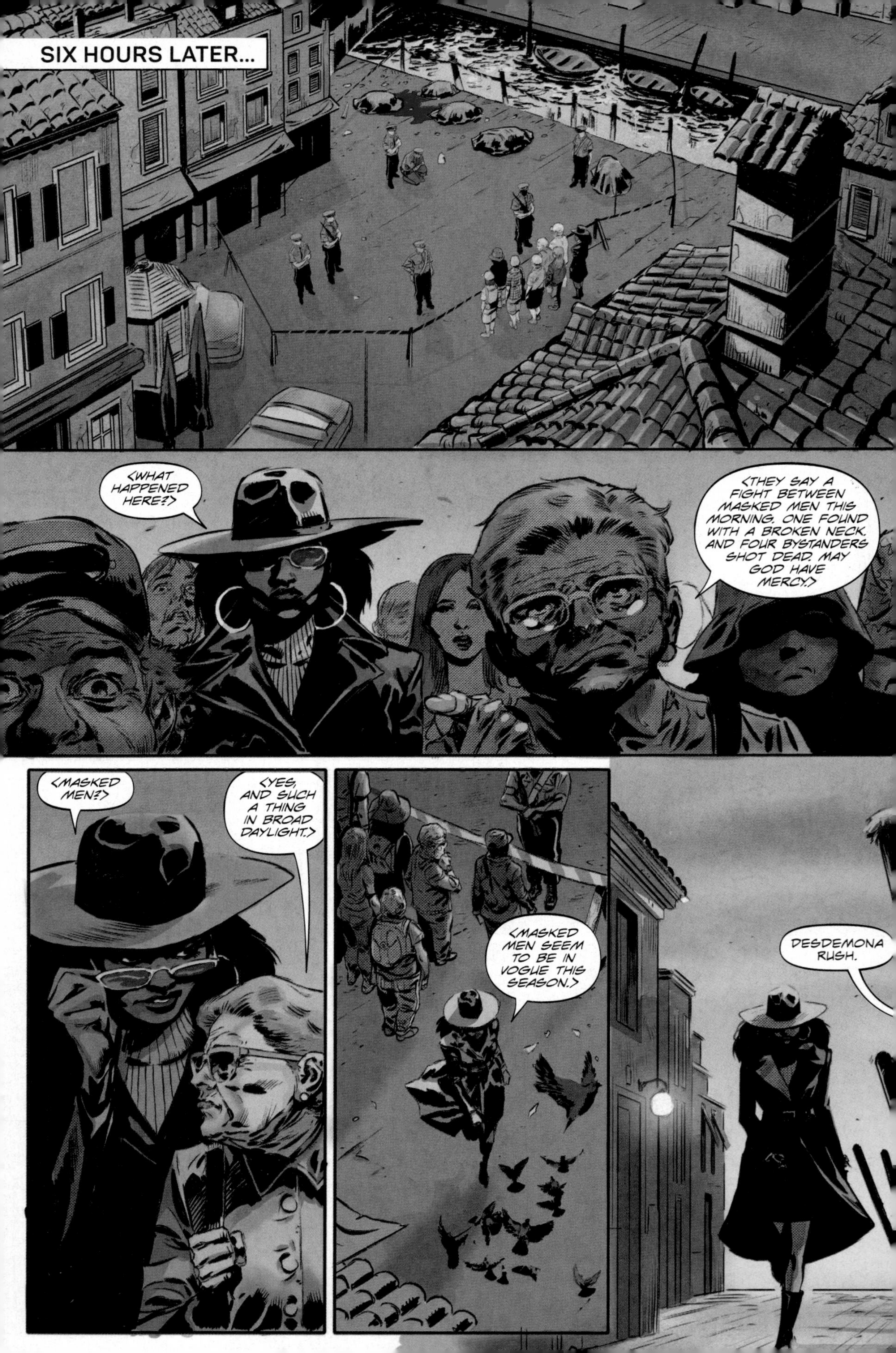
SIX HOURS LATER...
<WHAT HAPPENED HERE?>
<THEY SAY A FIGHT BETWEEN MASKED MEN THIS MORNING. ONE FOUND WITH A BROKEN NECK. AND FOUR BYSTANDERS SHOT DEAD. MAY GOD HAVE MERCY.>
<MASKED MEN?>
<YES, AND SUCH A THING IN BROAD DAYLIGHT.>
<MASKED MEN SEEM TO BE IN VOGUE THIS SEASON.>
DESDEMONA RUSH.

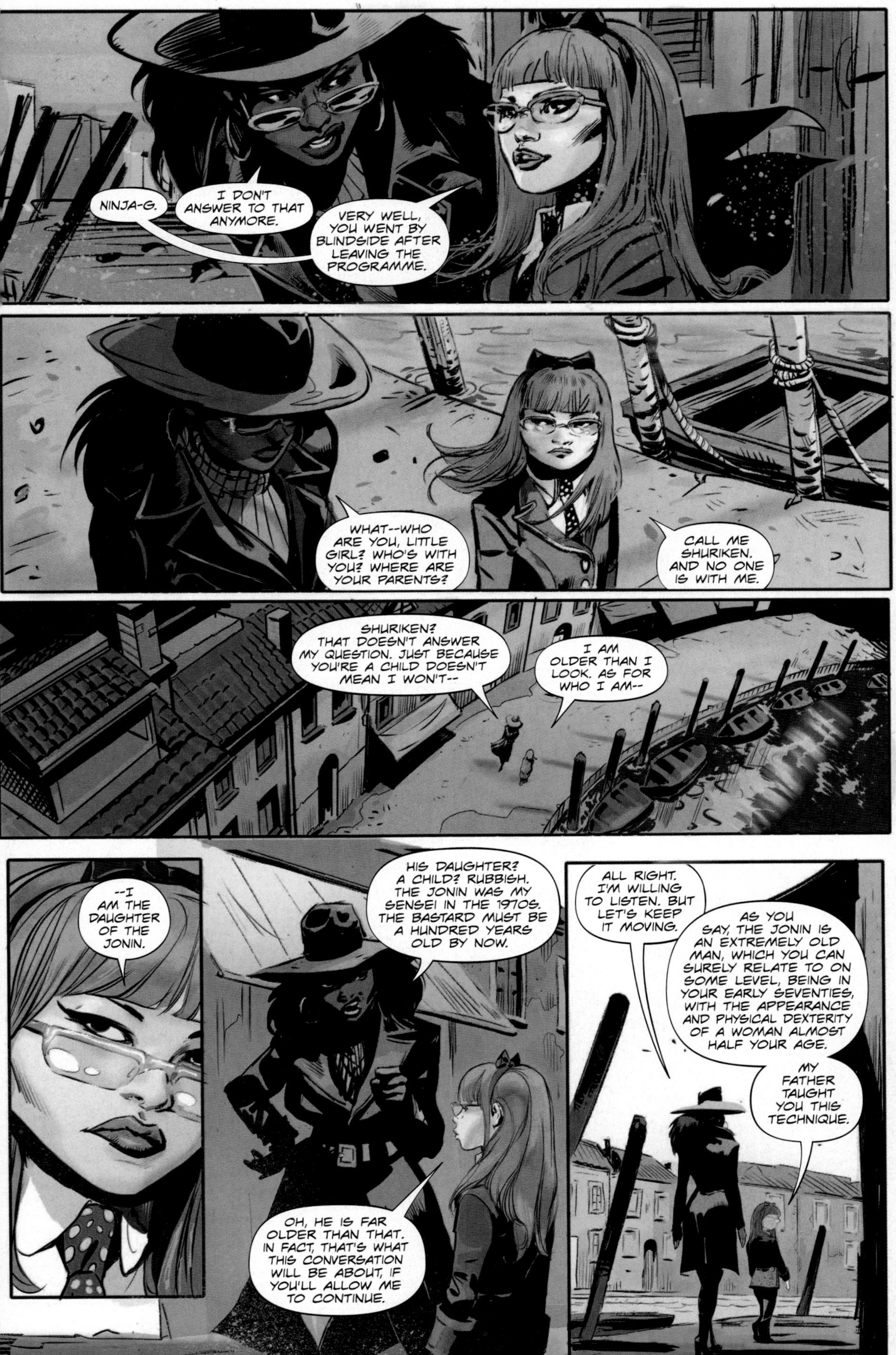
NINJA-G.
I DON'T ANSWER TO THAT ANYMORE.
VERY WELL, YOU WENT BY BLINDSIDE AFTER LEAVING THE PROGRAMME.
WHAT--WHO ARE YOU, LITTLE GIRL? WHO'S WITH YOU? WHERE ARE YOUR PARENTS?
CALL ME SHURIKEN. AND NO ONE IS WITH ME.
SHURIKEN? THAT DOESN'T ANSWER MY QUESTION. JUST BECAUSE YOU'RE A CHILD DOESN'T MEAN I WON'T--
I AM OLDER THAN I LOOK. AS FOR WHO I AM--
--I AM THE DAUGHTER OF THE JONIN.
HIS DAUGHTER? A CHILD? RUBBISH. THE JONIN WAS MY SENSEI IN THE 1970S. THE BASTARD MUST BE A HUNDRED YEARS OLD BY NOW.
OH, HE IS FAR OLDER THAN THAT. IN FACT, THAT'S WHAT THIS CONVERSATION WILL BE ABOUT, IF YOU'LL ALLOW ME TO CONTINUE.
ALL RIGHT. I'M WILLING TO LISTEN. BUT LET'S KEEP IT MOVING.
AS YOU SAY, THE JONIN IS AN EXTREMELY OLD MAN, WHICH YOU CAN SURELY RELATE TO ON SOME LEVEL, BEING IN YOUR EARLY SEVENTIES, WITH THE APPEARANCE AND PHYSICAL DEXTERITY OF A WOMAN ALMOST HALF YOUR AGE.
MY FATHER TAUGHT YOU THIS TECHNIQUE.

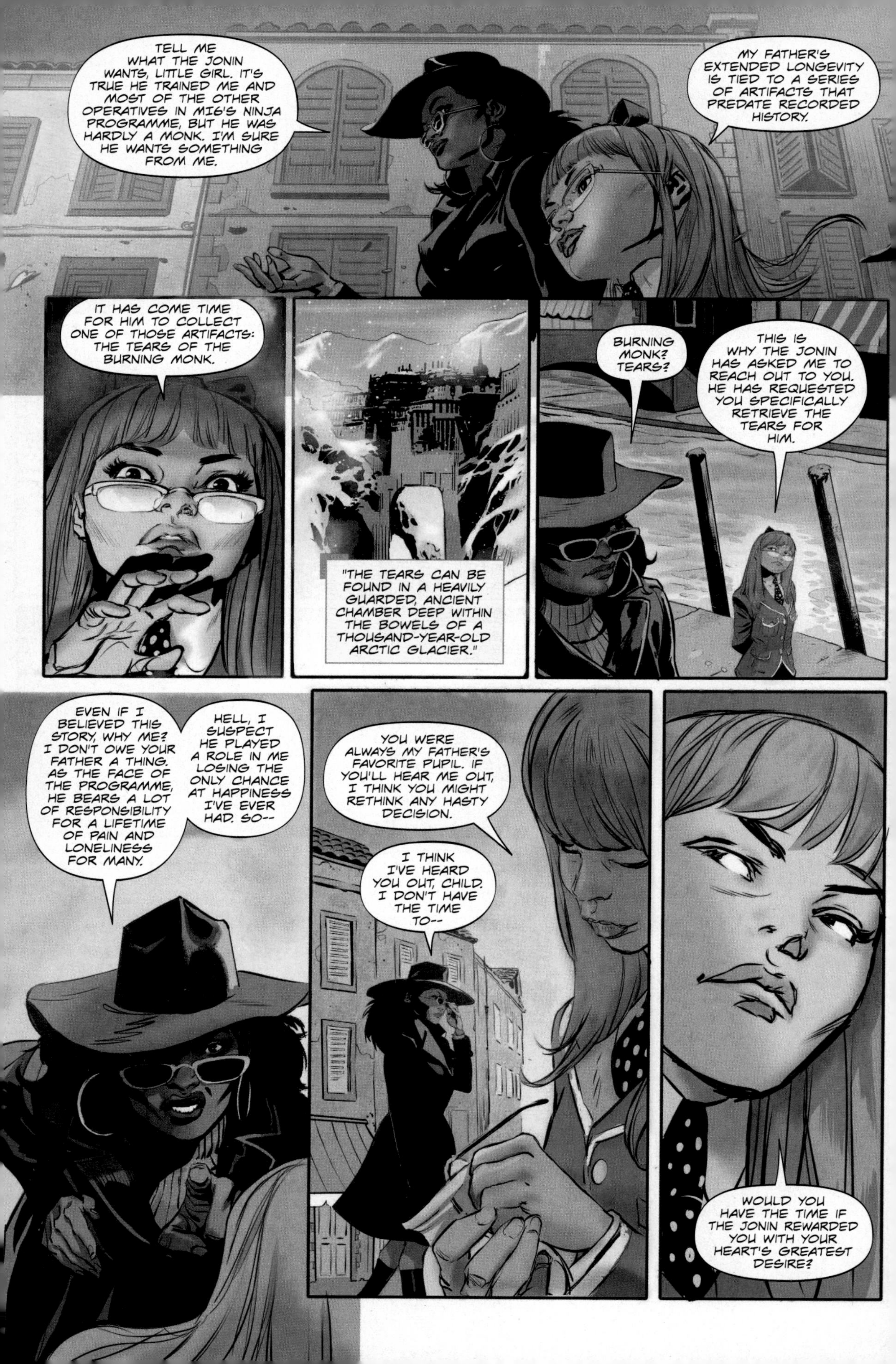
TELL ME WHAT THE JONIN WANTS, LITTLE GIRL. IT'S TRUE HE TRAINED ME AND MOST OF THE OTHER OPERATIVES IN MI6'S NINJA PROGRAMME, BUT HE WAS HARDLY A MONK. I'M SURE HE WANTS SOMETHING FROM ME.
MY FATHER'S EXTENDED LONGEVITY IS TIED TO A SERIES OF ARTIFACTS THAT PREDATE RECORDED HISTORY.
IT HAS COME TIME FOR HIM TO COLLECT ONE OF THOSE ARTIFACTS: THE TEARS OF THE BURNING MONK.
"THE TEARS CAN BE FOUND IN A HEAVILY GUARDED, ANCIENT CHAMBER DEEP WITHIN THE BOWELS OF A THOUSAND-YEAR-OLD ARCTIC GLACIER."
BURNING MONK? TEARS?
THIS IS WHY THE JONIN HAS ASKED ME TO REACH OUT TO YOU. HE HAS REQUESTED YOU SPECIFICALLY RETRIEVE THE TEARS FOR HIM.
EVEN IF I BELIEVED THIS STORY, WHY ME? I DON'T OWE YOUR FATHER A THING. AS THE FACE OF THE PROGRAMME, HE BEARS A LOT OF RESPONSIBILITY FOR A LIFETIME OF PAIN AND LONELINESS FOR MANY.
HELL, I SUSPECT HE PLAYED A ROLE IN ME LOSING THE ONLY CHANCE AT HAPPINESS I'VE EVER HAD. SO--
YOU WERE ALWAYS MY FATHER'S FAVORITE PUPIL. IF YOU'LL HEAR ME OUT, I THINK YOU MIGHT RETHINK ANY HASTY DECISION.
I THINK I'VE HEARD YOU OUT, CHILD. I DON'T HAVE THE TIME TO--
WOULD YOU HAVE THE TIME IF THE JONIN REWARDED YOU WITH YOUR HEART'S GREATEST DESIRE?

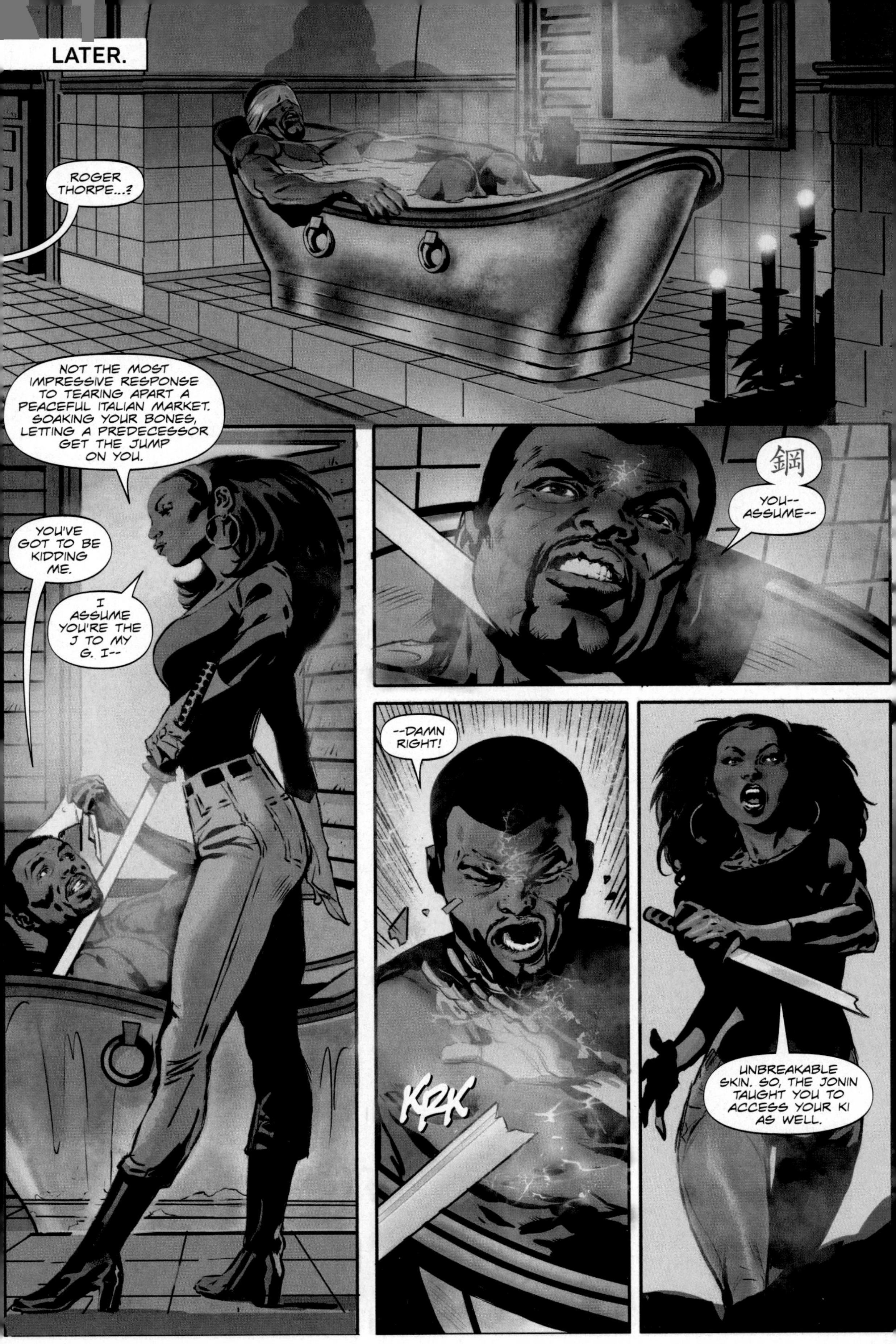
LATER.
ROGER THORPE...?
NOT THE MOST IMPRESSIVE RESPONSE TO TEARING APART A PEACEFUL ITALIAN MARKET. SOAKING YOUR BONES, LETTING A PREDECESSOR GET THE JUMP ON YOU.
YOU'VE GOT TO BE KIDDING ME.
I ASSUME YOU'RE THE J TO MY G. I--
鋼
YOU-- ASSUME--
--DAMN RIGHT!
KRK
UNBREAKABLE SKIN. SO, THE JONIN TAUGHT YOU TO ACCESS YOUR KI AS WELL.

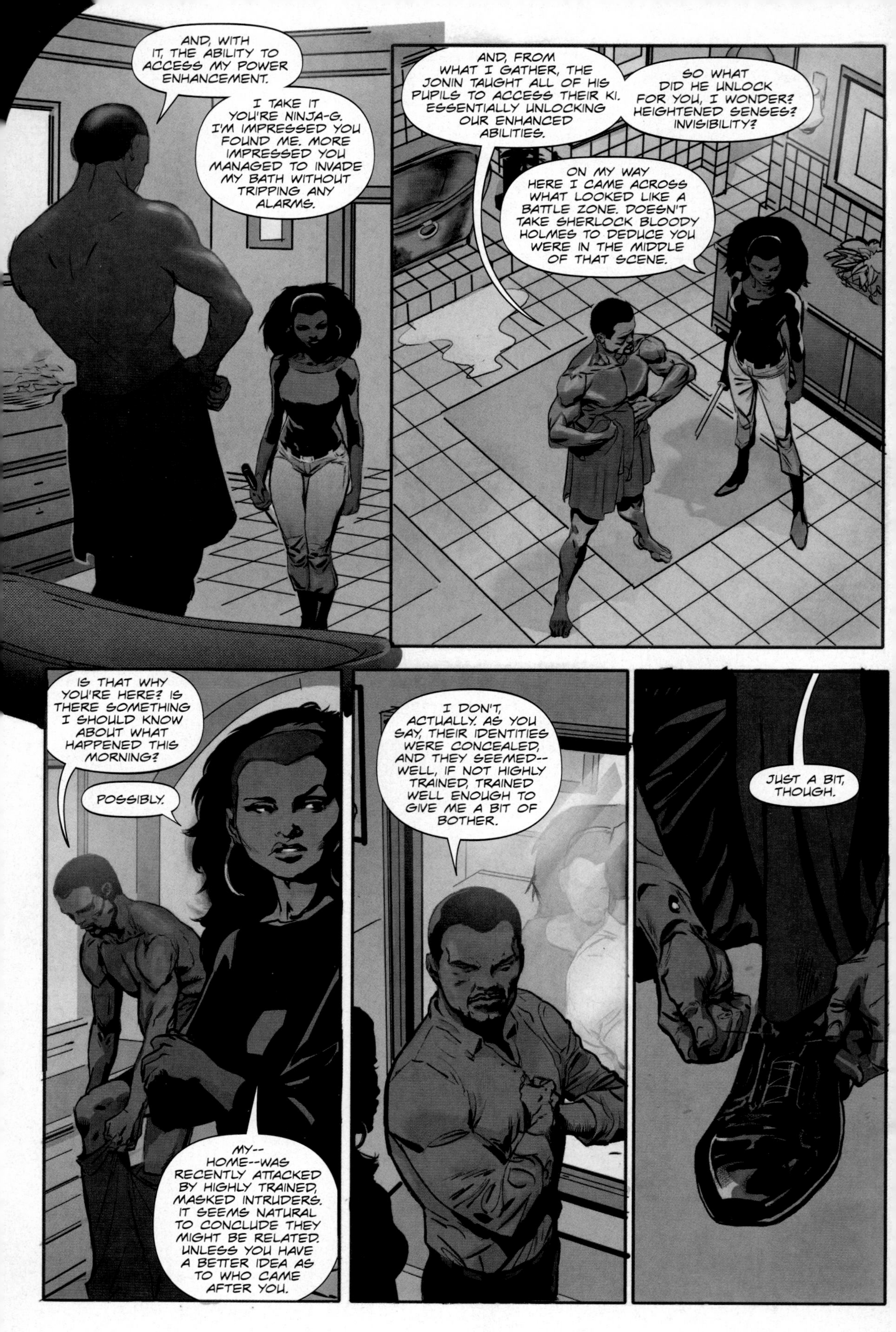
AND, WITH IT, THE ABILITY TO ACCESS MY POWER ENHANCEMENT.
I TAKE IT YOU'RE NINJA-G. I'M IMPRESSED YOU FOUND ME. MORE IMPRESSED YOU MANAGED TO INVADE MY BATH WITHOUT TRIPPING ANY ALARMS.
AND, FROM WHAT I GATHER, THE JONIN TAUGHT ALL OF HIS PUPILS TO ACCESS THEIR KI. ESSENTIALLY UNLOCKING OUR ENHANCED ABILITIES.
SO WHAT DID HE UNLOCK FOR YOU, I WONDER? HEIGHTENED SENSES? INVISIBILITY?
ON MY WAY HERE I CAME ACROSS WHAT LOOKED LIKE A BATTLE ZONE. DOESN'T TAKE SHERLOCK BLOODY HOLMES TO DEDUCE YOU WERE IN THE MIDDLE OF THAT SCENE.
IS THAT WHY YOU'RE HERE? IS THERE SOMETHING I SHOULD KNOW ABOUT WHAT HAPPENED THIS MORNING?
POSSIBLY.
MY--HOME--WAS RECENTLY ATTACKED BY HIGHLY TRAINED, MASKED INTRUDERS. IT SEEMS NATURAL TO CONCLUDE THEY MIGHT BE RELATED. UNLESS YOU HAVE A BETTER IDEA AS TO WHO CAME AFTER YOU.
I DON'T, ACTUALLY. AS YOU SAY, THEIR IDENTITIES WERE CONCEALED, AND THEY SEEMED--WELL, IF NOT HIGHLY TRAINED, TRAINED WELL ENOUGH TO GIVE ME A BIT OF BOTHER.
JUST A BIT, THOUGH.

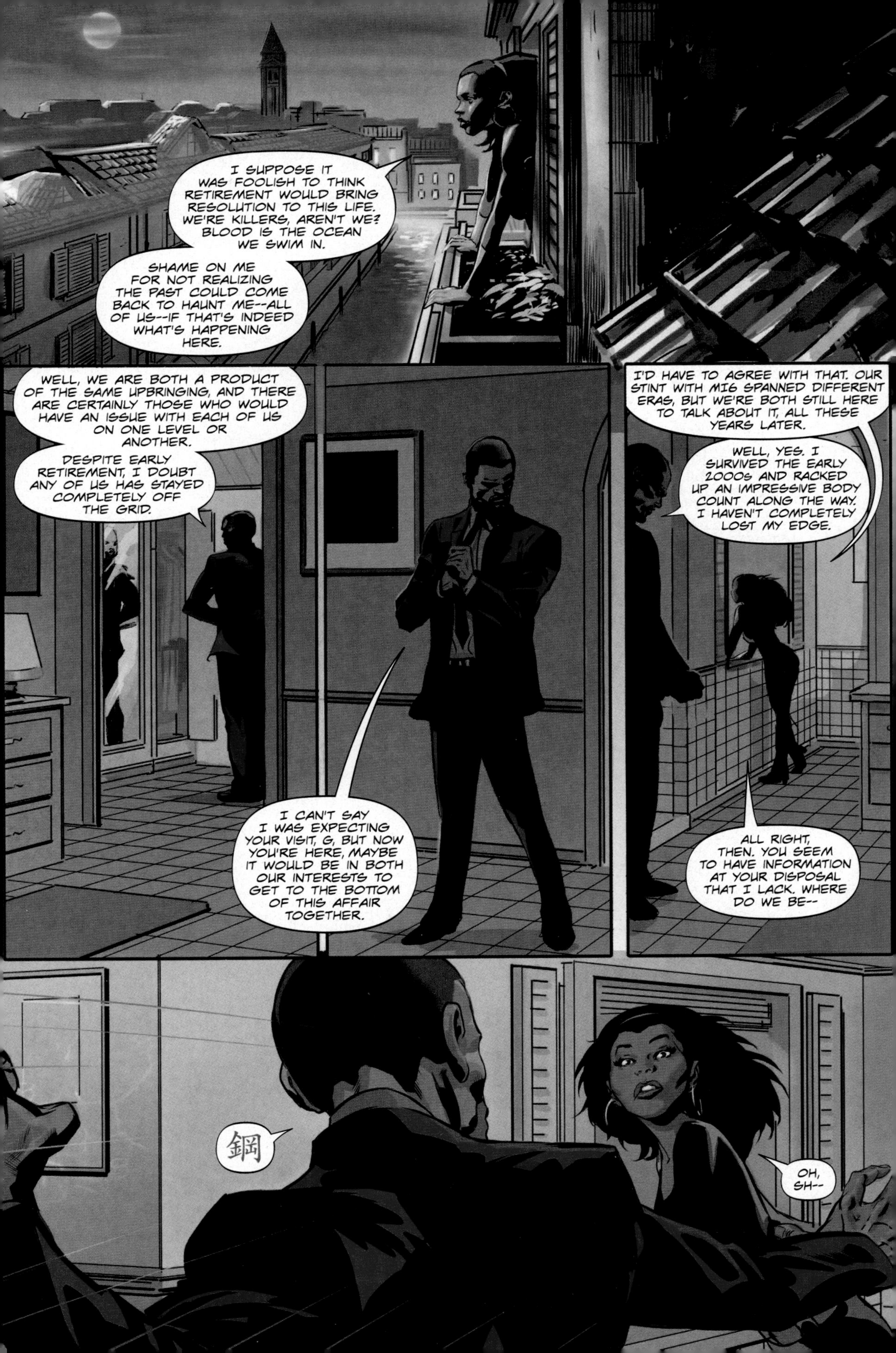

I SUPPOSE IT WAS FOOLISH TO THINK RETIREMENT WOULD BRING RESOLUTION TO THIS LIFE. WE'RE KILLERS, AREN'T WE? BLOOD IS THE OCEAN WE SWIM IN.
SHAME ON ME FOR NOT REALIZING THE PAST COULD COME BACK TO HAUNT ME--ALL OF US--IF THAT'S INDEED WHAT'S HAPPENING HERE.
WELL, WE ARE BOTH A PRODUCT OF THE SAME UPBRINGING, AND THERE ARE CERTAINLY THOSE WHO WOULD HAVE AN ISSUE WITH EACH OF US ON ONE LEVEL OR ANOTHER.
DESPITE EARLY RETIREMENT, I DOUBT ANY OF US HAS STAYED COMPLETELY OFF THE GRID.
I CAN'T SAY I WAS EXPECTING YOUR VISIT, G, BUT NOW YOU'RE HERE, MAYBE IT WOULD BE IN BOTH OUR INTERESTS TO GET TO THE BOTTOM OF THIS AFFAIR TOGETHER.
I'D HAVE TO AGREE WITH THAT. OUR STINT WITH MI6 SPANNED DIFFERENT ERAS, BUT WE'RE BOTH STILL HERE TO TALK ABOUT IT, ALL THESE YEARS LATER.
WELL, YES. I SURVIVED THE EARLY 2000s AND RACKED UP AN IMPRESSIVE BODY COUNT ALONG THE WAY. I HAVEN'T COMPLETELY LOST MY EDGE.
ALL RIGHT, THEN. YOU SEEM TO HAVE INFORMATION AT YOUR DISPOSAL THAT I LACK. WHERE DO WE BE--
鋼
OH, SH--

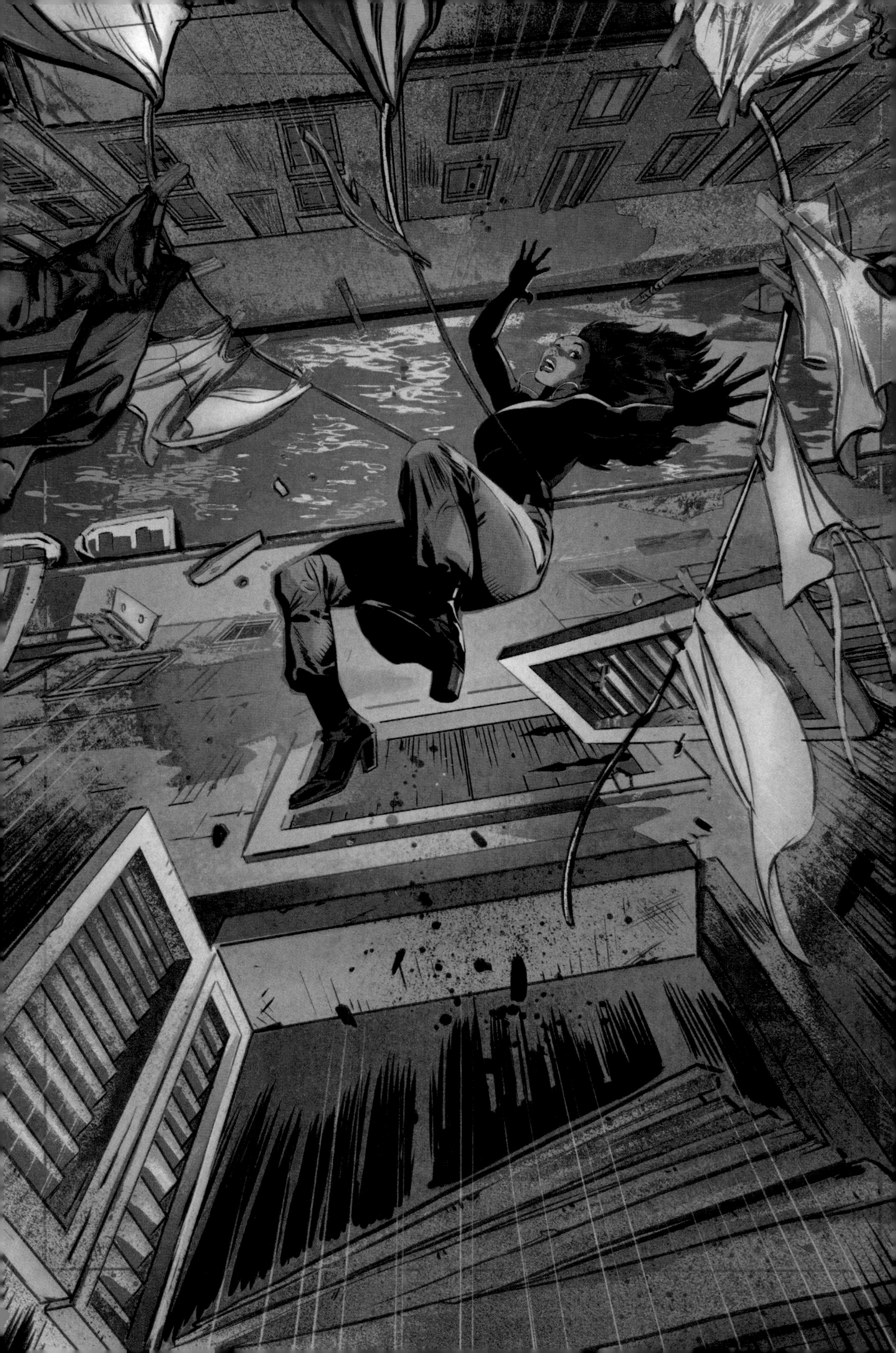

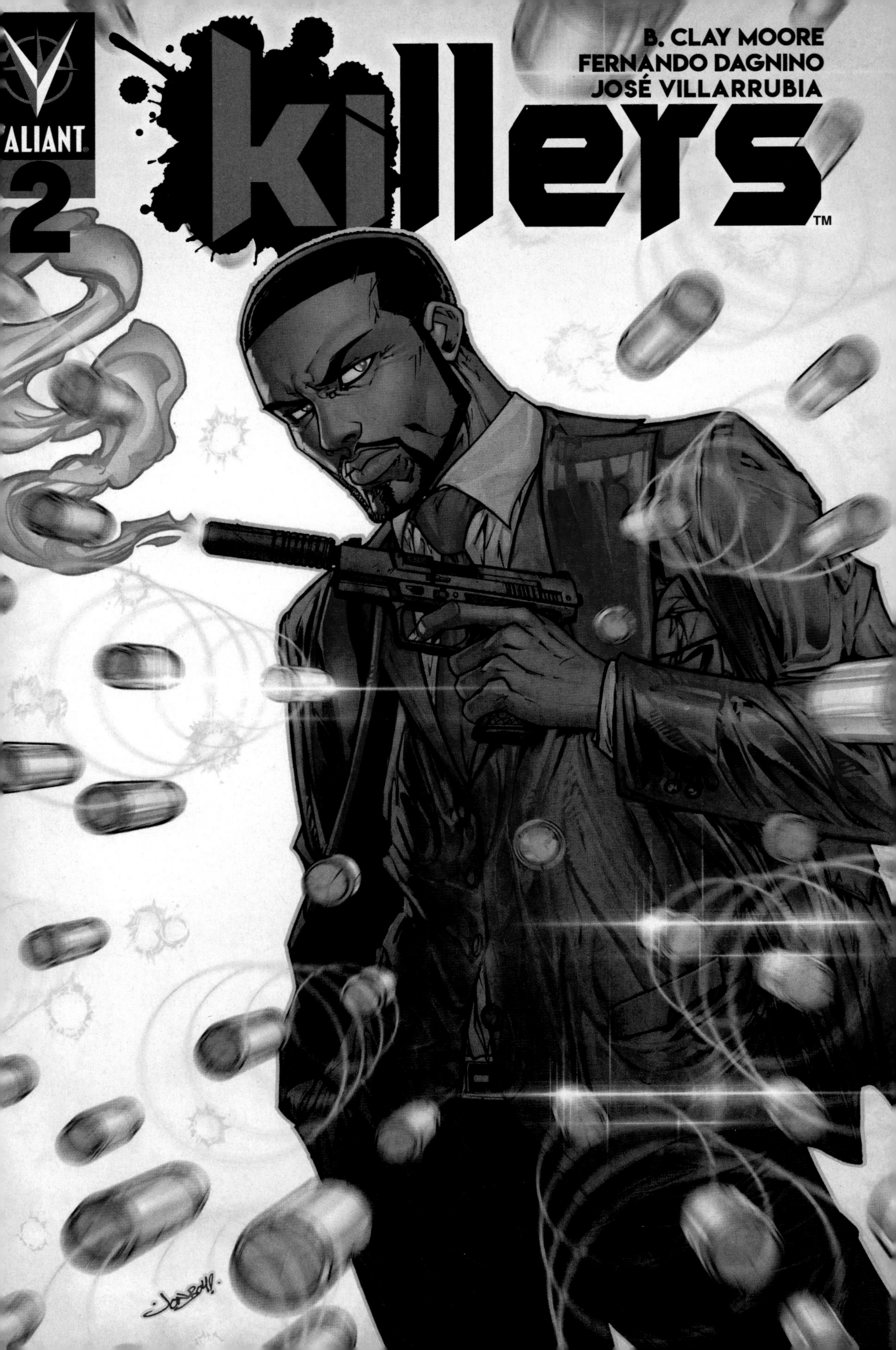
ALIANT
2
killers
TM
B. CLAY MOORE
FERNANDO DAGNINO
JOSÉ VILLARRUBIA

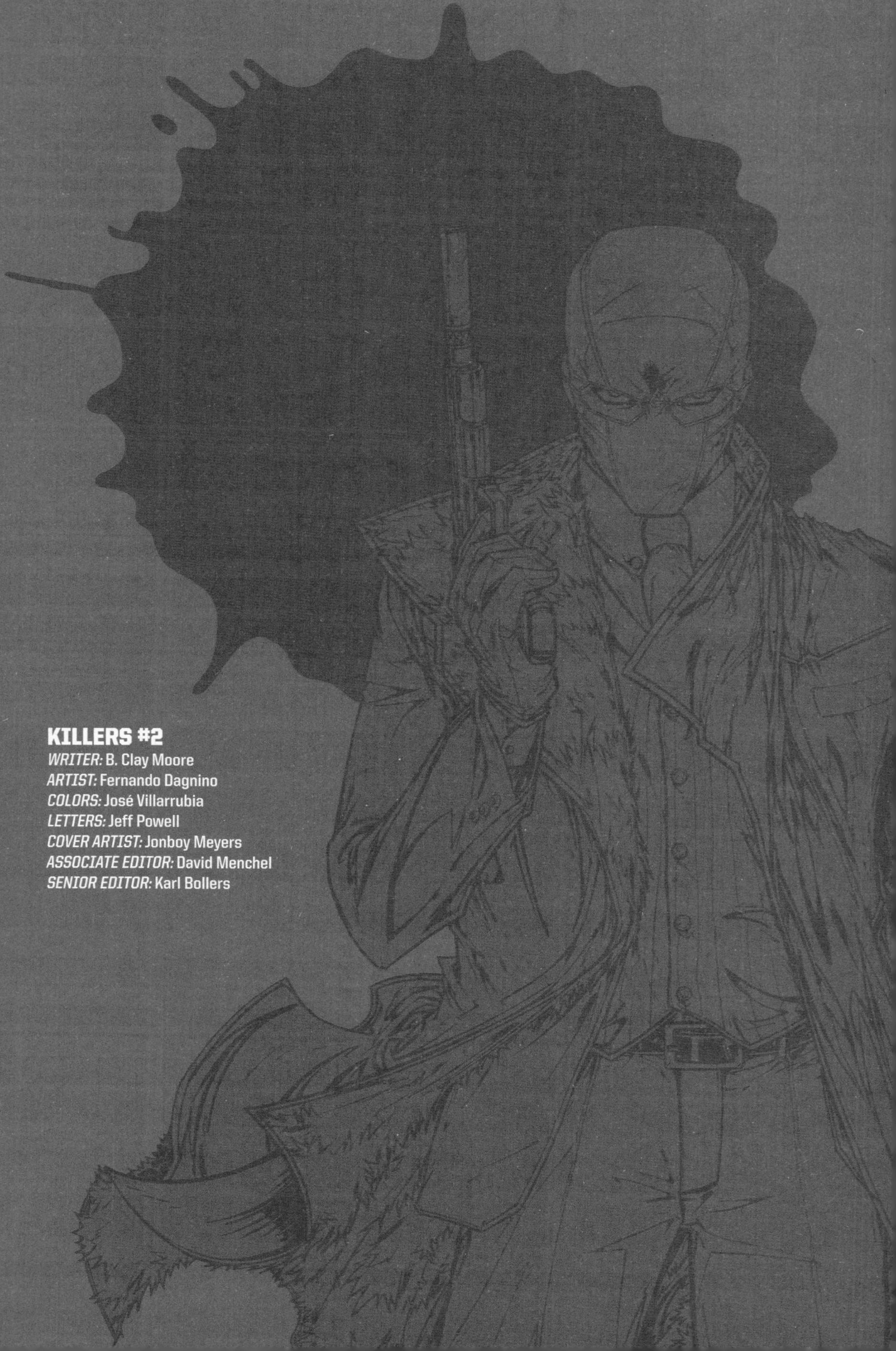

KILLERS #2

WRITER: B. Clay Moore
ARTIST: Fernando Dagnino
COLORS: José Villarrubia
LETTERS: Jeff Powell
COVER ARTIST: Jonboy Meyers
ASSOCIATE EDITOR: David Menchel
SENIOR EDITOR: Karl Bollers

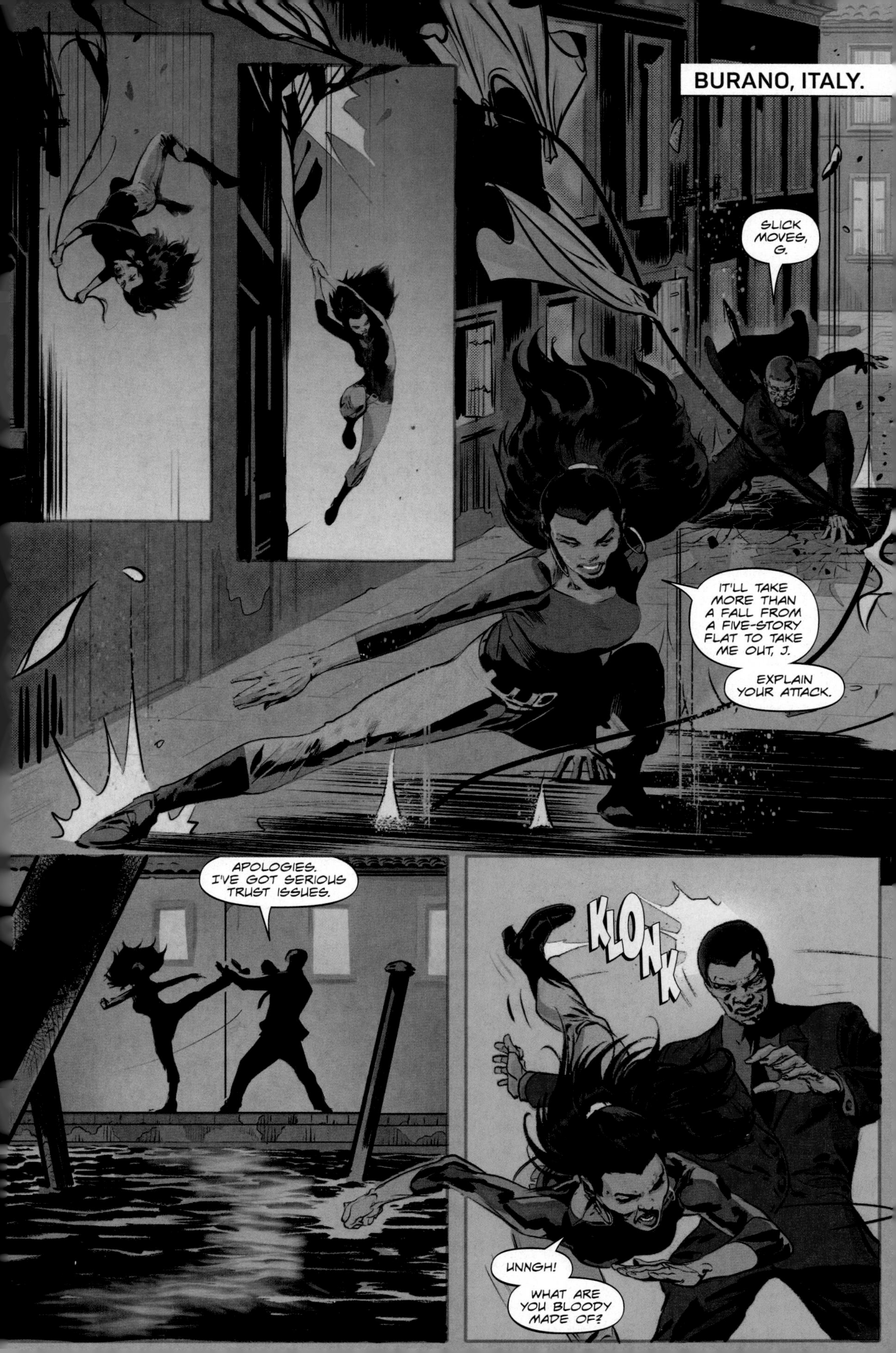
BURANO, ITALY.
SLICK MOVES, G.
IT'LL TAKE MORE THAN A FALL FROM A FIVE-STORY FLAT TO TAKE ME OUT, J.
EXPLAIN YOUR ATTACK.
APOLOGIES. I'VE GOT SERIOUS TRUST ISSUES.
KLONK
UNNGH!
WHAT ARE YOU BLOODY MADE OF?

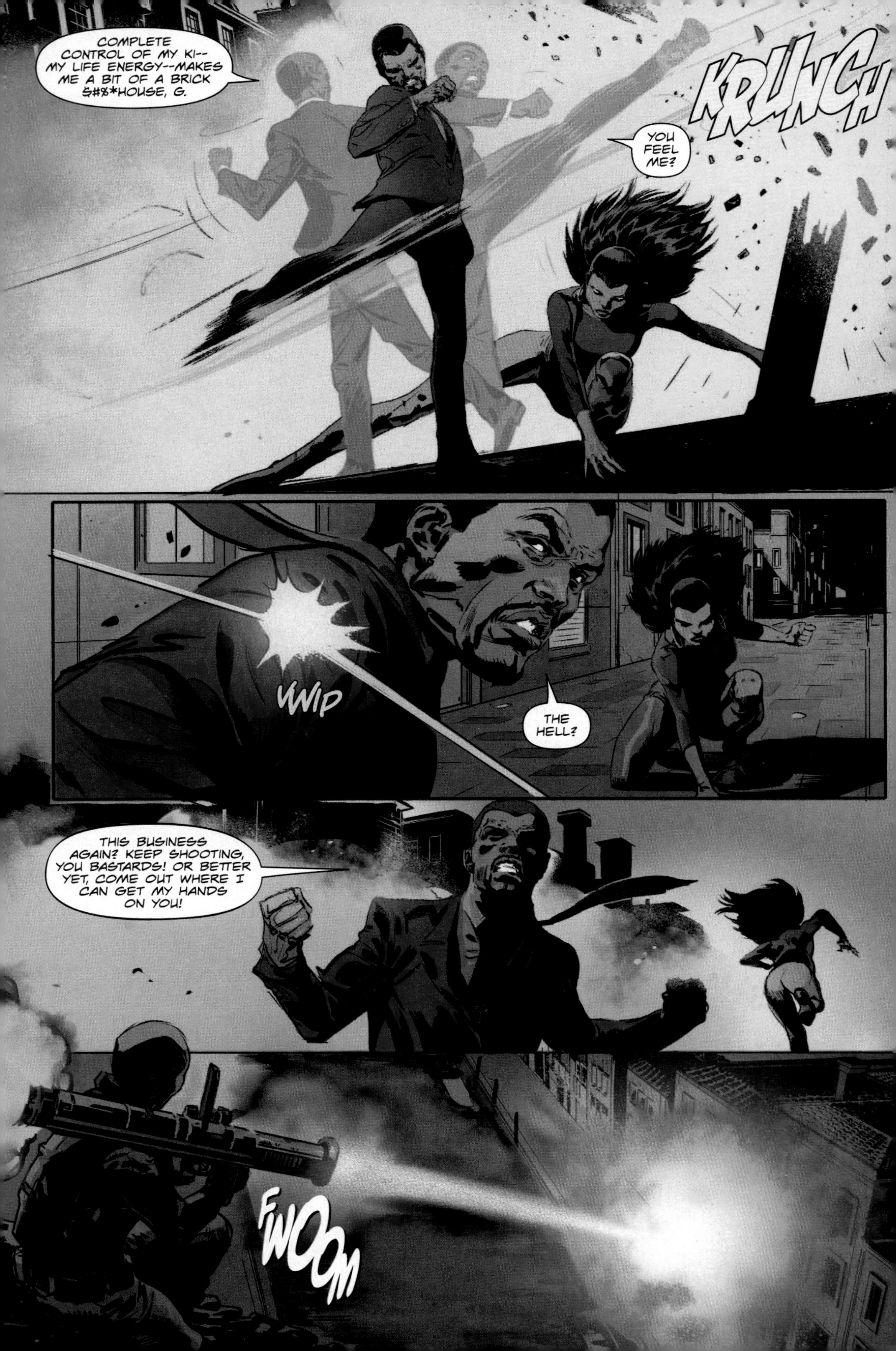
COMPLETE CONTROL OF MY KI-- MY LIFE ENERGY--MAKES ME A BIT OF A BRICK $#&*HOUSE, G.
KRUNCH
YOU FEEL ME?
VWIP
THE HELL?
THIS BUSINESS AGAIN? KEEP SHOOTING, YOU BASTARDS! OR BETTER YET, COME OUT WHERE I CAN GET MY HANDS ON YOU!
FWOOM

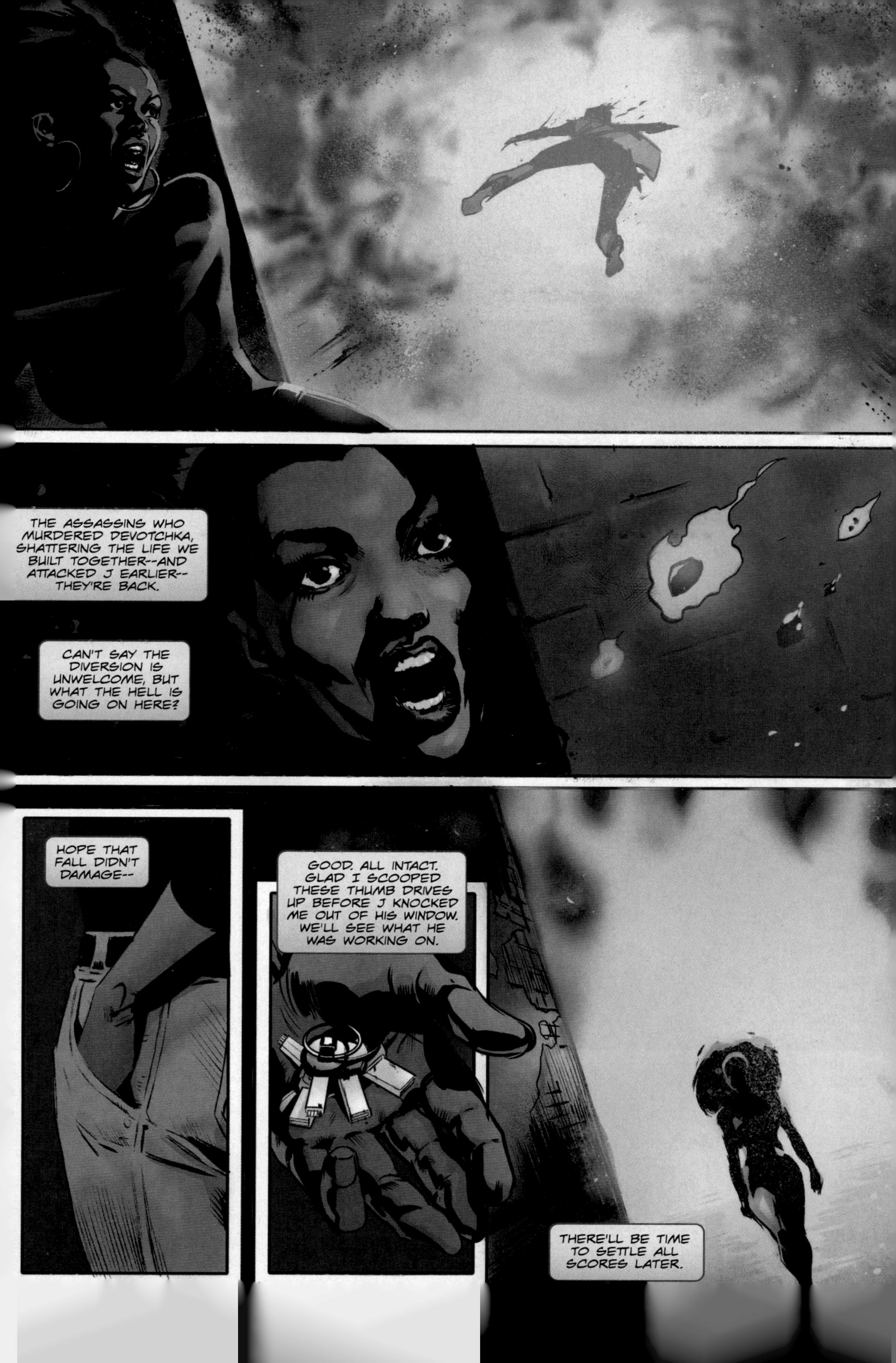
THE ASSASSINS WHO MURDERED DEVOTCHKA, SHATTERING THE LIFE WE BUILT TOGETHER--AND ATTACKED J EARLIER--THEY'RE BACK.
CAN'T SAY THE DIVERSION IS UNWELCOME, BUT WHAT THE HELL IS GOING ON HERE?
HOPE THAT FALL DIDN'T DAMAGE--
GOOD. ALL INTACT. GLAD I SCOOPED THESE THUMB DRIVES UP BEFORE J KNOCKED ME OUT OF HIS WINDOW. WE'LL SEE WHAT HE WAS WORKING ON.
THERE'LL BE TIME TO SETTLE ALL SCORES LATER.

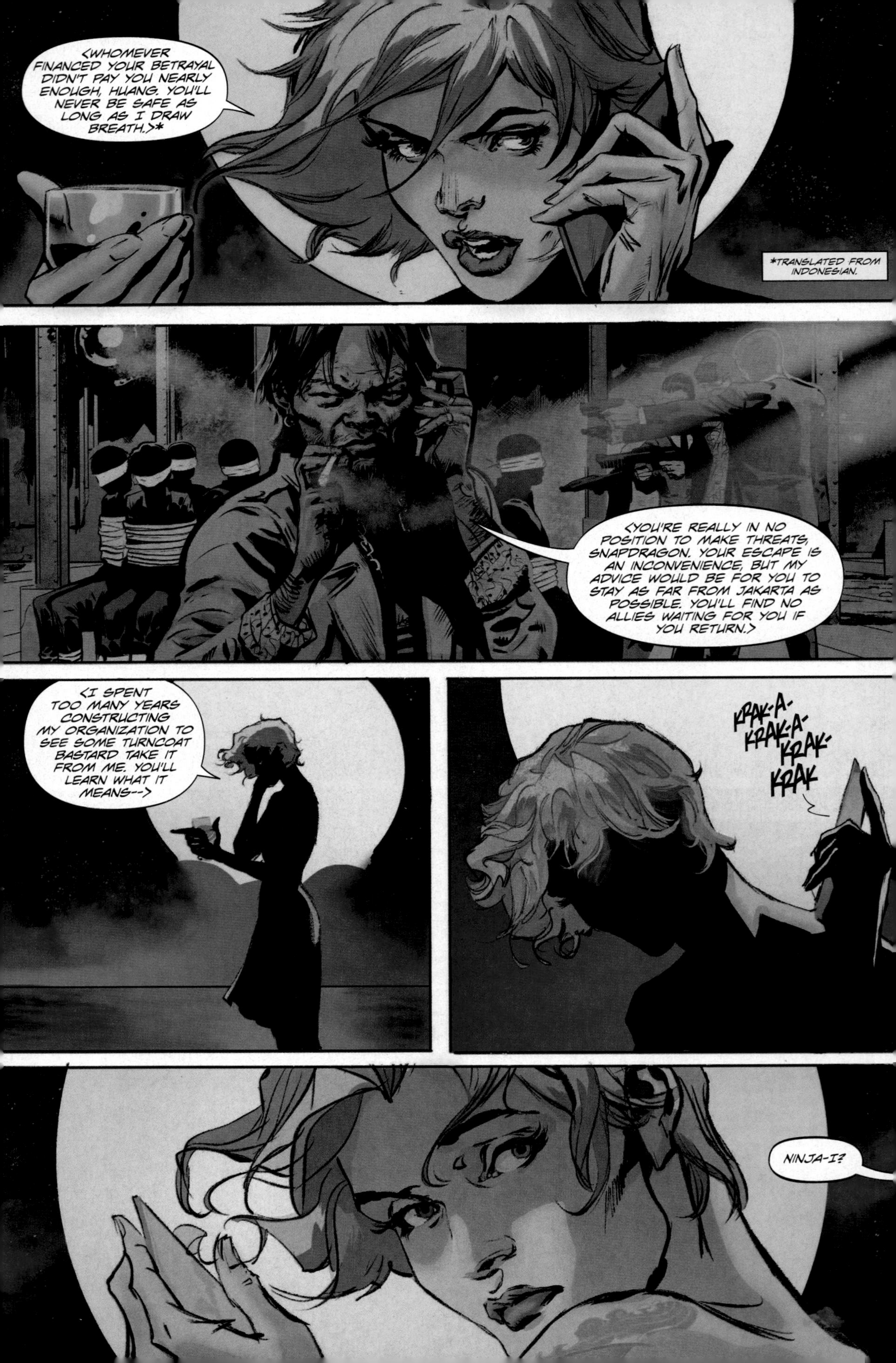
<WHOMEVER FINANCED YOUR BETRAYAL DIDN'T PAY YOU NEARLY ENOUGH, HUANG. YOU'LL NEVER BE SAFE AS LONG AS I DRAW BREATH.>*
*TRANSLATED FROM INDONESIAN.
<YOU'RE REALLY IN NO POSITION TO MAKE THREATS, SNAPDRAGON. YOUR ESCAPE IS AN INCONVENIENCE, BUT MY ADVICE WOULD BE FOR YOU TO STAY AS FAR FROM JAKARTA AS POSSIBLE. YOU'LL FIND NO ALLIES WAITING FOR YOU IF YOU RETURN.>
<I SPENT TOO MANY YEARS CONSTRUCTING MY ORGANIZATION TO SEE SOME TURNCOAT BASTARD TAKE IT FROM ME. YOU'LL LEARN WHAT IT MEANS-->
KRAK-A-KRAK-A-KRAK-KRAK
NINJA-I?

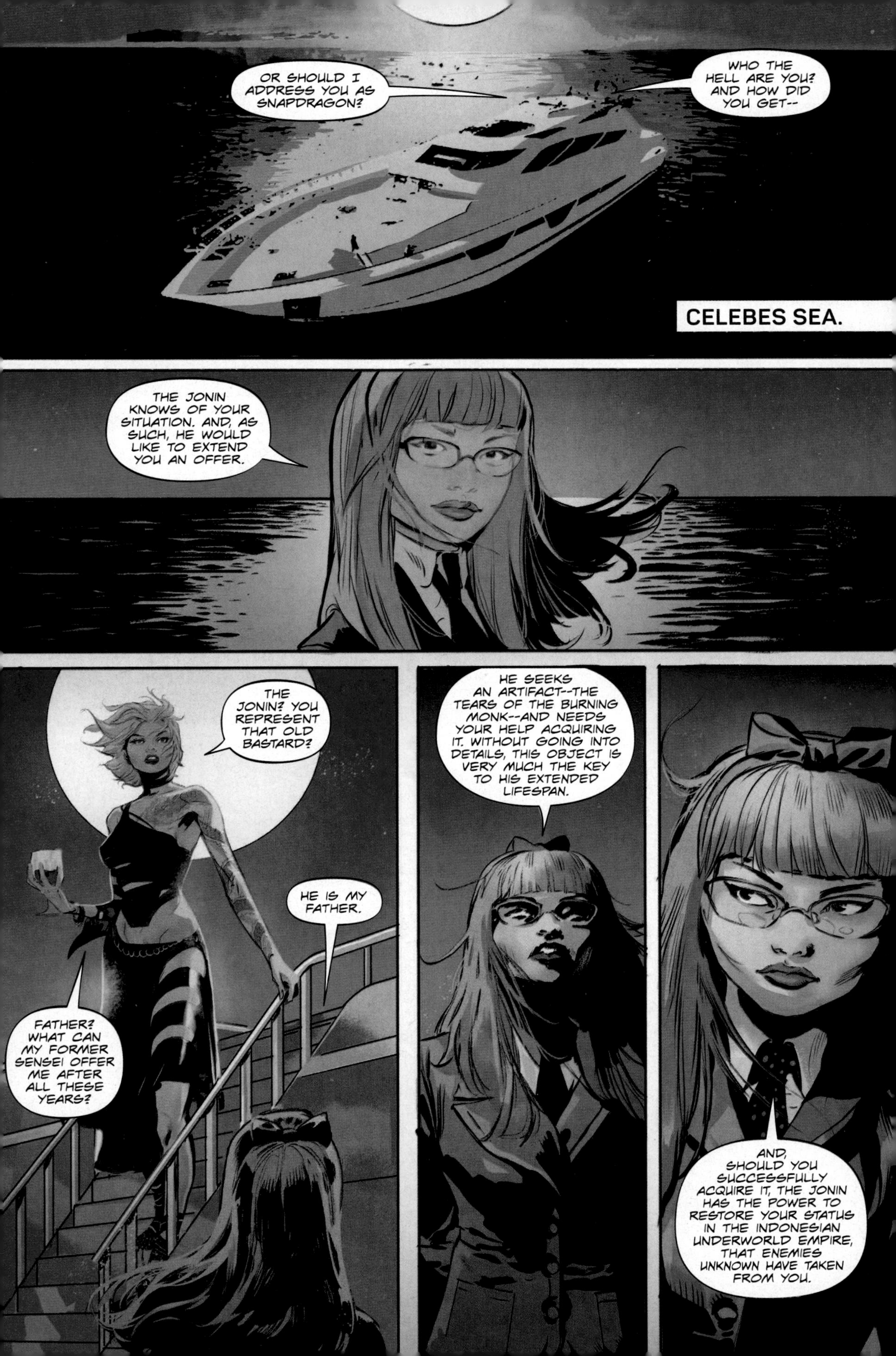
OR SHOULD I ADDRESS YOU AS SNAPDRAGON?
WHO THE HELL ARE YOU? AND HOW DID YOU GET--
CELEBES SEA.
THE JONIN KNOWS OF YOUR SITUATION. AND, AS SUCH, HE WOULD LIKE TO EXTEND YOU AN OFFER.
THE JONIN? YOU REPRESENT THAT OLD BASTARD?
HE IS MY FATHER.
FATHER? WHAT CAN MY FORMER SENSEI OFFER ME AFTER ALL THESE YEARS?
HE SEEKS AN ARTIFACT--THE TEARS OF THE BURNING MONK--AND NEEDS YOUR HELP ACQUIRING IT. WITHOUT GOING INTO DETAILS, THIS OBJECT IS VERY MUCH THE KEY TO HIS EXTENDED LIFESPAN.
AND, SHOULD YOU SUCCESSFULLY ACQUIRE IT, THE JONIN HAS THE POWER TO RESTORE YOUR STATUS IN THE INDONESIAN UNDERWORLD EMPIRE, THAT ENEMIES UNKNOWN HAVE TAKEN FROM YOU.

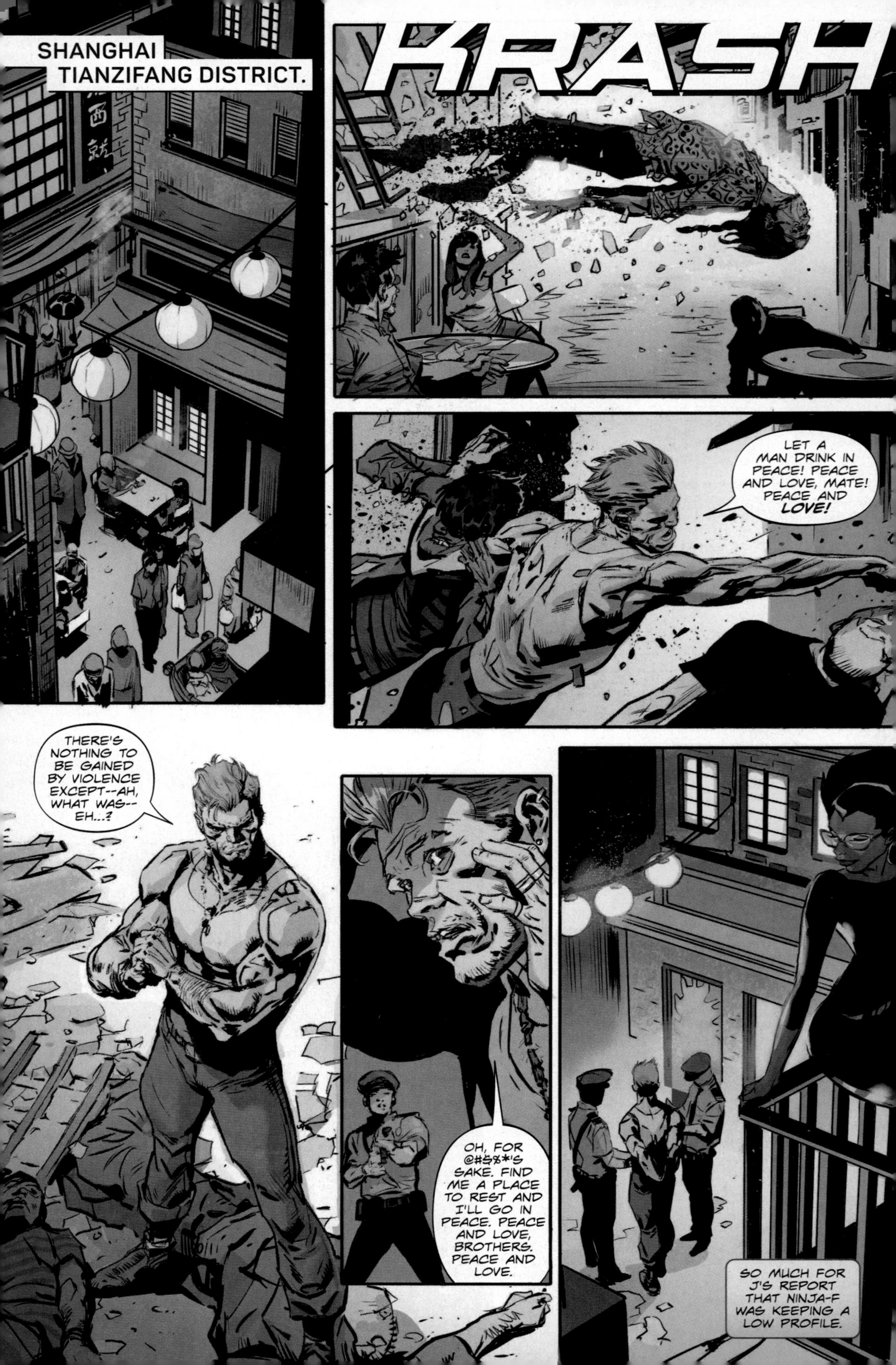
SHANGHAI TIANZIFANG DISTRICT.
KRASH
LET A MAN DRINK IN PEACE! PEACE AND LOVE, MATE! PEACE AND ***LOVE!***
THERE'S NOTHING TO BE GAINED BY VIOLENCE EXCEPT--AH, WHAT WAS--EH...?
OH, FOR @#$%*'S SAKE. FIND ME A PLACE TO REST AND I'LL GO IN PEACE. PEACE AND LOVE, BROTHERS. PEACE AND LOVE.
SO MUCH FOR J'S REPORT THAT NINJA-F WAS KEEPING A LOW PROFILE.

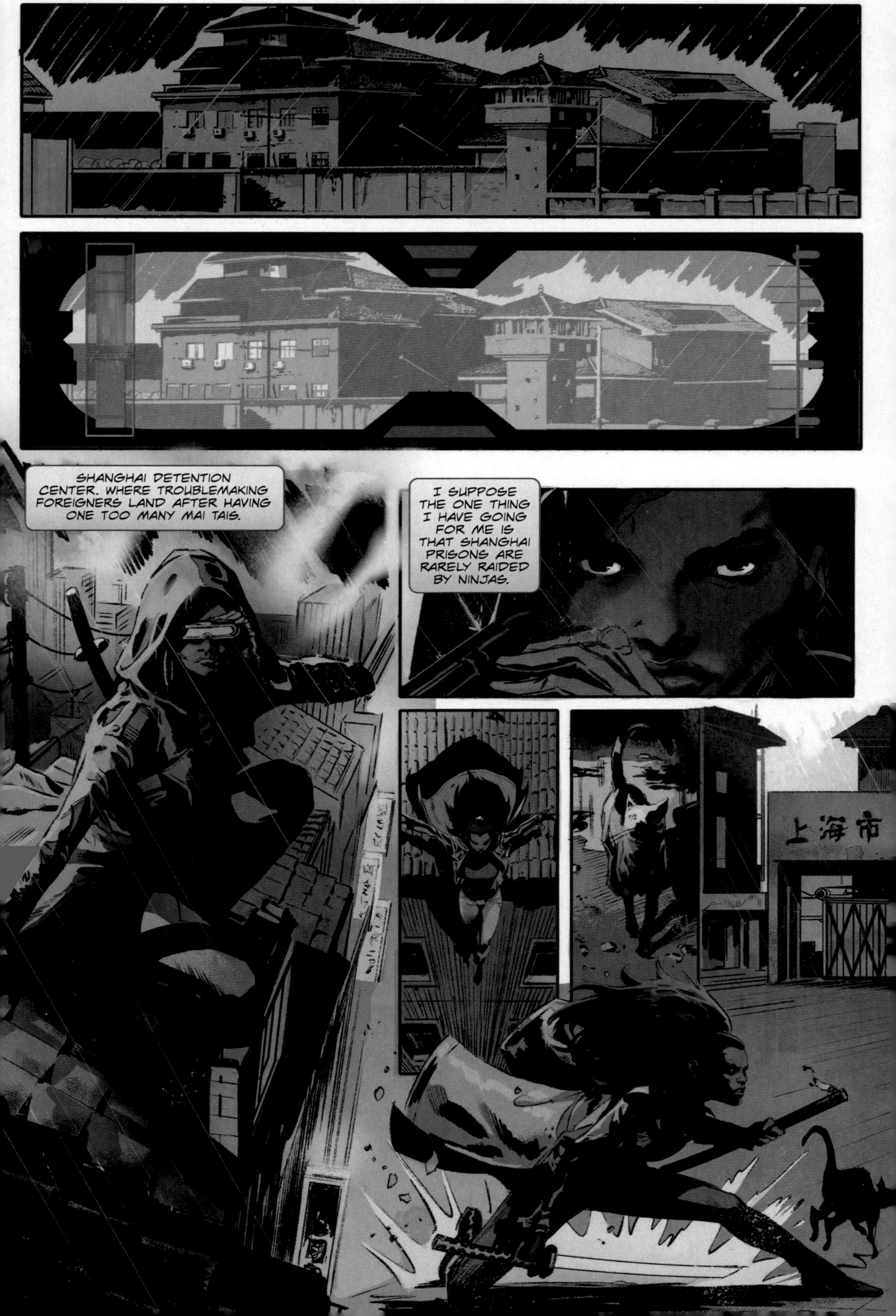
SHANGHAI DETENTION CENTER. WHERE TROUBLEMAKING FOREIGNERS LAND AFTER HAVING ONE TOO MANY MAI TAIS.
I SUPPOSE THE ONE THING I HAVE GOING FOR ME IS THAT SHANGHAI PRISONS ARE RARELY RAIDED BY NINJAS.
上海市

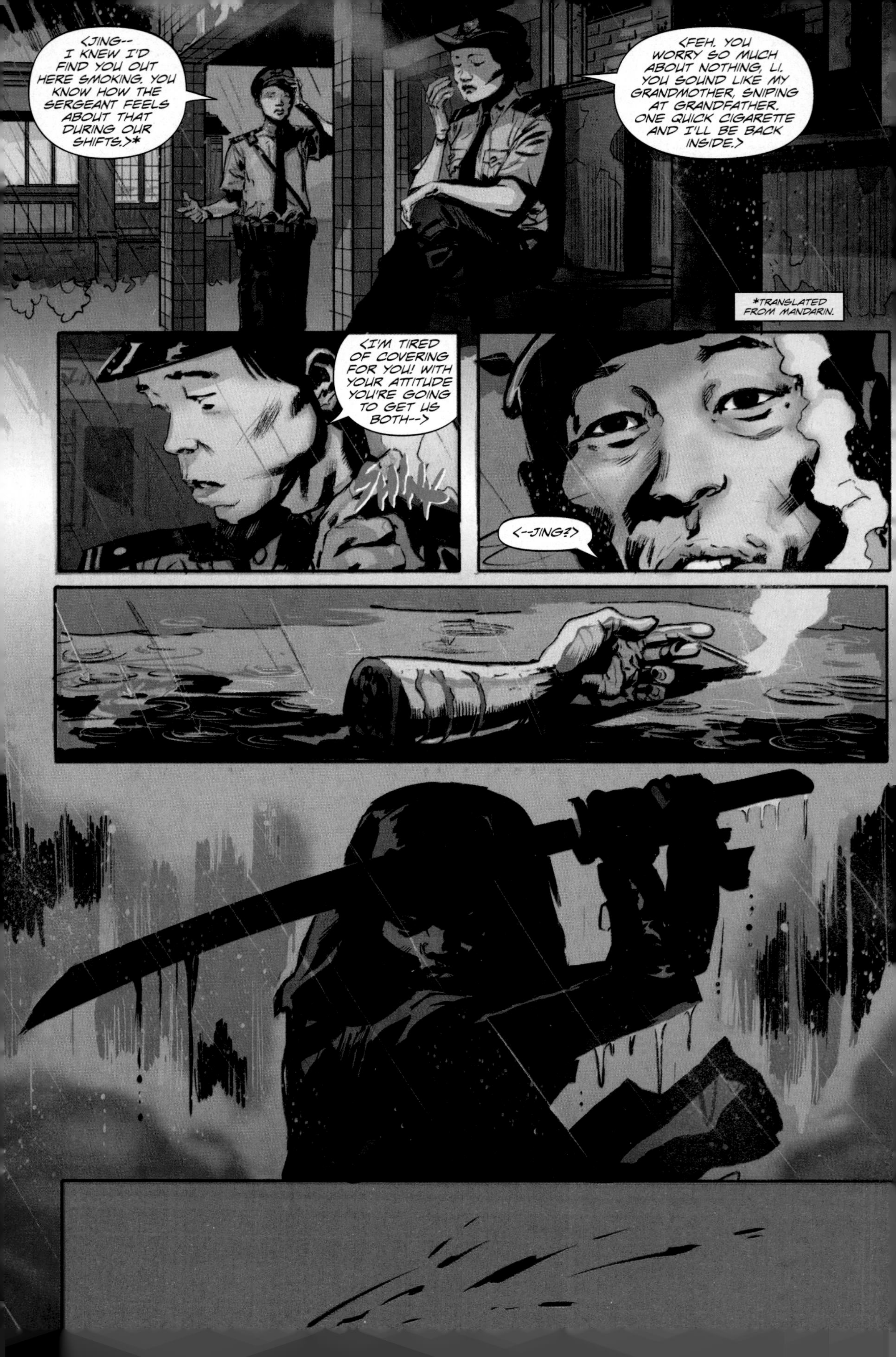
<JING-- I KNEW I'D FIND YOU OUT HERE SMOKING. YOU KNOW HOW THE SERGEANT FEELS ABOUT THAT DURING OUR SHIFTS.>*
<FEH. YOU WORRY SO MUCH ABOUT NOTHING, LI. YOU SOUND LIKE MY GRANDMOTHER, SNIPING AT GRANDFATHER. ONE QUICK CIGARETTE AND I'LL BE BACK INSIDE.>
*TRANSLATED FROM MANDARIN.
<I'M TIRED OF COVERING FOR YOU! WITH YOUR ATTITUDE YOU'RE GOING TO GET US BOTH-->
SHINK
<--JING?>

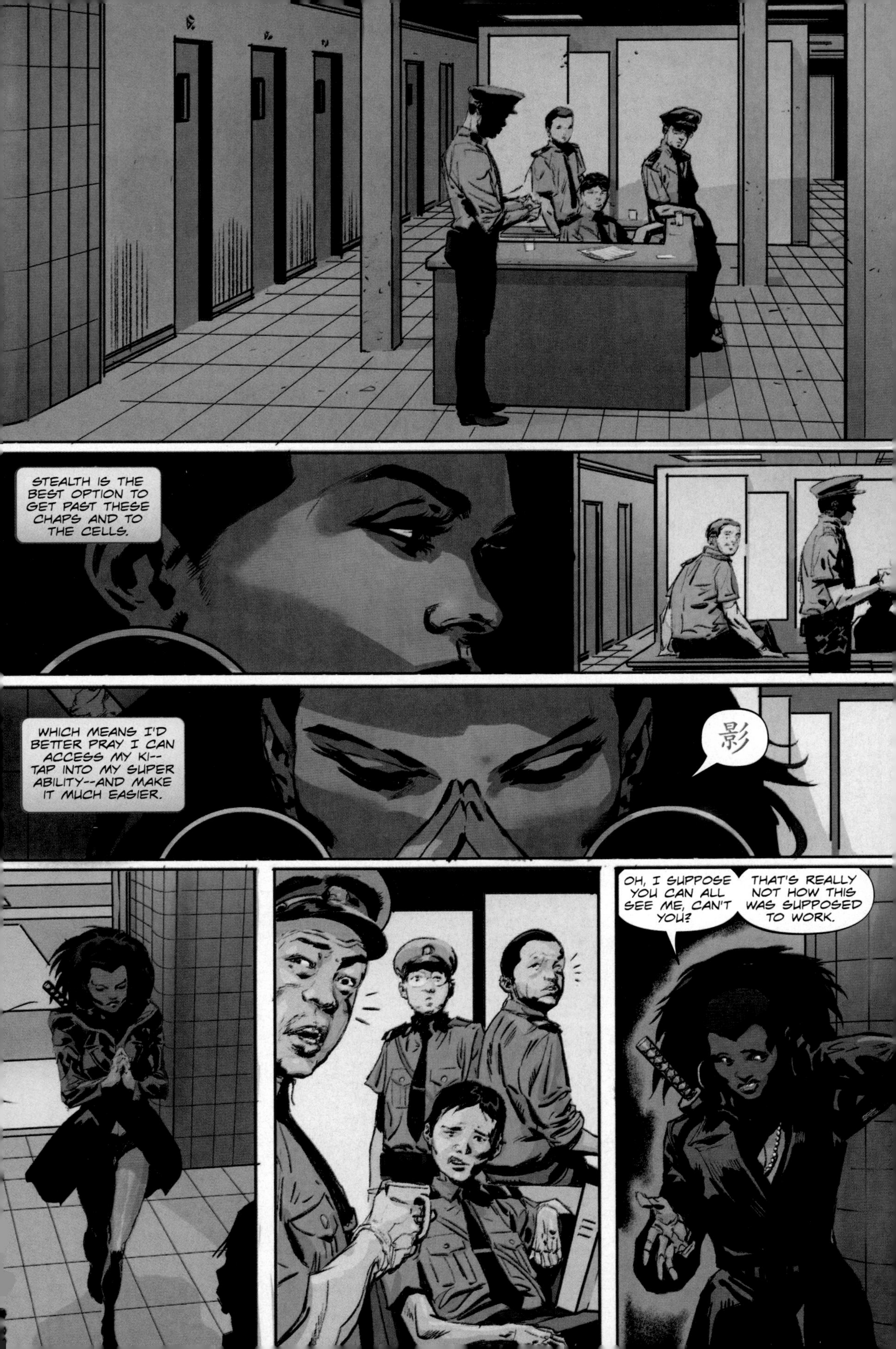
STEALTH IS THE BEST OPTION TO GET PAST THESE CHAPS AND TO THE CELLS.
WHICH MEANS I'D BETTER PRAY I CAN ACCESS MY KI--TAP INTO MY SUPER ABILITY--AND MAKE IT MUCH EASIER.
影
OH, I SUPPOSE YOU CAN ALL SEE ME, CAN'T YOU?
THAT'S REALLY NOT HOW THIS WAS SUPPOSED TO WORK.

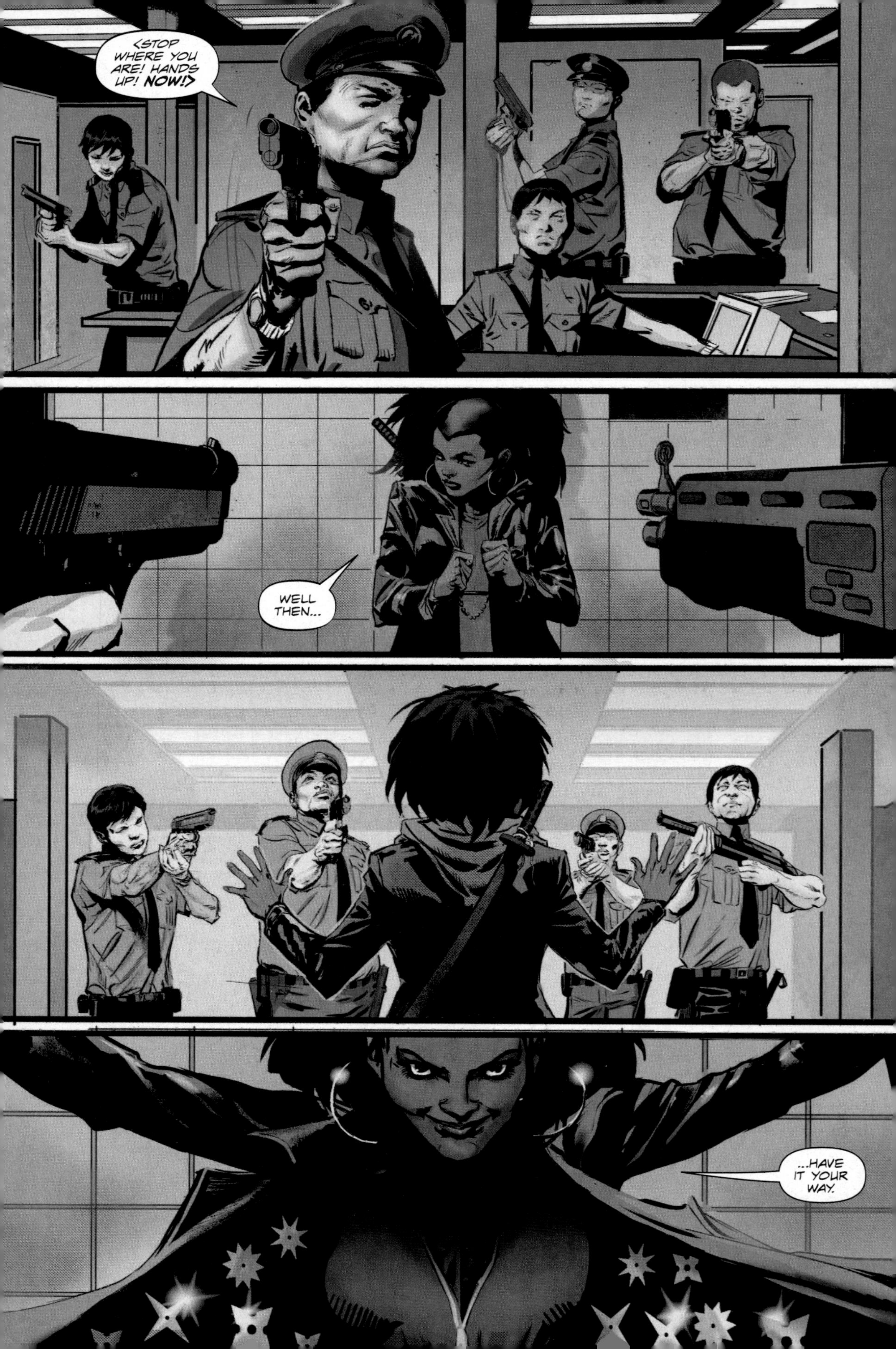
<STOP WHERE YOU ARE! HANDS UP! **NOW!**>
WELL THEN...
...HAVE IT YOUR WAY.

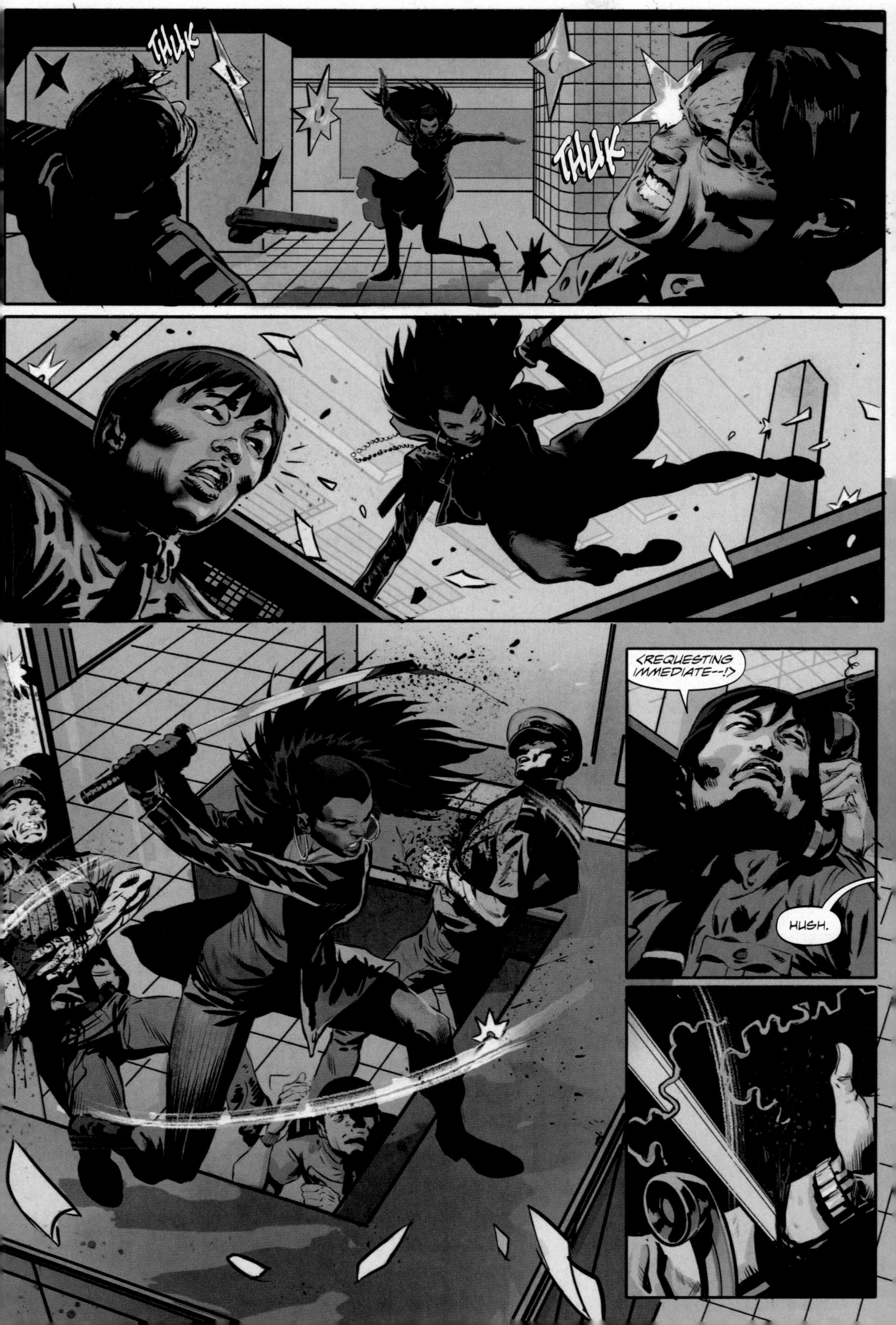
THUK
THUK
<REQUESTING IMMEDIATE--!>
HUSH.

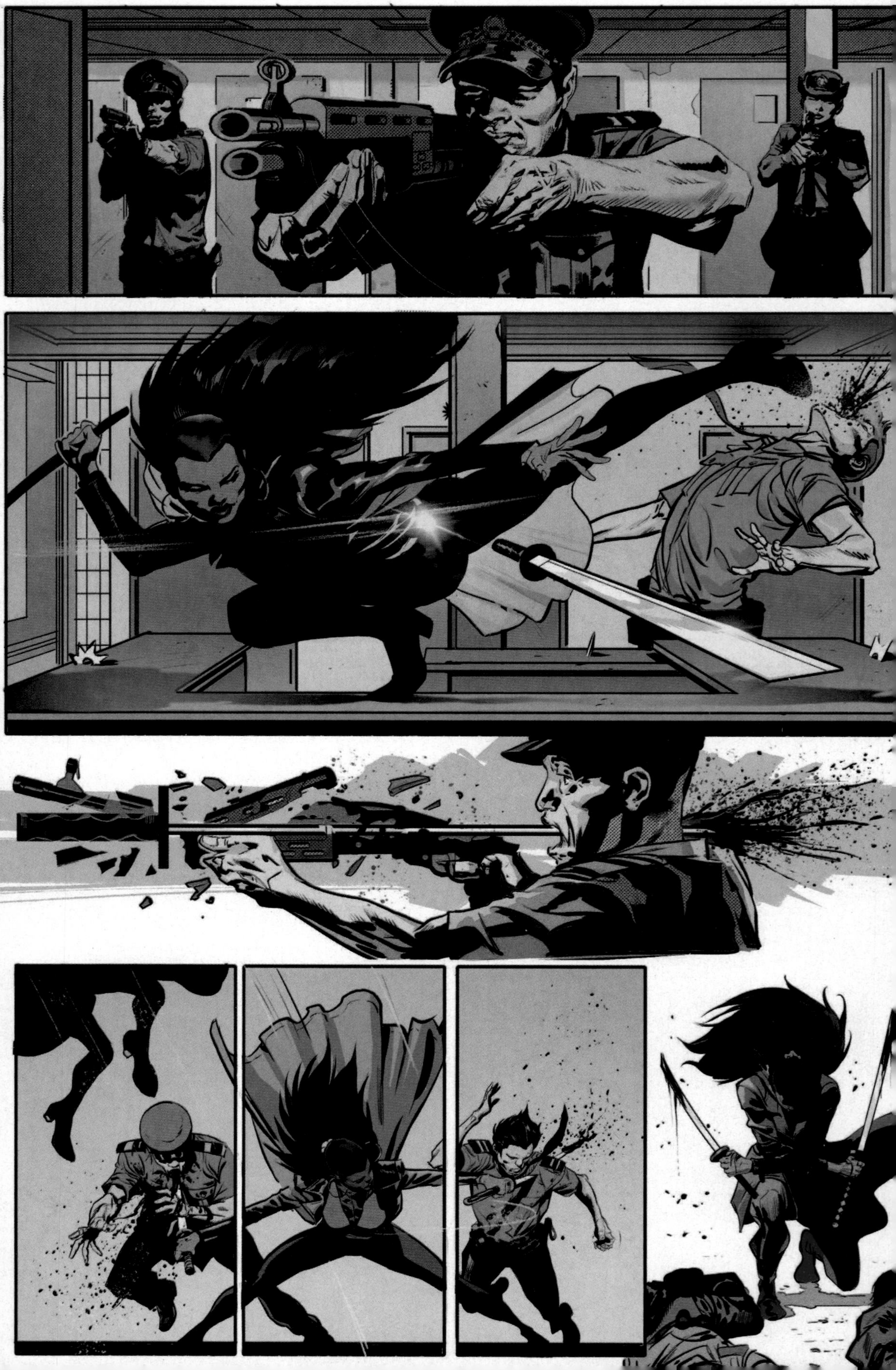

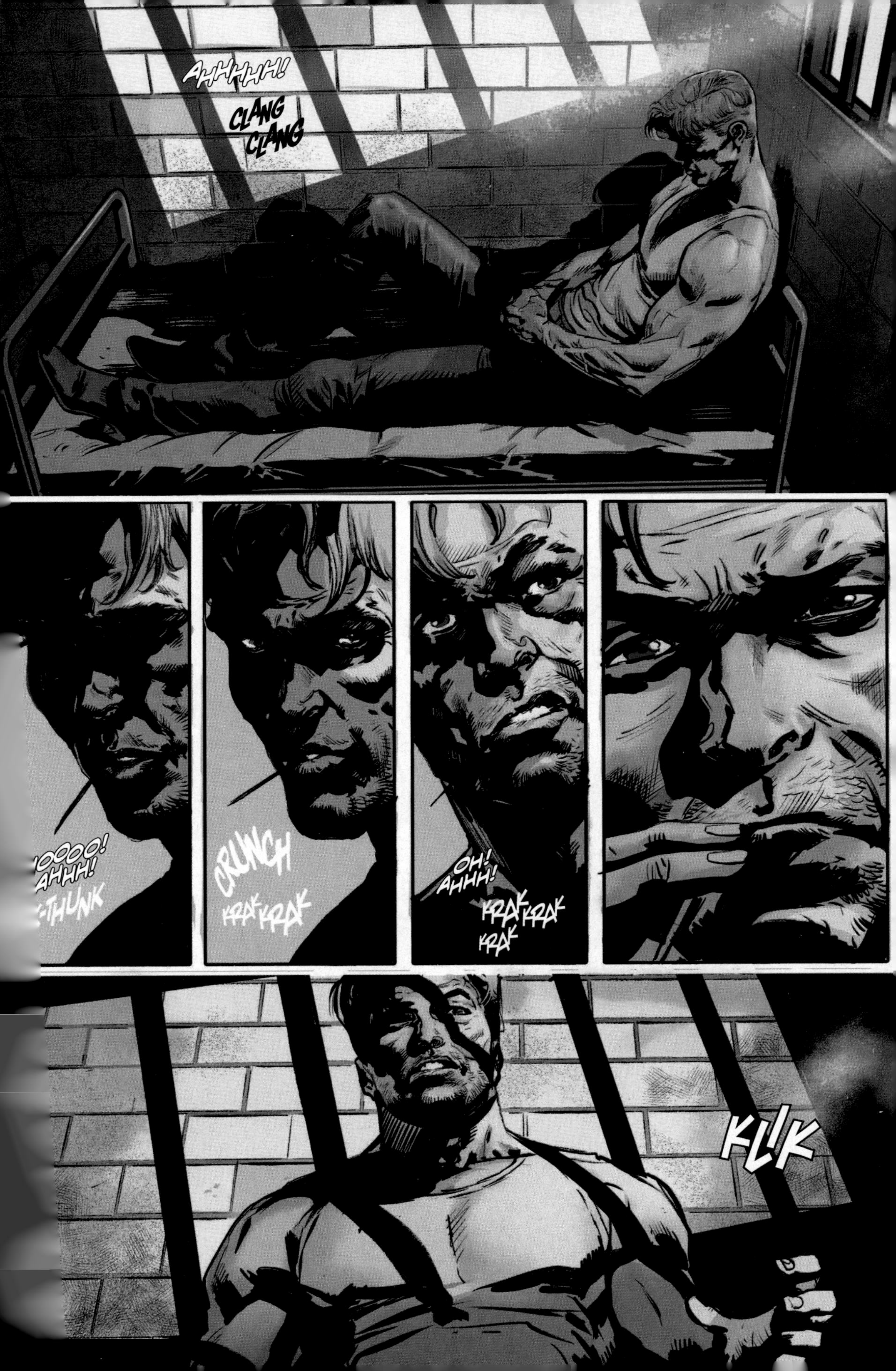
AHHHHH!
CLANG
CLANG
OOOO!
AHHH!
-THUNK
CRUNCH
KRAK KRAK
OH!
AHHH!
KRAK KRAK
KRAK
KLIK

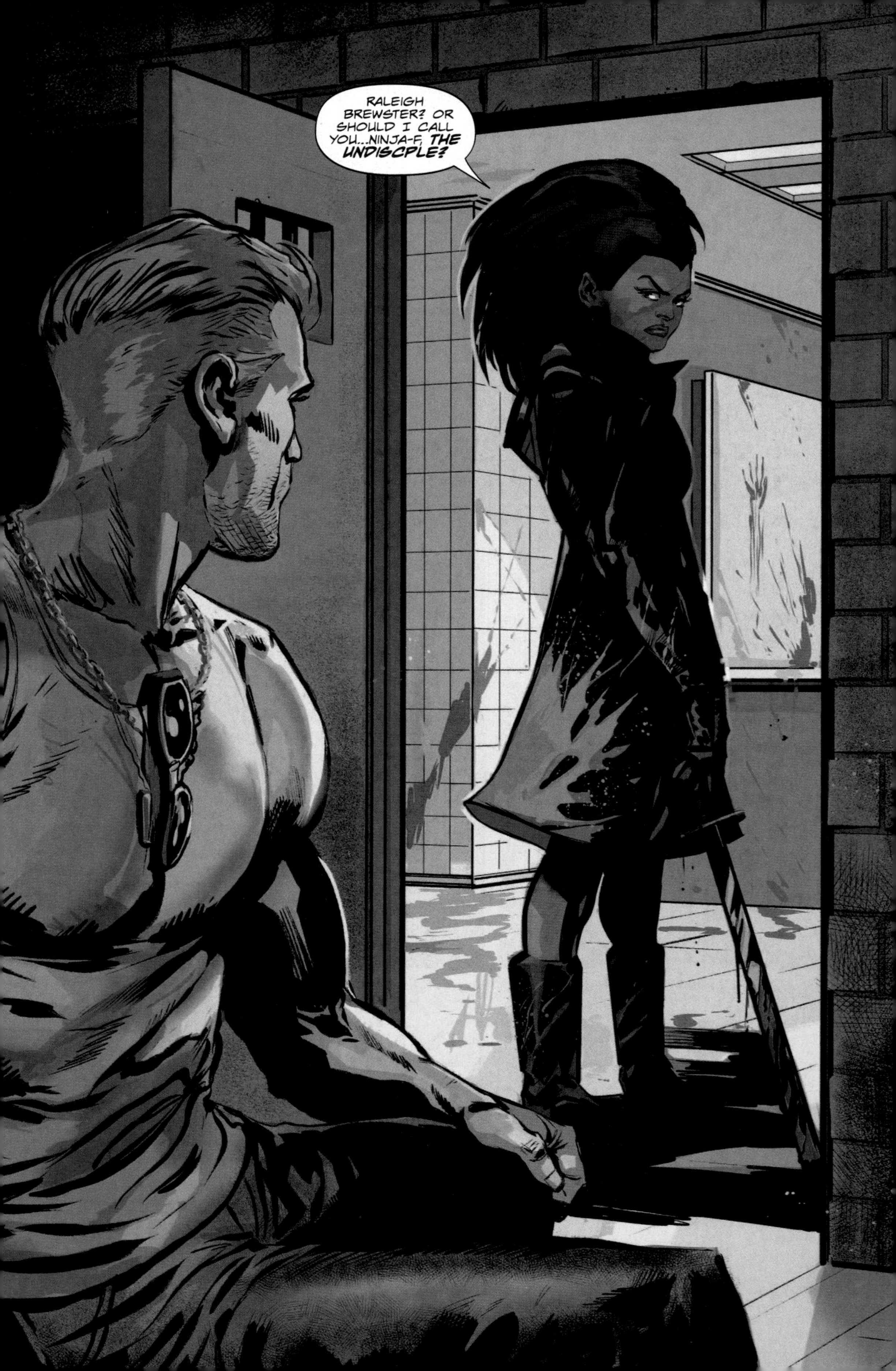
RALEIGH BREWSTER? OR SHOULD I CALL YOU...NINJA-F, THE UNDISCPLE?

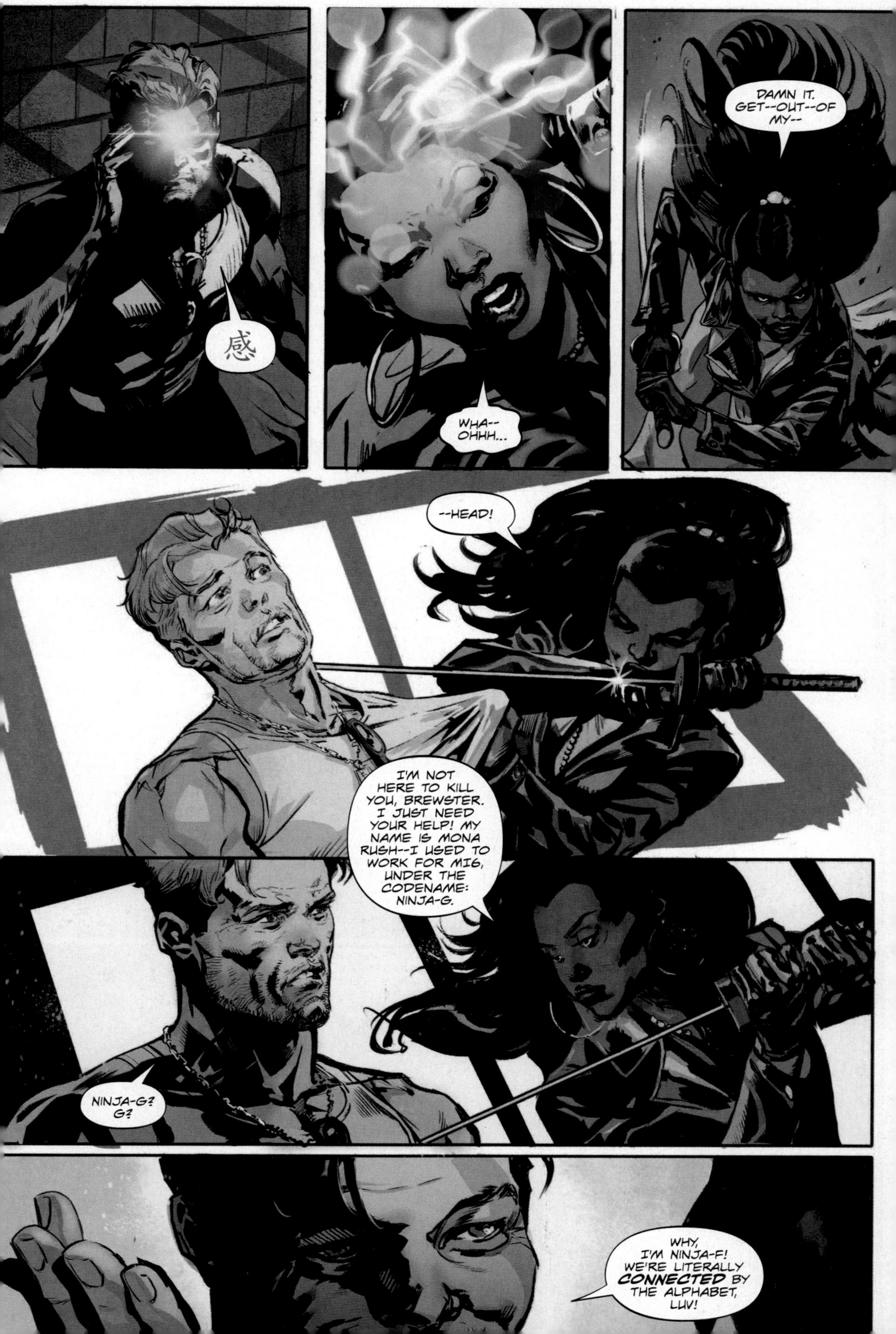
感
WHA--
OHHH...
DAMN IT. GET--OUT--OF MY--
--HEAD!
I'M NOT HERE TO KILL YOU, BREWSTER. I JUST NEED YOUR HELP! MY NAME IS MONA RUSH--I USED TO WORK FOR MI6, UNDER THE CODENAME: NINJA-G.
NINJA-G? G?
WHY, I'M NINJA-F! WE'RE LITERALLY **CONNECTED** BY THE ALPHABET, LUV!

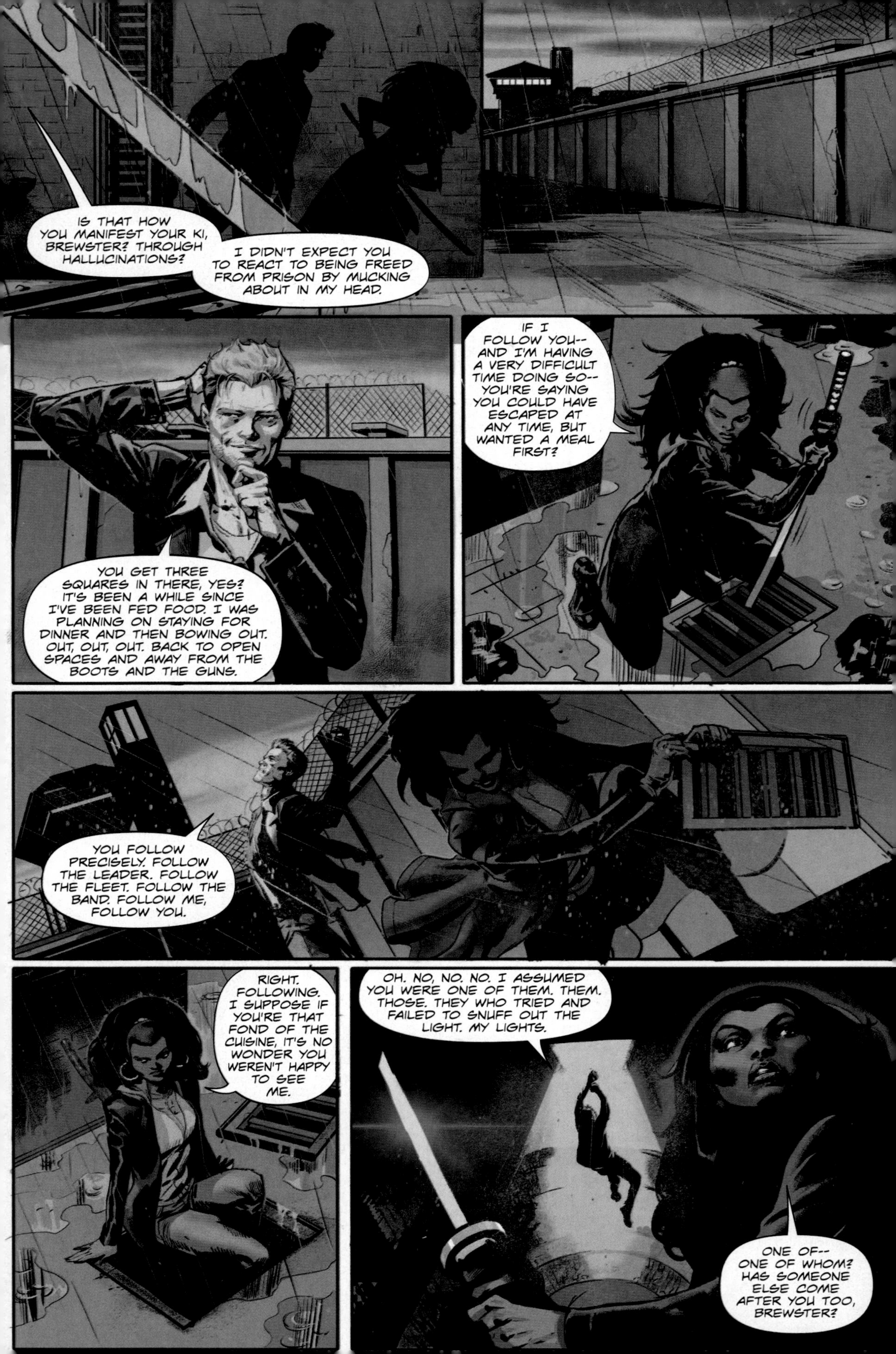
IS THAT HOW YOU MANIFEST YOUR KI, BREWSTER? THROUGH HALLUCINATIONS?
I DIDN'T EXPECT YOU TO REACT TO BEING FREED FROM PRISON BY MUCKING ABOUT IN MY HEAD.
YOU GET THREE SQUARES IN THERE, YES? IT'S BEEN A WHILE SINCE I'VE BEEN FED FOOD. I WAS PLANNING ON STAYING FOR DINNER AND THEN BOWING OUT. OUT, OUT, OUT. BACK TO OPEN SPACES AND AWAY FROM THE BOOTS AND THE GUNS.
IF I FOLLOW YOU-- AND I'M HAVING A VERY DIFFICULT TIME DOING SO-- YOU'RE SAYING YOU COULD HAVE ESCAPED AT ANY TIME, BUT WANTED A MEAL FIRST?
YOU FOLLOW PRECISELY. FOLLOW THE LEADER. FOLLOW THE FLEET. FOLLOW THE BAND. FOLLOW ME, FOLLOW YOU.
RIGHT. FOLLOWING. I SUPPOSE IF YOU'RE THAT FOND OF THE CUISINE, IT'S NO WONDER YOU WEREN'T HAPPY TO SEE ME.
OH. NO, NO. NO. I ASSUMED YOU WERE ONE OF THEM. THEM. THOSE. THEY WHO TRIED AND FAILED TO SNUFF OUT THE LIGHT. MY LIGHTS.
ONE OF-- ONE OF WHOM? HAS SOMEONE ELSE COME AFTER YOU TOO, BREWSTER?

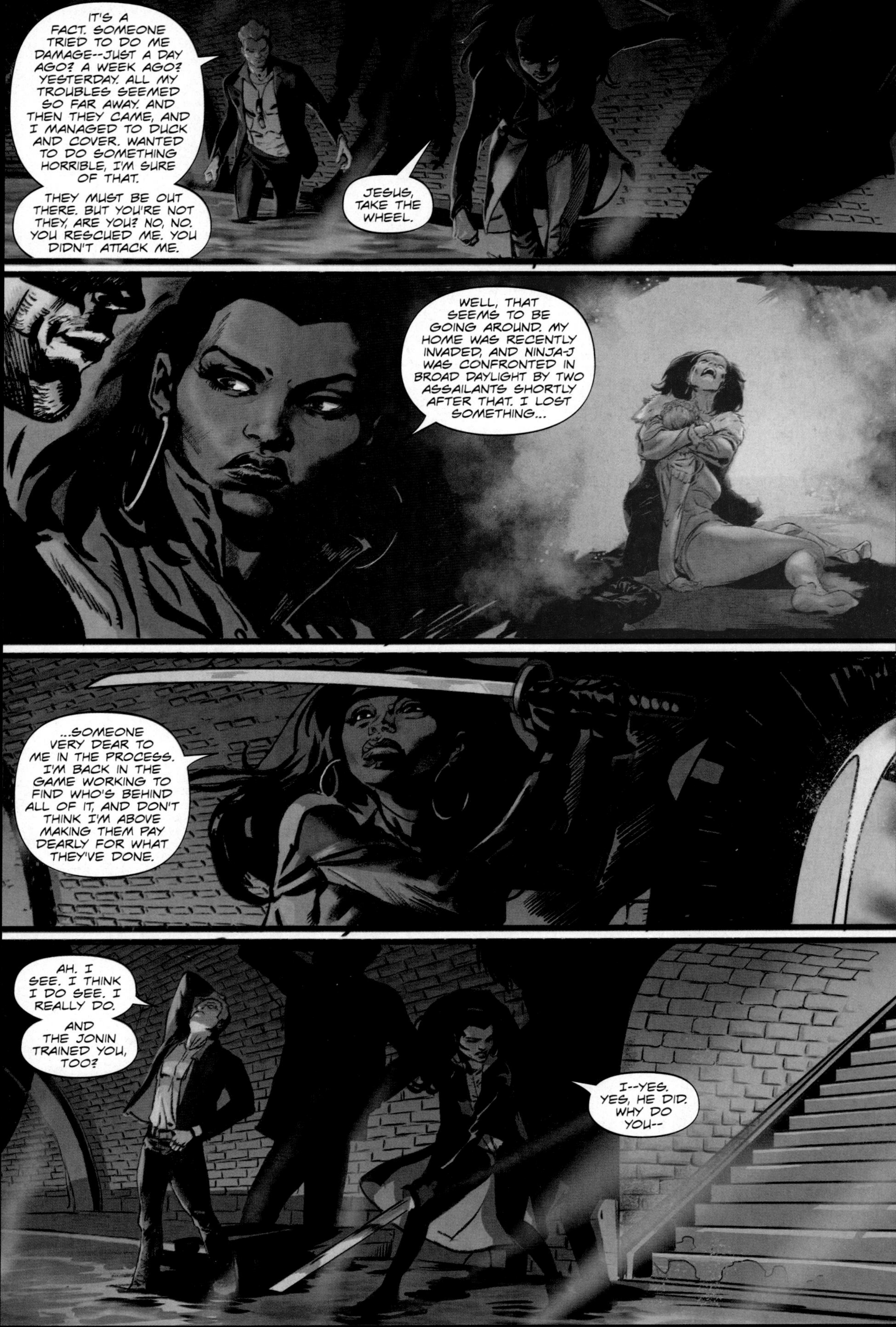
IT'S A FACT. SOMEONE TRIED TO DO ME DAMAGE--JUST A DAY AGO? A WEEK AGO? YESTERDAY. ALL MY TROUBLES SEEMED SO FAR AWAY. AND THEN THEY CAME, AND I MANAGED TO DUCK AND COVER. WANTED TO DO SOMETHING HORRIBLE, I'M SURE OF THAT.
THEY MUST BE OUT THERE. BUT YOU'RE NOT THEY, ARE YOU? NO, NO. YOU RESCUED ME. YOU DIDN'T ATTACK ME.
JESUS, TAKE THE WHEEL.
WELL, THAT SEEMS TO BE GOING AROUND. MY HOME WAS RECENTLY INVADED, AND NINJA-J WAS CONFRONTED IN BROAD DAYLIGHT BY TWO ASSAILANTS SHORTLY AFTER THAT. I LOST SOMETHING...
...SOMEONE VERY DEAR TO ME IN THE PROCESS. I'M BACK IN THE GAME WORKING TO FIND WHO'S BEHIND ALL OF IT, AND DON'T THINK I'M ABOVE MAKING THEM PAY DEARLY FOR WHAT THEY'VE DONE.
AH. I SEE. I THINK I DO SEE. I REALLY DO.
AND THE JONIN TRAINED YOU, TOO?
I--YES. YES, HE DID. WHY DO YOU--

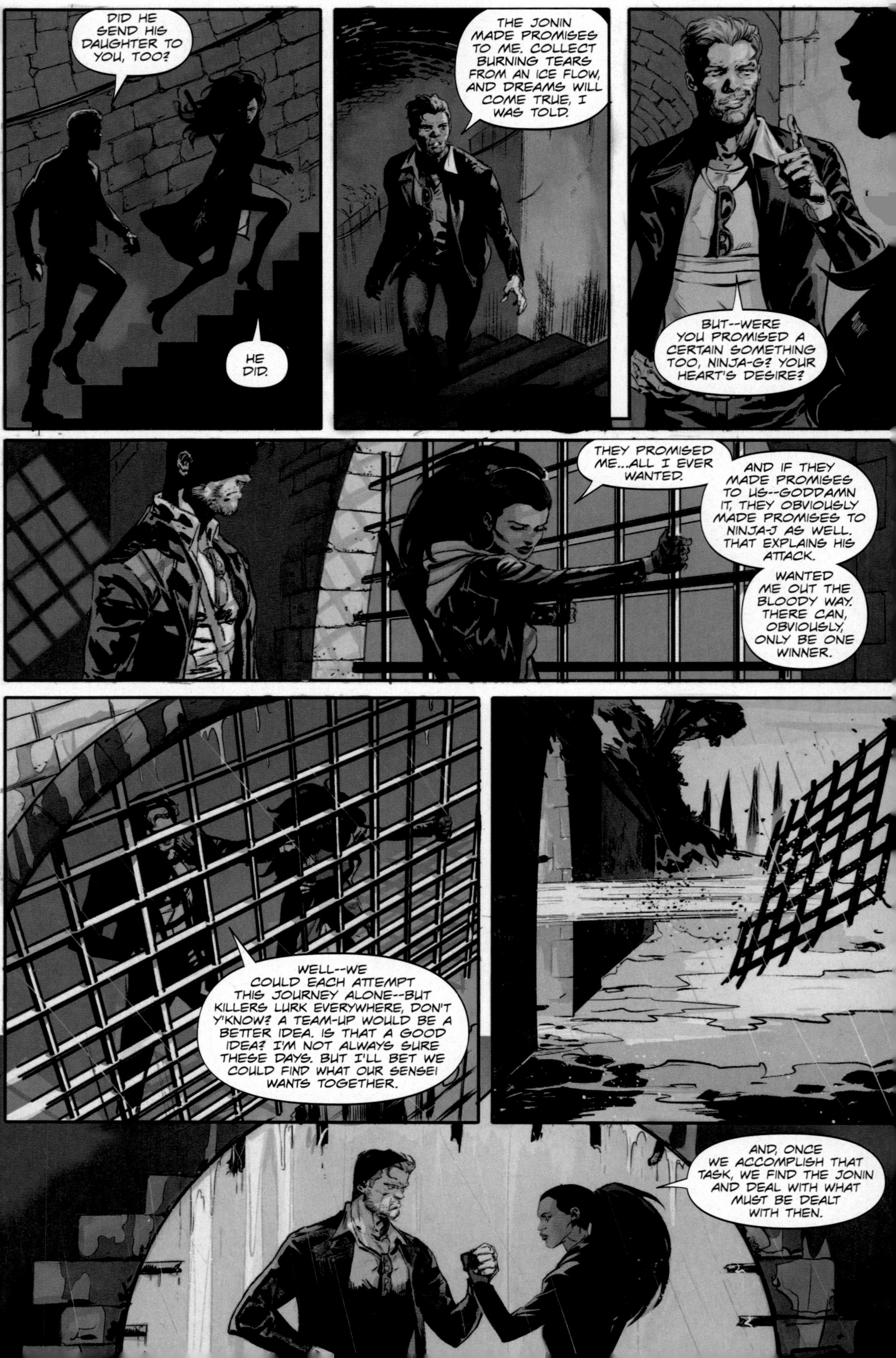
DID HE SEND HIS DAUGHTER TO YOU, TOO?
HE DID.
THE JONIN MADE PROMISES TO ME. COLLECT BURNING TEARS FROM AN ICE FLOW, AND DREAMS WILL COME TRUE, I WAS TOLD.
BUT--WERE YOU PROMISED A CERTAIN SOMETHING TOO, NINJA-G? YOUR HEART'S DESIRE?
THEY PROMISED ME...ALL I EVER WANTED.
AND IF THEY MADE PROMISES TO US--GODDAMN IT, THEY OBVIOUSLY MADE PROMISES TO NINJA-J AS WELL. THAT EXPLAINS HIS ATTACK.
WANTED ME OUT THE BLOODY WAY. THERE CAN, OBVIOUSLY, ONLY BE ONE WINNER.
WELL--WE COULD EACH ATTEMPT THIS JOURNEY ALONE--BUT KILLERS LURK EVERYWHERE, DON'T Y'KNOW? A TEAM-UP WOULD BE A BETTER IDEA. IS THAT A GOOD IDEA? I'M NOT ALWAYS SURE THESE DAYS. BUT I'LL BET WE COULD FIND WHAT OUR SENSEI WANTS TOGETHER.
AND, ONCE WE ACCOMPLISH THAT TASK, WE FIND THE JONIN AND DEAL WITH WHAT MUST BE DEALT WITH THEN.

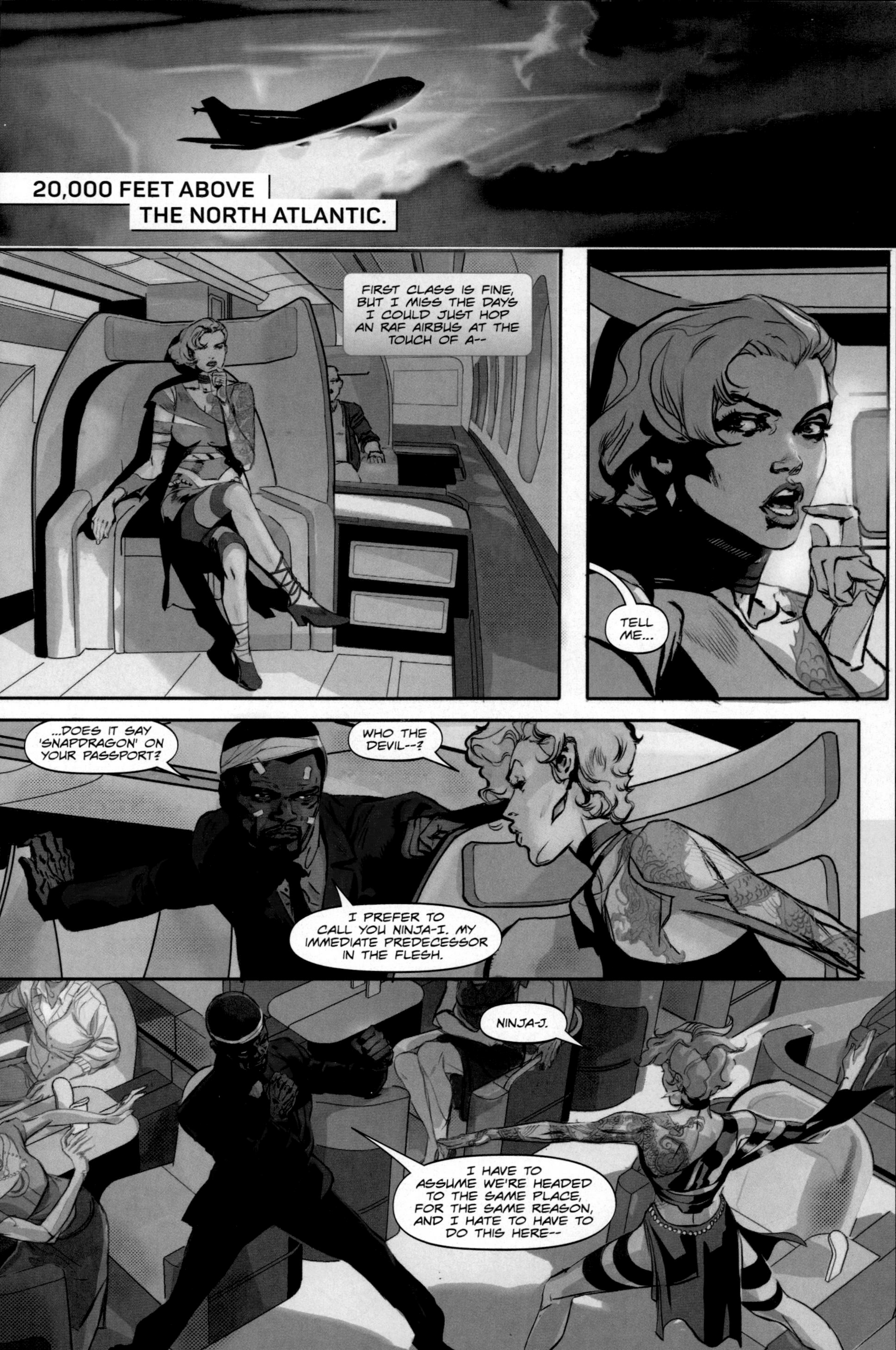
20,000 FEET ABOVE
THE NORTH ATLANTIC.
FIRST CLASS IS FINE, BUT I MISS THE DAYS I COULD JUST HOP AN RAF AIRBUS AT THE TOUCH OF A--
TELL ME...
...DOES IT SAY 'SNAPDRAGON' ON YOUR PASSPORT?
WHO THE DEVIL--?
I PREFER TO CALL YOU NINJA-I. MY IMMEDIATE PREDECESSOR IN THE FLESH.
NINJA-J.
I HAVE TO ASSUME WE'RE HEADED TO THE SAME PLACE, FOR THE SAME REASON, AND I HATE TO HAVE TO DO THIS HERE--

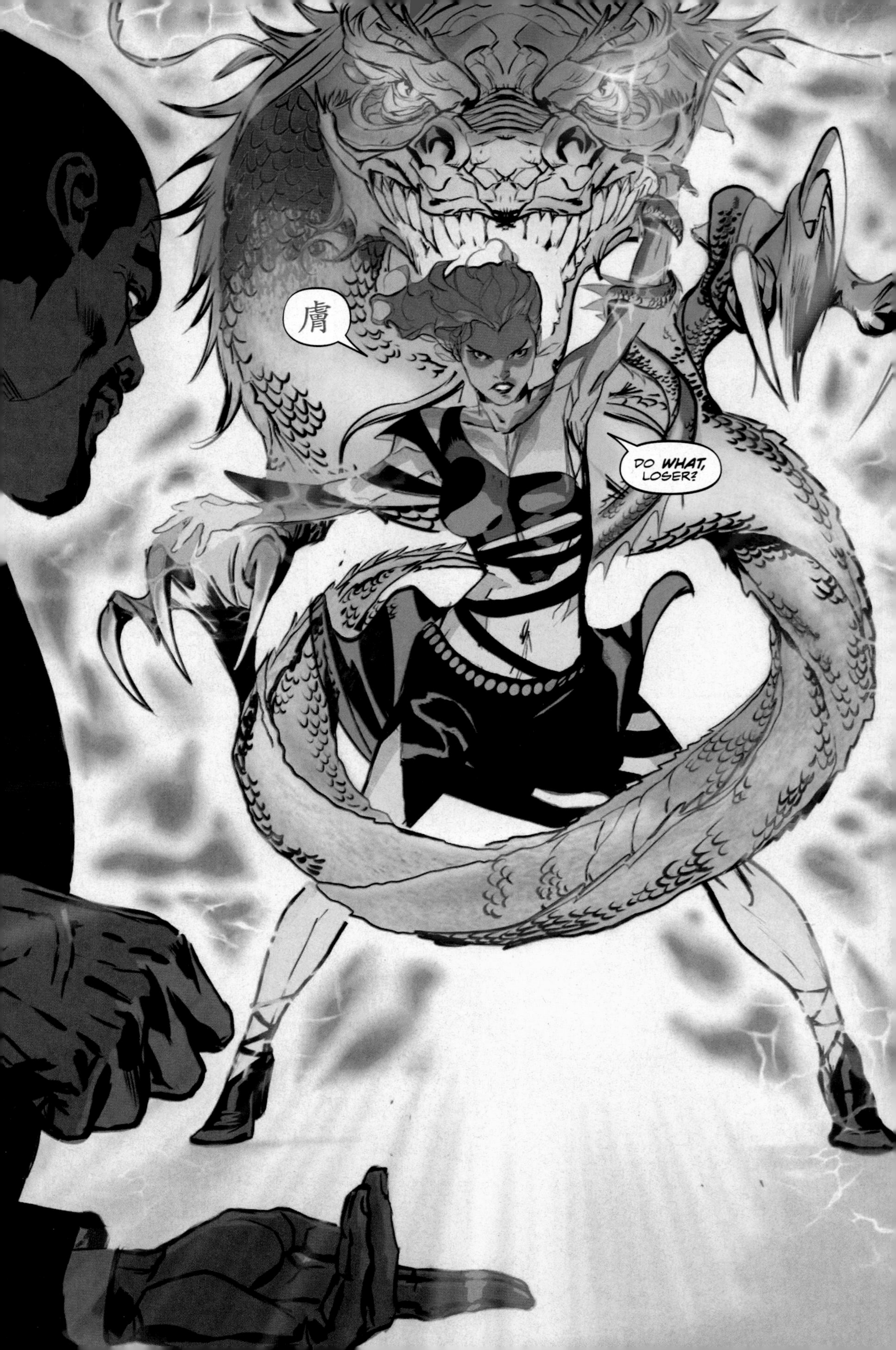
膚
DO WHAT, LOSER?

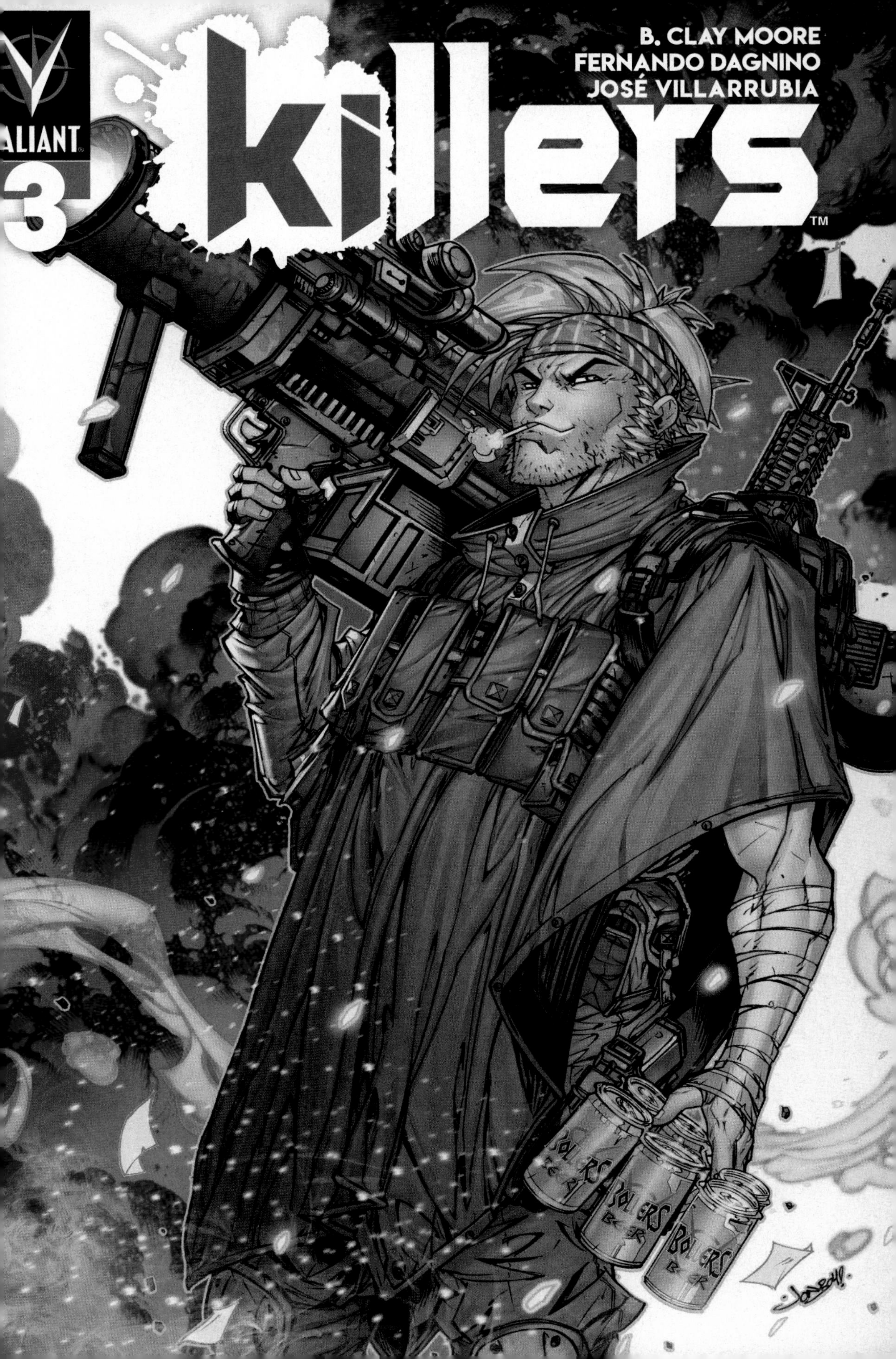
VALIANT
3
killers
TM
B. CLAY MOORE
FERNANDO DAGNINO
JOSÉ VILLARRUBIA

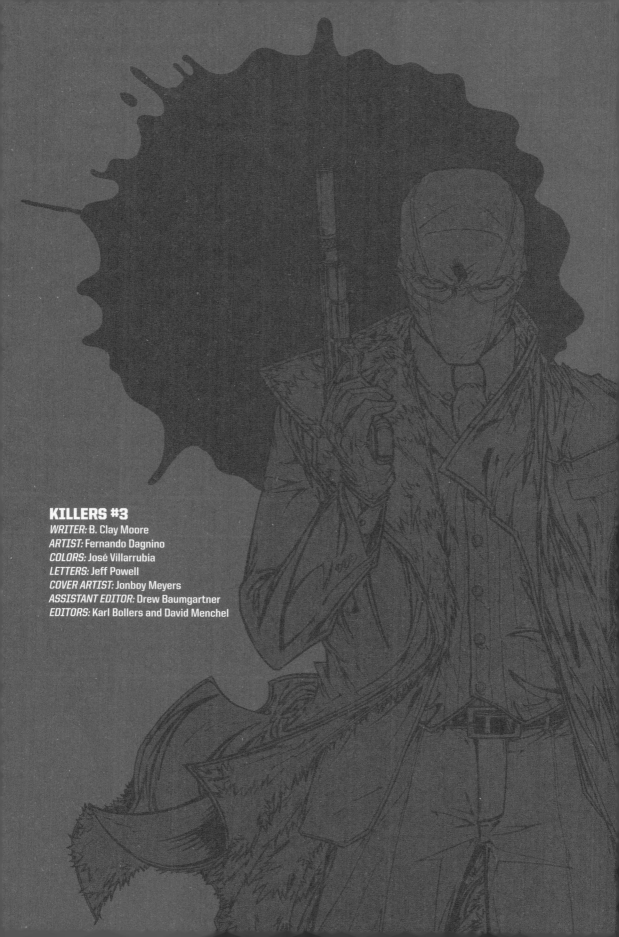

KILLERS #3
WRITER: B. Clay Moore
ARTIST: Fernando Dagnino
COLORS: José Villarrubia
LETTERS: Jeff Powell
COVER ARTIST: Jonboy Meyers
ASSISTANT EDITOR: Drew Baumgartner
EDITORS: Karl Bollers and David Menchel

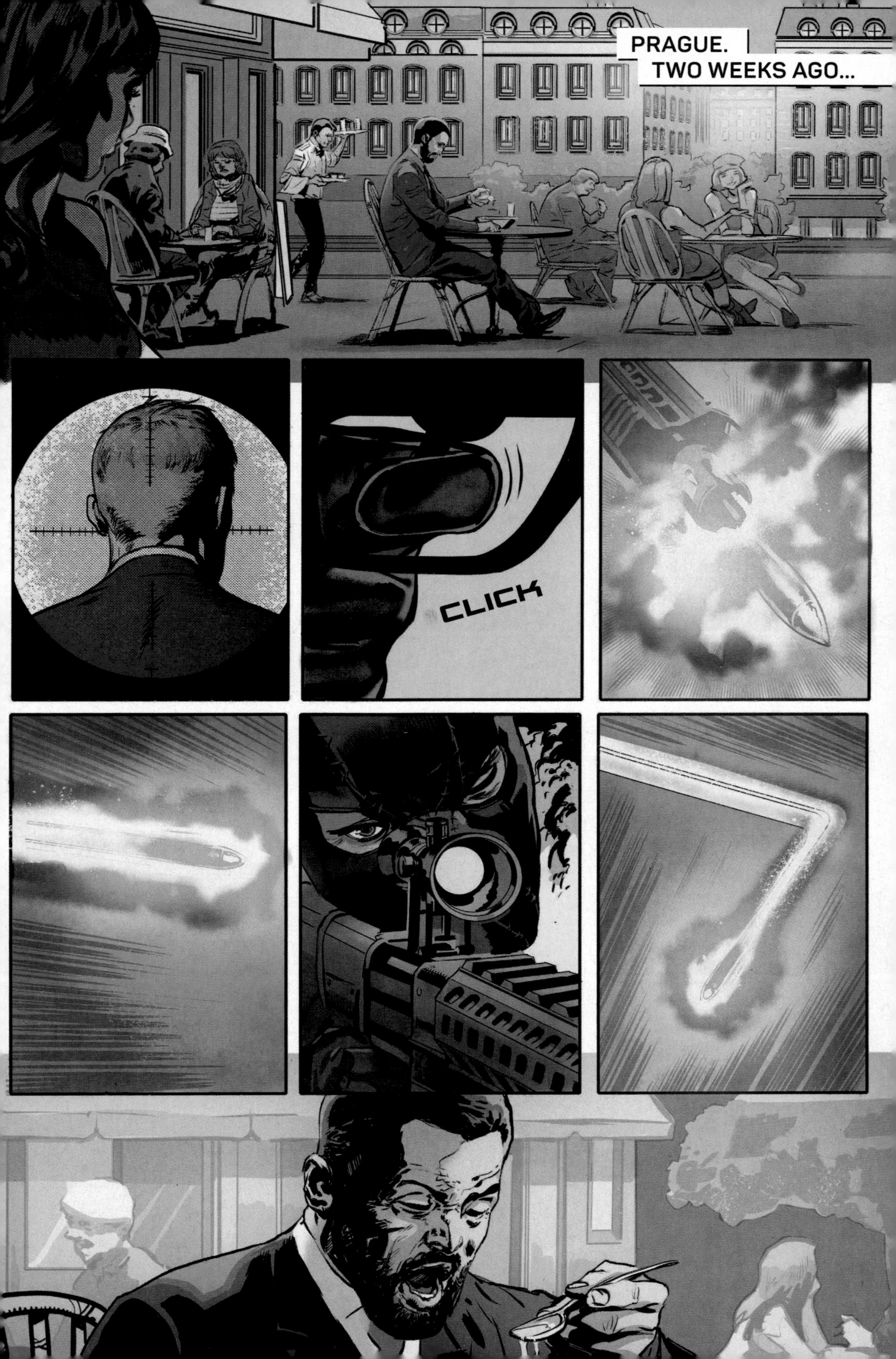
PRAGUE.
TWO WEEKS AGO...
CLICK

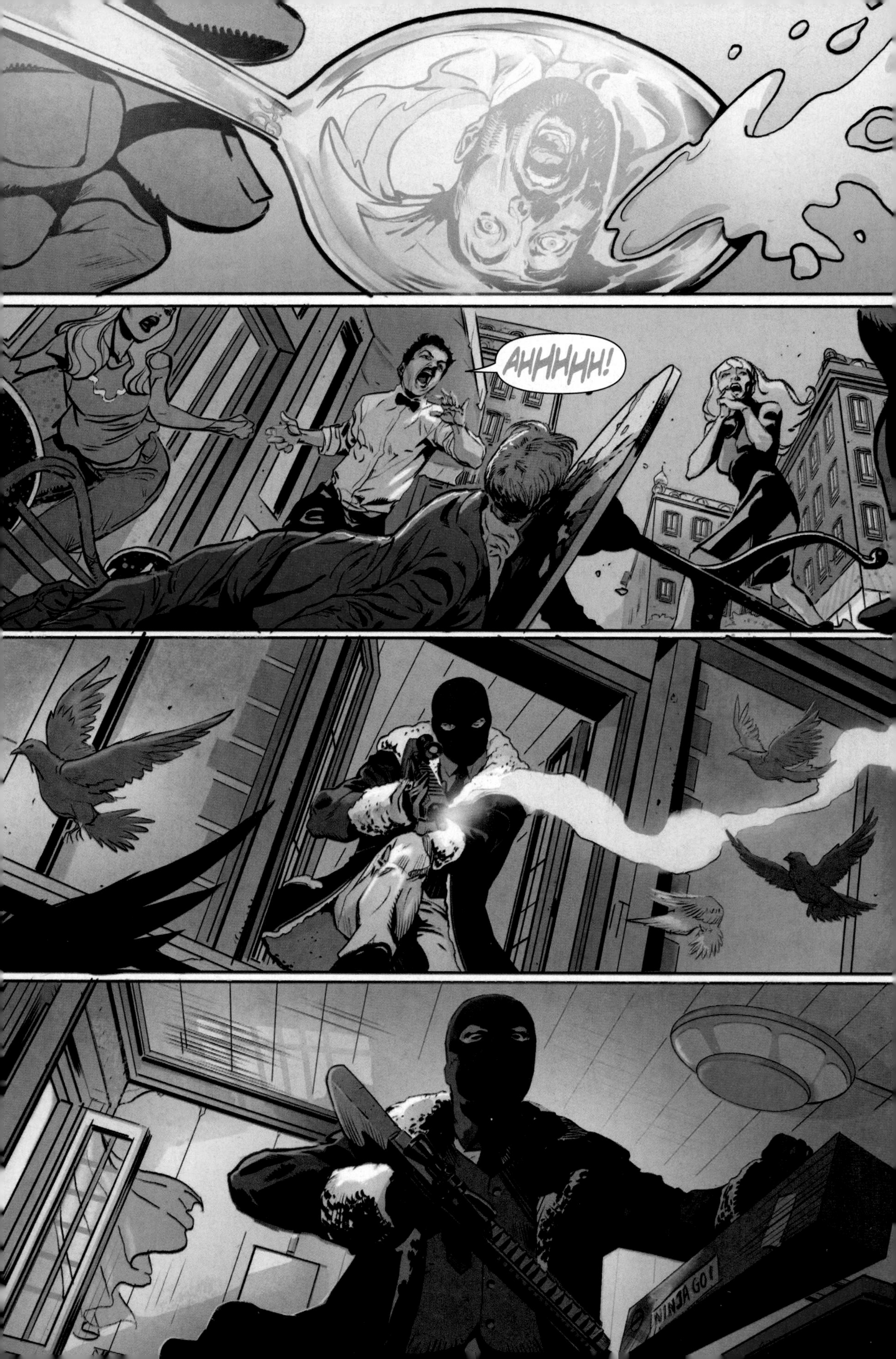
AHHHHH!
NINJA GO!

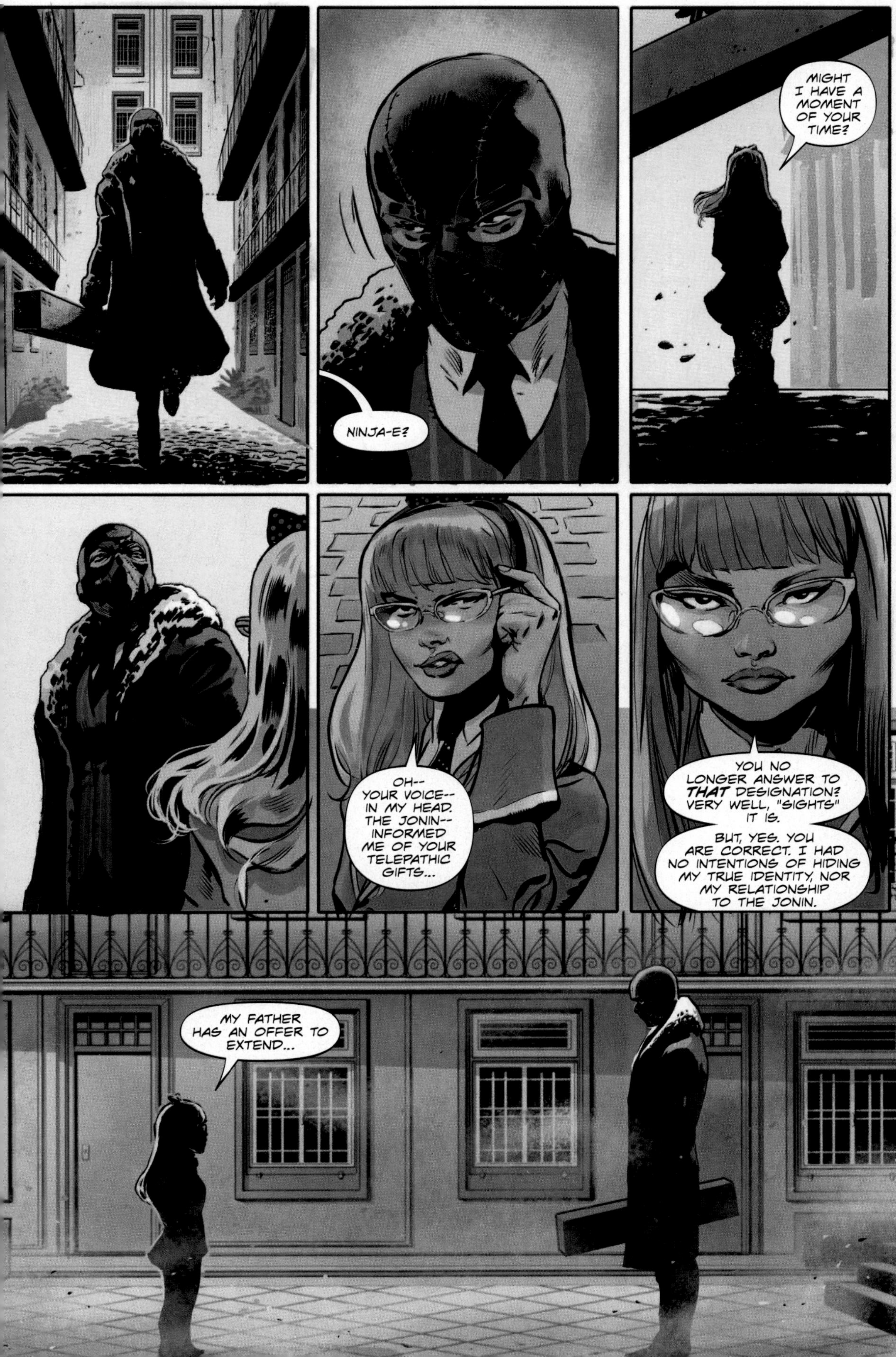
NINJA-E?
MIGHT I HAVE A MOMENT OF YOUR TIME?
OH-- YOUR VOICE-- IN MY HEAD. THE JONIN-- INFORMED ME OF YOUR TELEPATHIC GIFTS...
YOU NO LONGER ANSWER TO *THAT* DESIGNATION? VERY WELL, "SIGHTS" IT IS.
BUT, YES. YOU ARE CORRECT. I HAD NO INTENTIONS OF HIDING MY TRUE IDENTITY, NOR MY RELATIONSHIP TO THE JONIN.
MY FATHER HAS AN OFFER TO EXTEND...

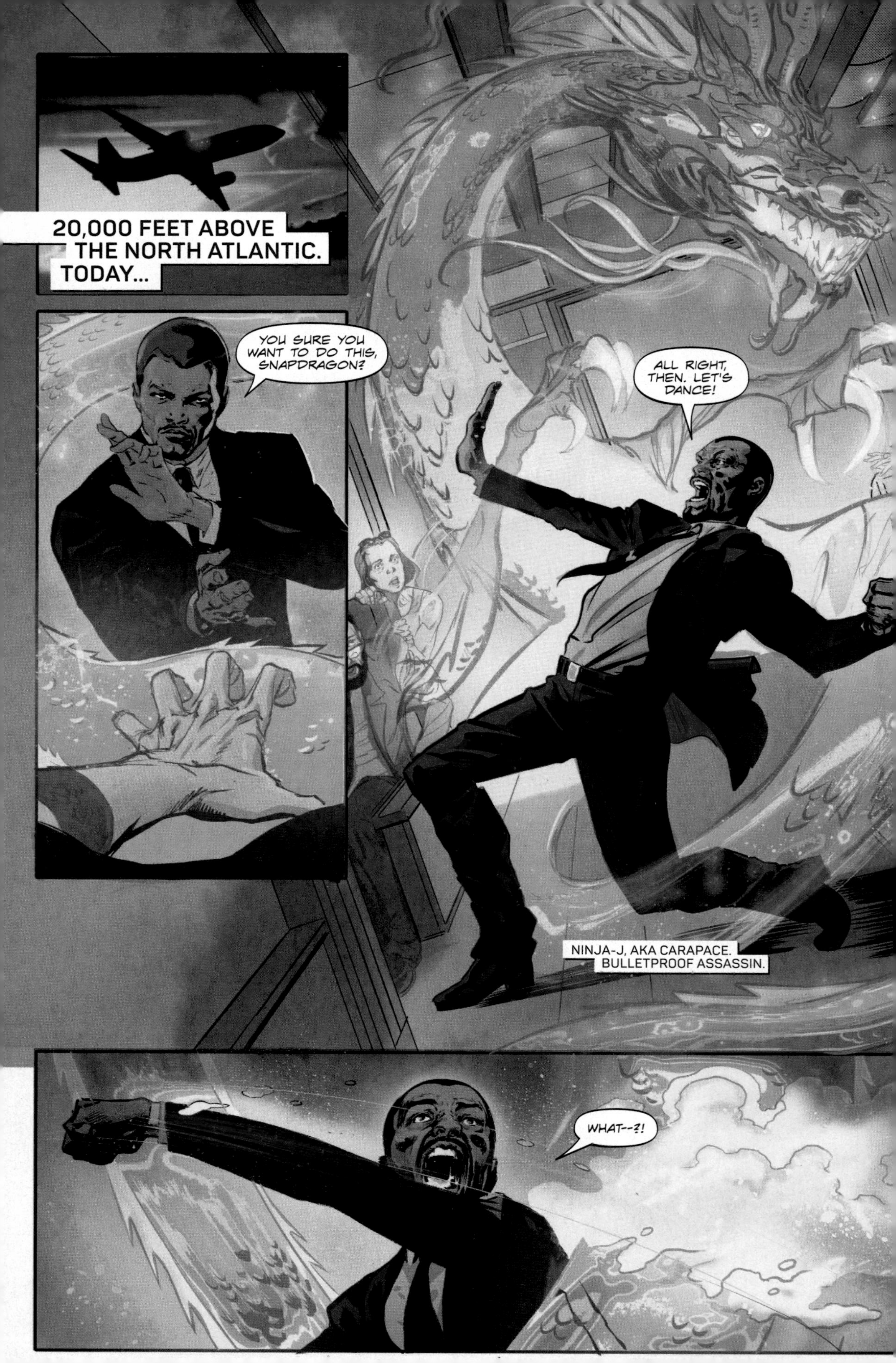
20,000 FEET ABOVE THE NORTH ATLANTIC. TODAY...
YOU SURE YOU WANT TO DO THIS, SNAPDRAGON?
ALL RIGHT, THEN. LET'S DANCE!
NINJA-J, AKA CARAPACE. BULLETPROOF ASSASSIN.
WHAT--?!

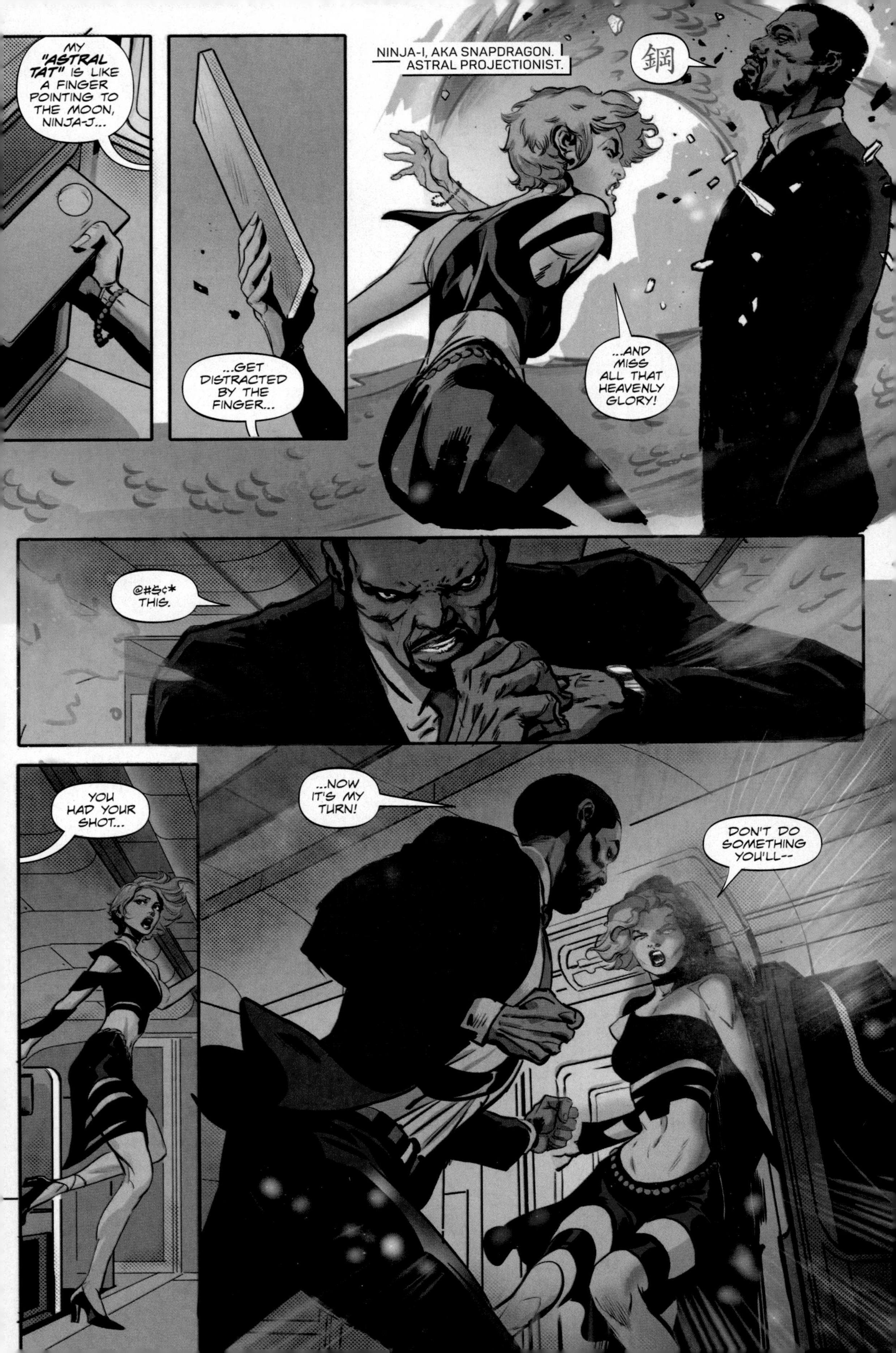
MY "ASTRAL TAT" IS LIKE A FINGER POINTING TO THE MOON, NINJA-J...
...GET DISTRACTED BY THE FINGER...
NINJA-I, AKA SNAPDRAGON. ASTRAL PROJECTIONIST.
鋼
...AND MISS ALL THAT HEAVENLY GLORY!
@#$¢* THIS.
YOU HAD YOUR SHOT...
...NOW IT'S MY TURN!
DON'T DO SOMETHING YOU'LL--

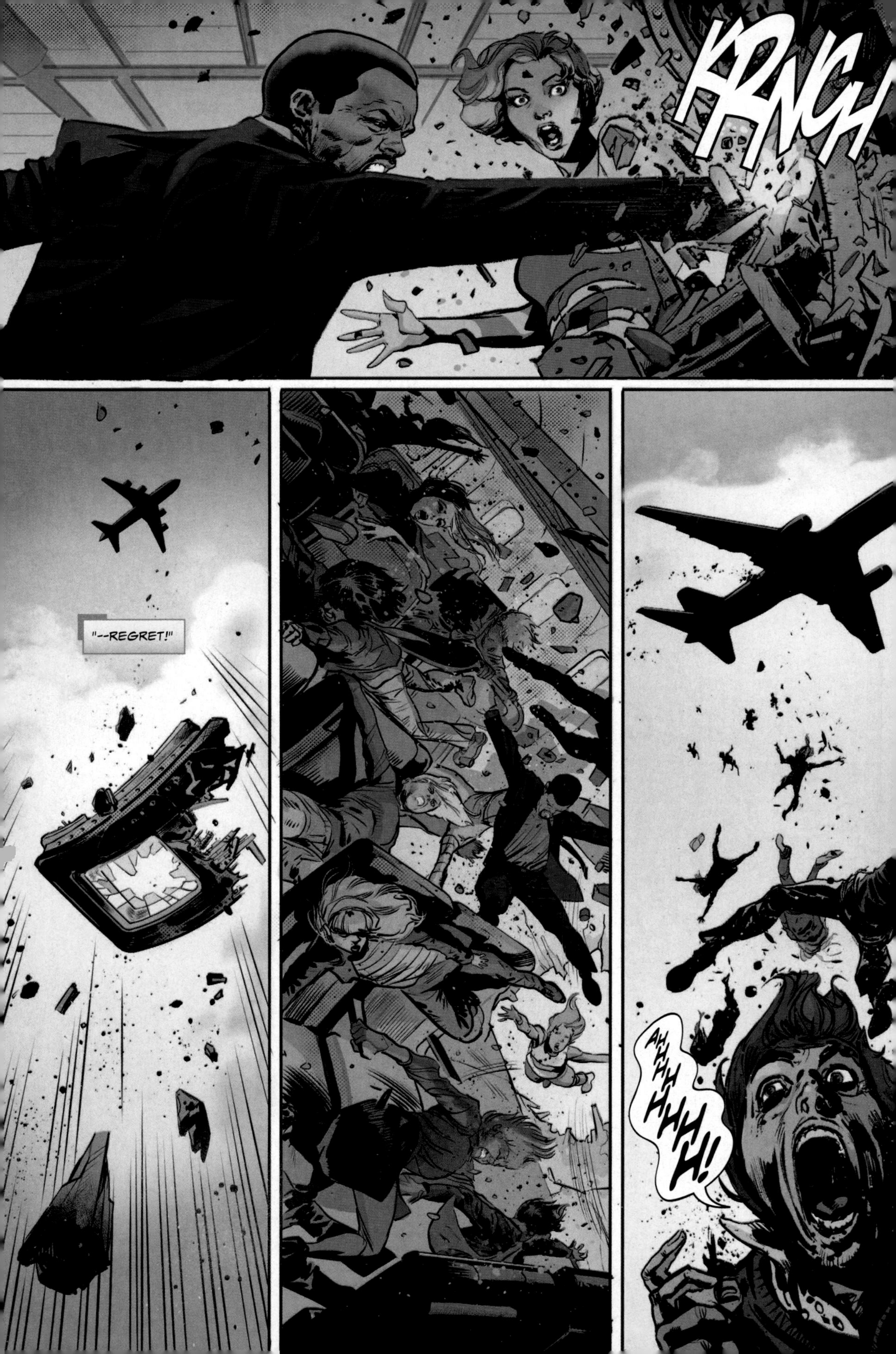
KRUNCH
"--REGRET!"
AHHHHHHH!

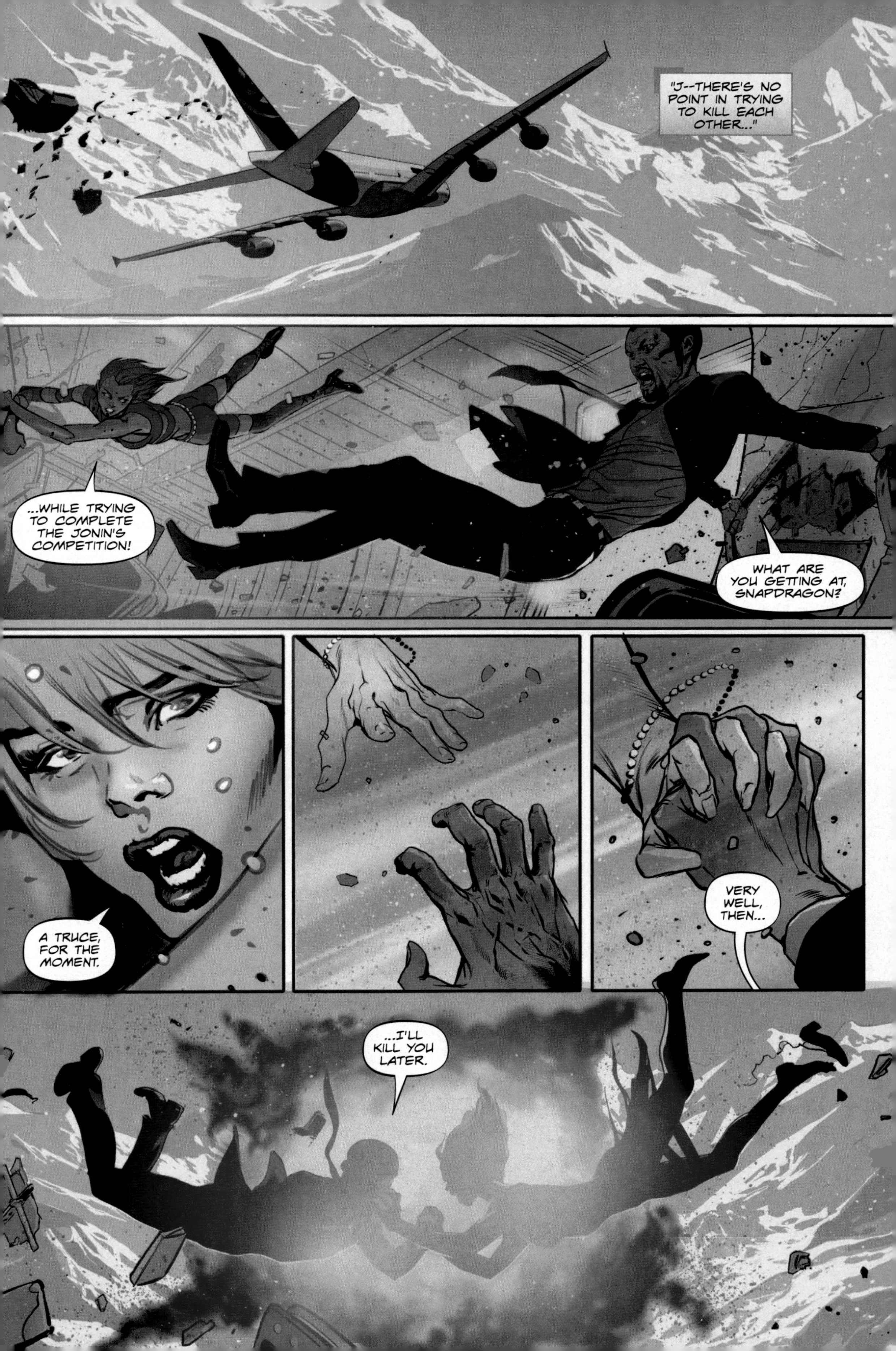
"J--THERE'S NO POINT IN TRYING TO KILL EACH OTHER..."
...WHILE TRYING TO COMPLETE THE JONIN'S COMPETITION!
WHAT ARE YOU GETTING AT, SNAPDRAGON?
A TRUCE, FOR THE MOMENT.
VERY WELL, THEN...
...I'LL KILL YOU LATER.

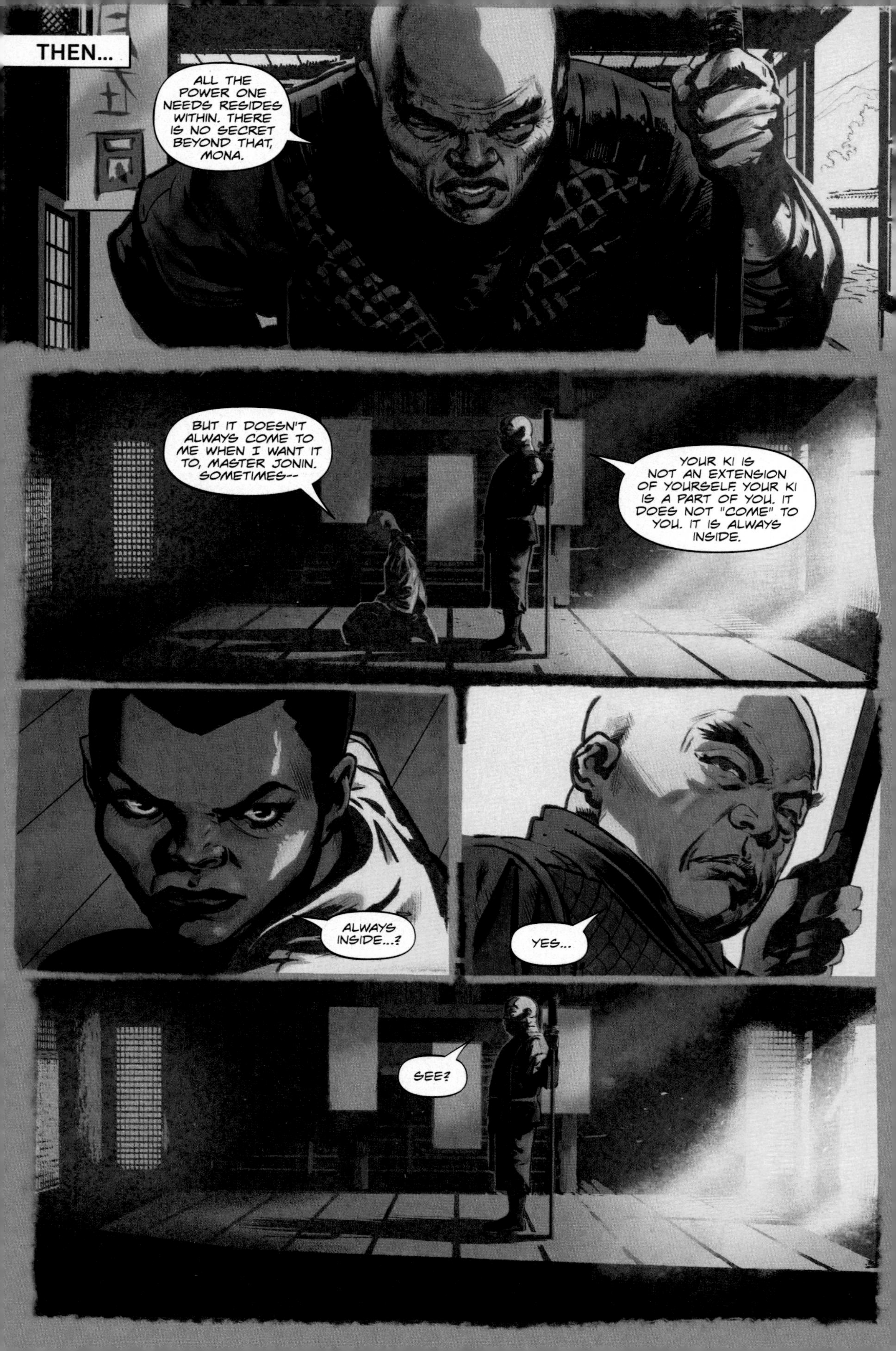
THEN...
ALL THE POWER ONE NEEDS RESIDES WITHIN. THERE IS NO SECRET BEYOND THAT, MONA.
BUT IT DOESN'T ALWAYS COME TO ME WHEN I WANT IT TO, MASTER JONIN. SOMETIMES--
YOUR KI IS NOT AN EXTENSION OF YOURSELF. YOUR KI IS A PART OF YOU. IT DOES NOT "COME" TO YOU. IT IS ALWAYS INSIDE.
ALWAYS INSIDE...?
YES...
SEE?

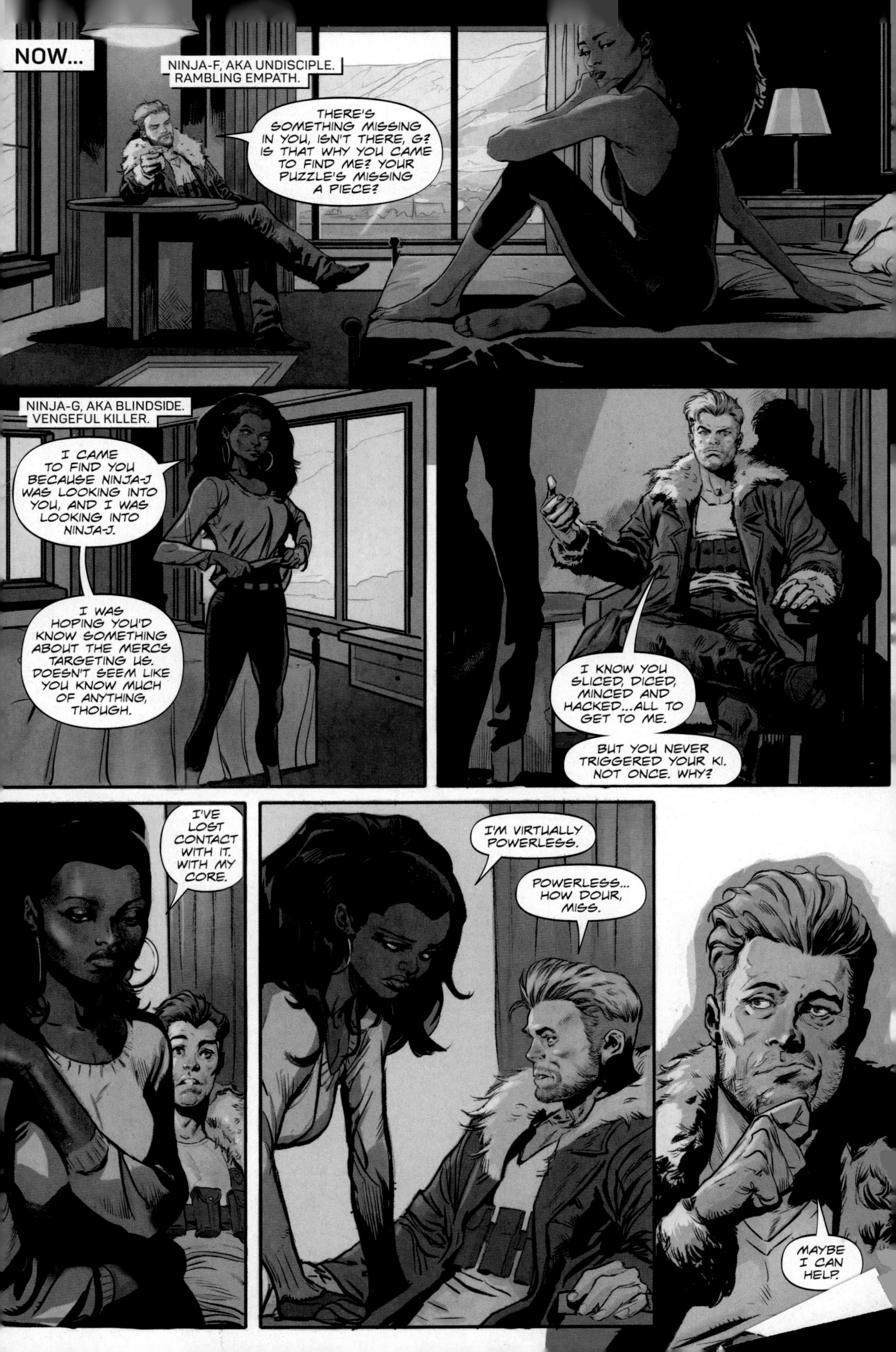
NOW...
NINJA-F, AKA UNDISCIPLE. RAMBLING EMPATH.
THERE'S SOMETHING MISSING IN YOU, ISN'T THERE, G? IS THAT WHY YOU CAME TO FIND ME? YOUR PUZZLE'S MISSING A PIECE?
NINJA-G, AKA BLINDSIDE. VENGEFUL KILLER.
I CAME TO FIND YOU BECAUSE NINJA-J WAS LOOKING INTO YOU, AND I WAS LOOKING INTO NINJA-J.
I WAS HOPING YOU'D KNOW SOMETHING ABOUT THE MERCS TARGETING US. DOESN'T SEEM LIKE YOU KNOW MUCH OF ANYTHING, THOUGH.
I KNOW YOU SLICED, DICED, MINCED AND HACKED...ALL TO GET TO ME.
BUT YOU NEVER TRIGGERED YOUR KI. NOT ONCE. WHY?
I'VE LOST CONTACT WITH IT. WITH MY CORE.
I'M VIRTUALLY POWERLESS.
POWERLESS... HOW DOUR, MISS.
MAYBE I CAN HELP.

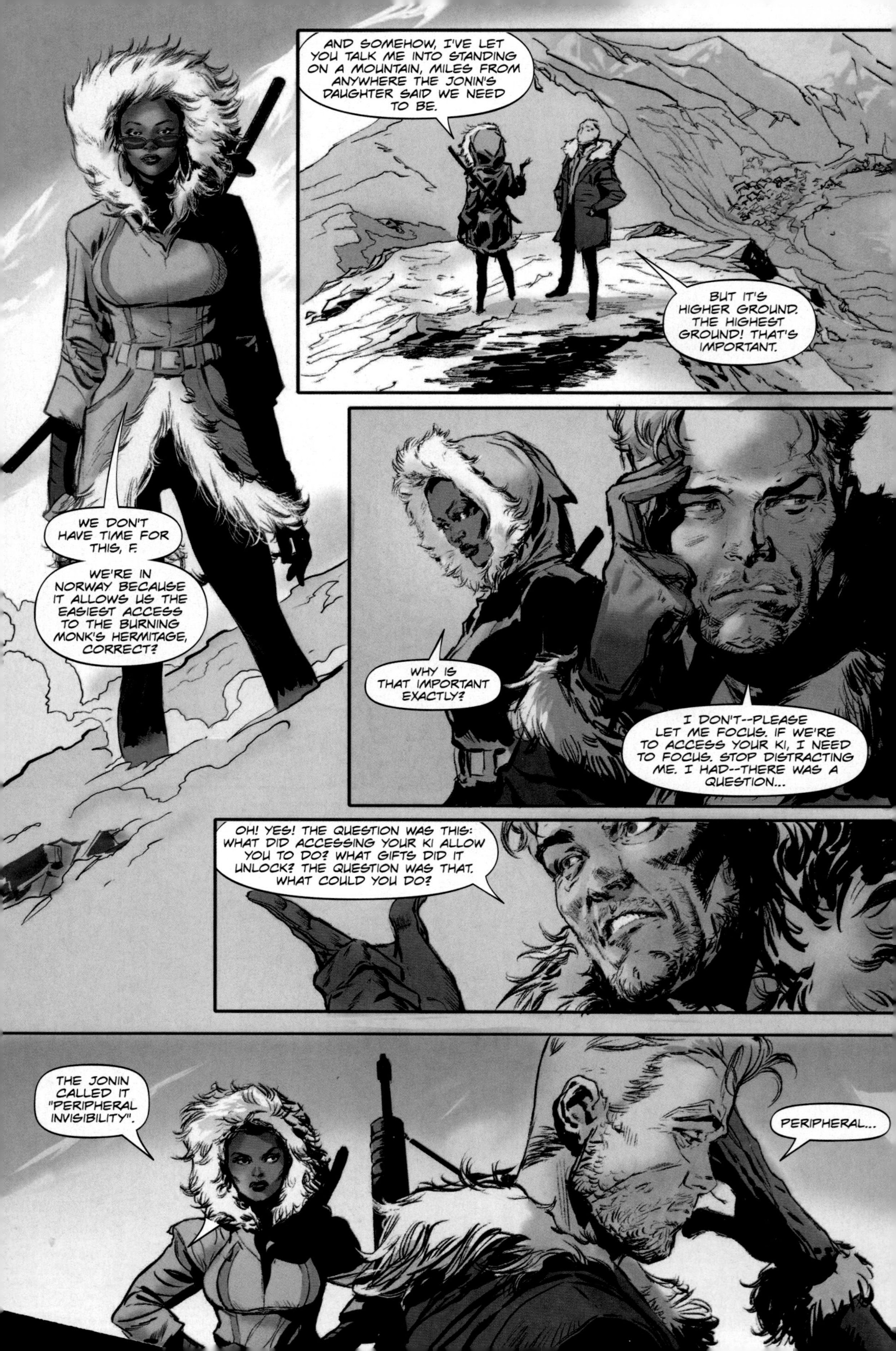
AND SOMEHOW, I'VE LET YOU TALK ME INTO STANDING ON A MOUNTAIN, MILES FROM ANYWHERE THE JONIN'S DAUGHTER SAID WE NEED TO BE.
BUT IT'S HIGHER GROUND. THE HIGHEST GROUND! THAT'S IMPORTANT.
WE DON'T HAVE TIME FOR THIS, F.
WE'RE IN NORWAY BECAUSE IT ALLOWS US THE EASIEST ACCESS TO THE BURNING MONK'S HERMITAGE, CORRECT?
WHY IS THAT IMPORTANT EXACTLY?
I DON'T--PLEASE LET ME FOCUS. IF WE'RE TO ACCESS YOUR KI, I NEED TO FOCUS. STOP DISTRACTING ME. I HAD--THERE WAS A QUESTION...
OH! YES! THE QUESTION WAS THIS: WHAT DID ACCESSING YOUR KI ALLOW YOU TO DO? WHAT GIFTS DID IT UNLOCK? THE QUESTION WAS THAT. WHAT COULD YOU DO?
THE JONIN CALLED IT "PERIPHERAL INVISIBILITY".
PERIPHERAL...

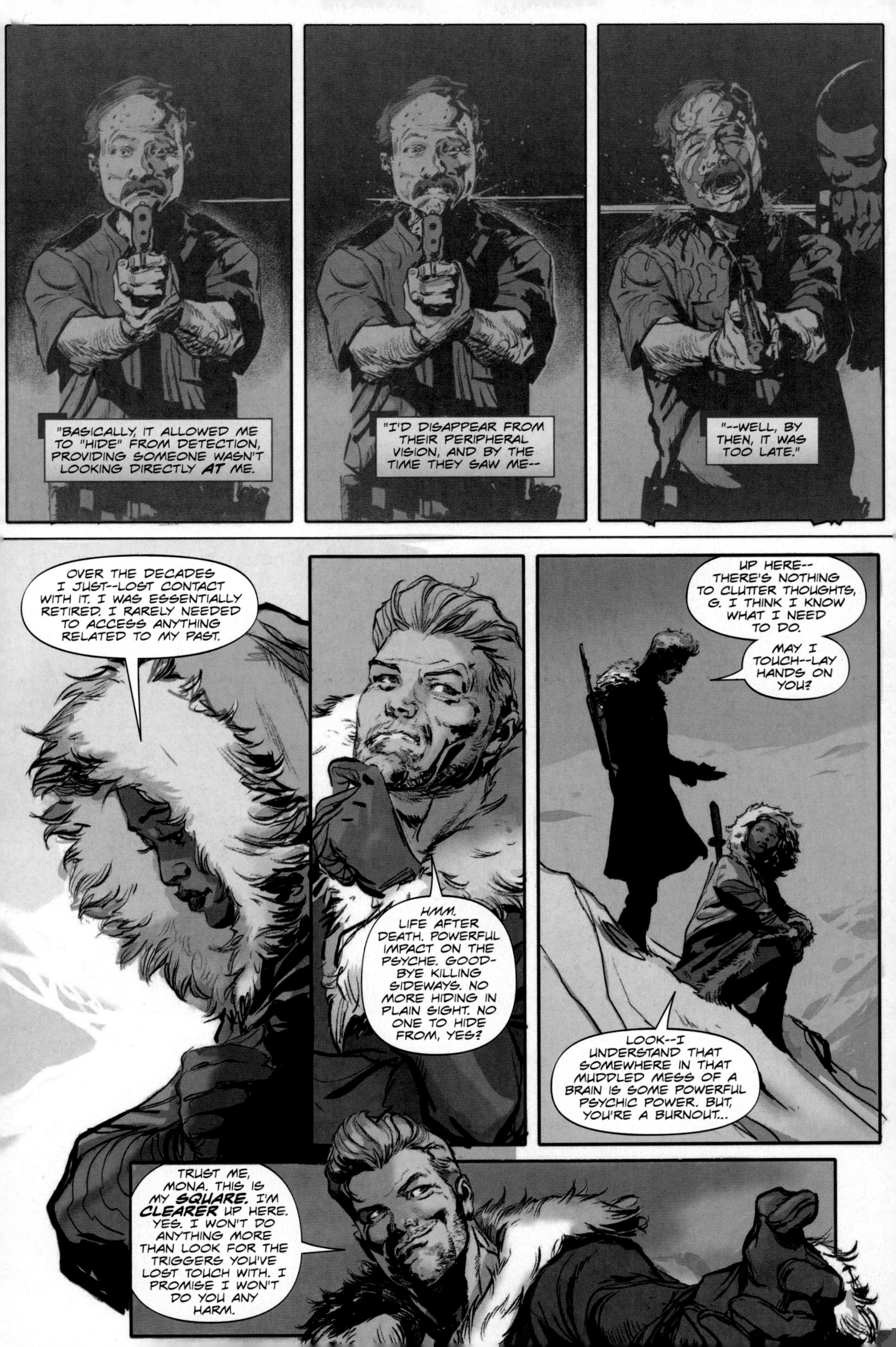
"BASICALLY, IT ALLOWED ME TO "HIDE" FROM DETECTION, PROVIDING SOMEONE WASN'T LOOKING DIRECTLY AT ME.
"I'D DISAPPEAR FROM THEIR PERIPHERAL VISION, AND BY THE TIME THEY SAW ME--
"--WELL, BY THEN, IT WAS TOO LATE."
OVER THE DECADES I JUST--LOST CONTACT WITH IT. I WAS ESSENTIALLY RETIRED. I RARELY NEEDED TO ACCESS ANYTHING RELATED TO MY PAST.
HMM. LIFE AFTER DEATH. POWERFUL IMPACT ON THE PSYCHE. GOOD-BYE KILLING SIDEWAYS. NO MORE HIDING IN PLAIN SIGHT. NO ONE TO HIDE FROM, YES?
UP HERE--THERE'S NOTHING TO CLUTTER THOUGHTS, G. I THINK I KNOW WHAT I NEED TO DO.
MAY I TOUCH--LAY HANDS ON YOU?
LOOK--I UNDERSTAND THAT SOMEWHERE IN THAT MUDDLED MESS OF A BRAIN IS SOME POWERFUL PSYCHIC POWER. BUT, YOU'RE A BURNOUT...
TRUST ME, MONA. THIS IS MY SQUARE. I'M CLEARER UP HERE. YES. I WON'T DO ANYTHING MORE THAN LOOK FOR THE TRIGGERS YOU'VE LOST TOUCH WITH. I PROMISE I WON'T DO YOU ANY HARM.

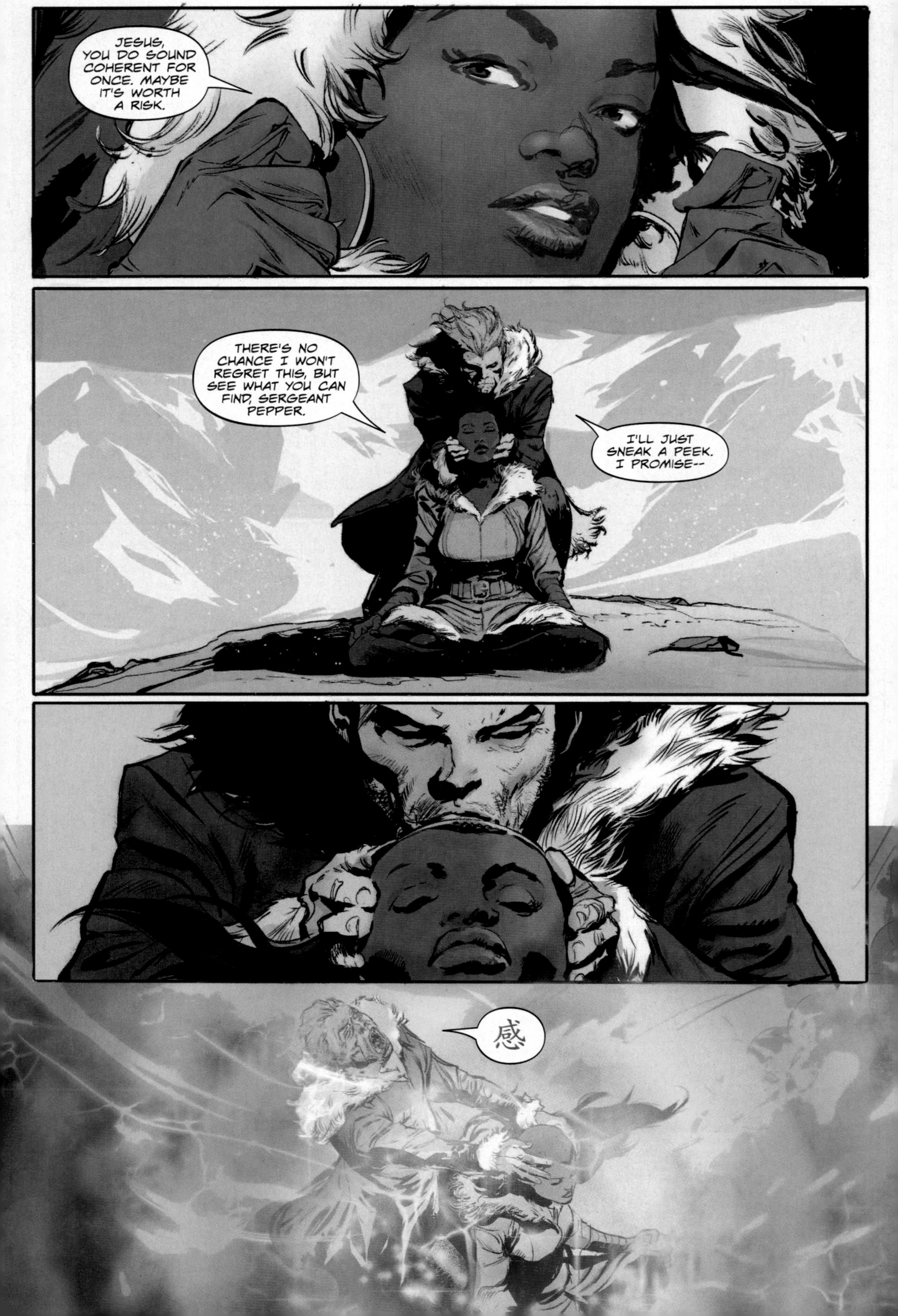
JESUS, YOU DO SOUND COHERENT FOR ONCE. MAYBE IT'S WORTH A RISK.
THERE'S NO CHANCE I WON'T REGRET THIS, BUT SEE WHAT YOU CAN FIND, SERGEANT PEPPER.
I'LL JUST SNEAK A PEEK. I PROMISE--
感

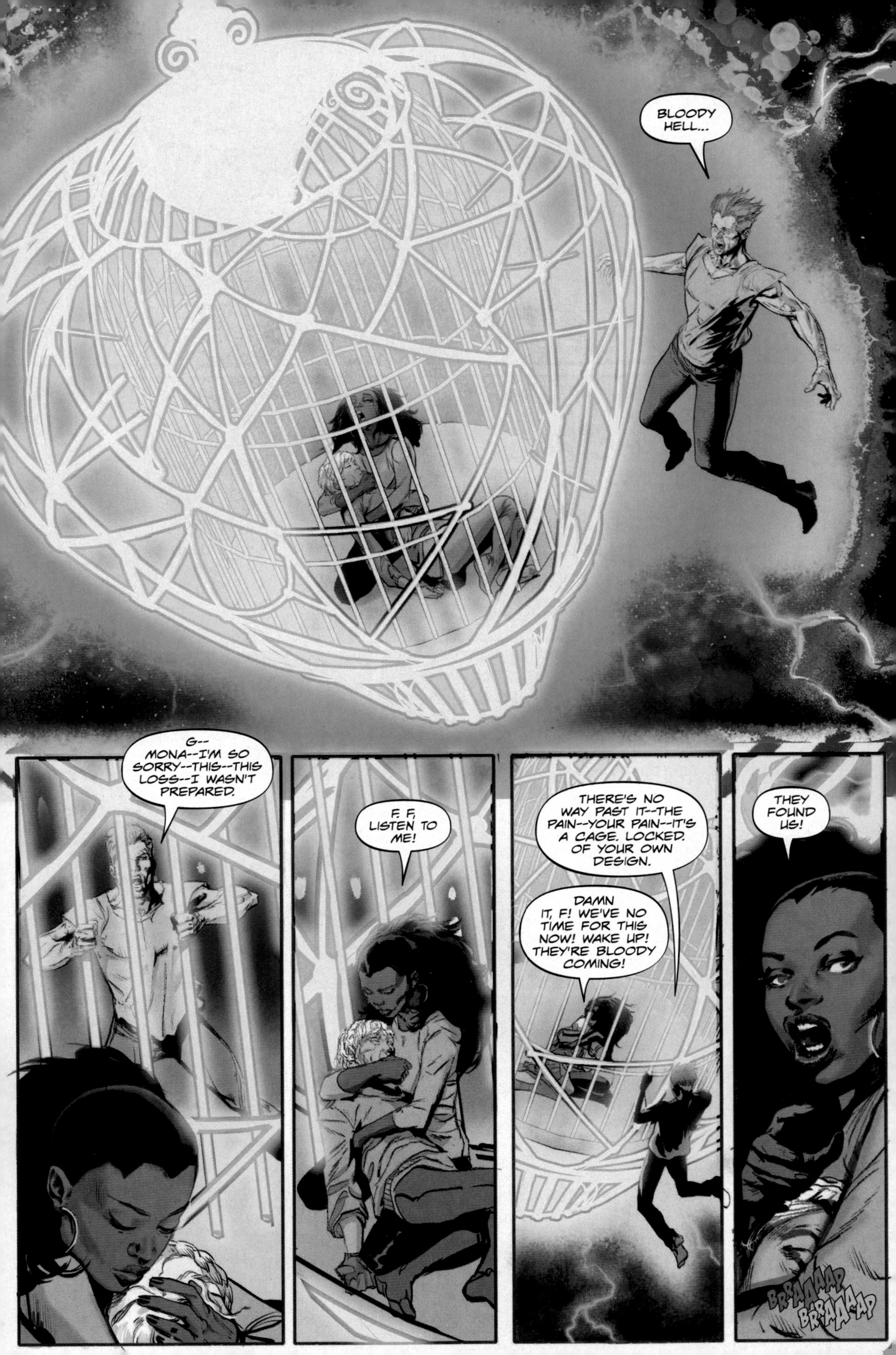
BLOODY HELL...
G-- MONA--I'M SO SORRY--THIS--THIS LOSS--I WASN'T PREPARED.
F, F, LISTEN TO ME!
THERE'S NO WAY PAST IT--THE PAIN--YOUR PAIN--IT'S A CAGE. LOCKED. OF YOUR OWN DESIGN.
DAMN IT, F! WE'VE NO TIME FOR THIS NOW! WAKE UP! THEY'RE BLOODY COMING!
THEY FOUND US!
BRAAAAP
BRAAAAP

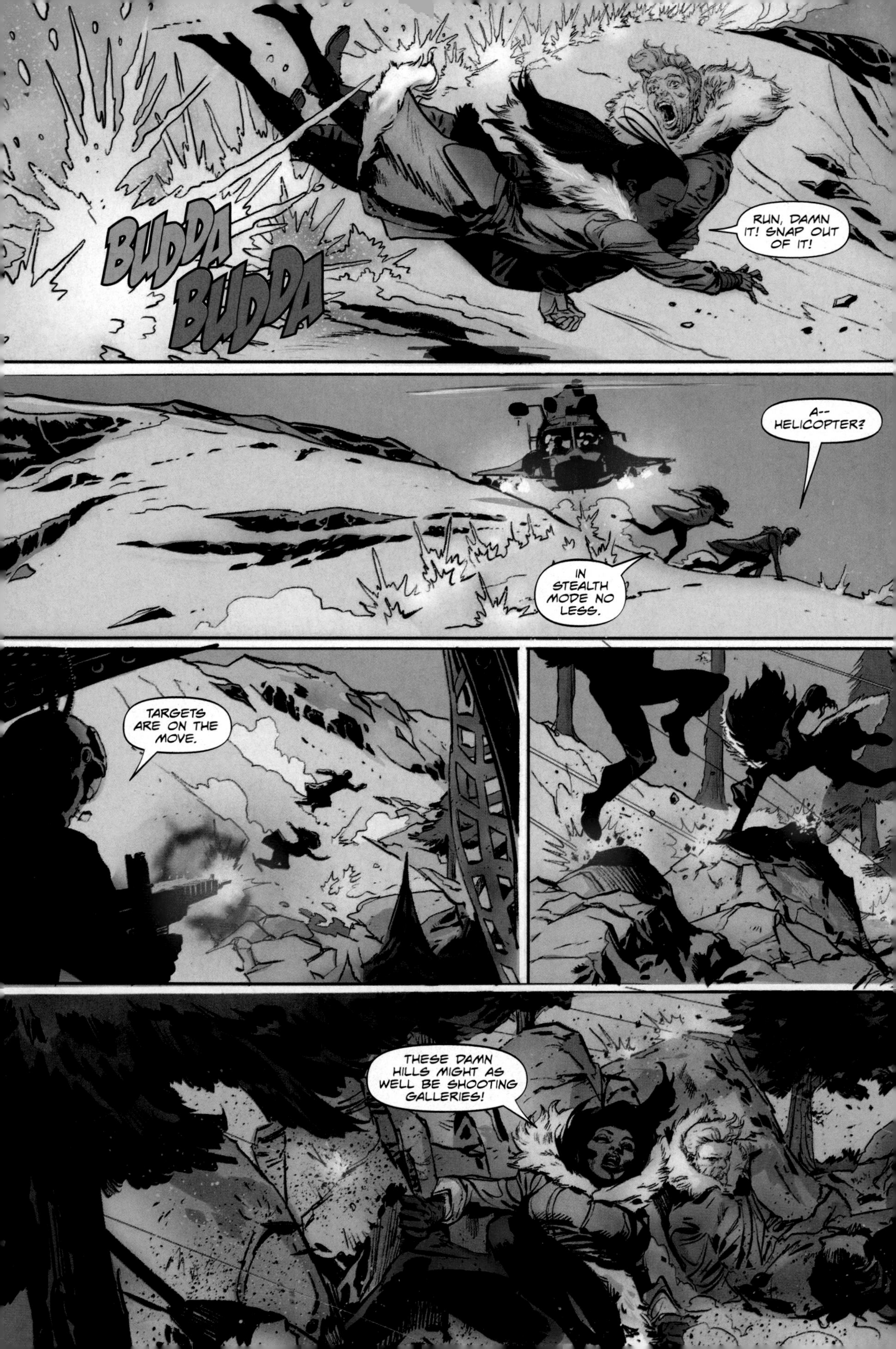
BUDDA BUDDA
RUN, DAMN IT! SNAP OUT OF IT!
A-- HELICOPTER?
IN STEALTH MODE NO LESS.
TARGETS ARE ON THE MOVE.
THESE DAMN HILLS MIGHT AS WELL BE SHOOTING GALLERIES!

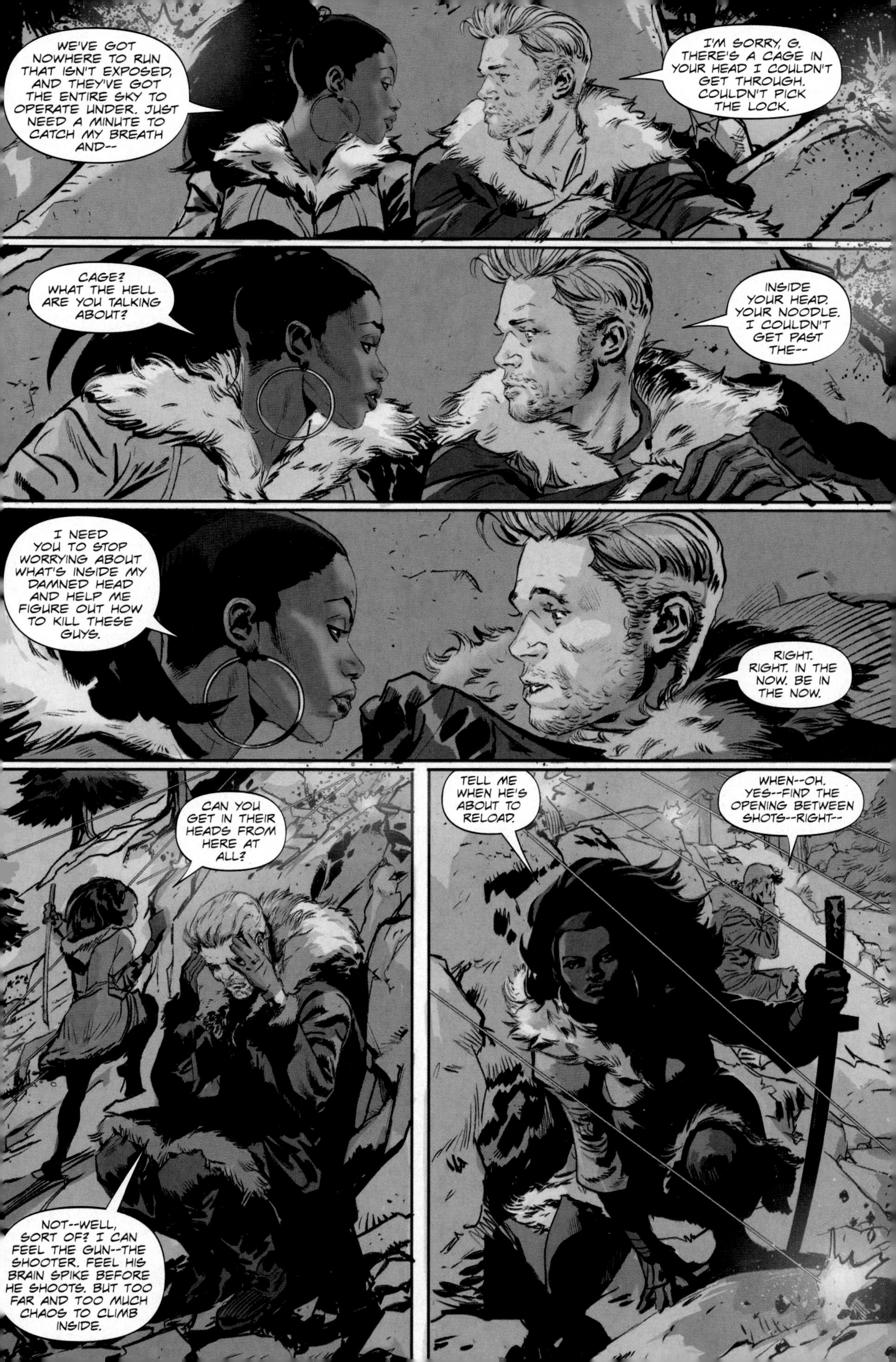
WE'VE GOT NOWHERE TO RUN THAT ISN'T EXPOSED, AND THEY'VE GOT THE ENTIRE SKY TO OPERATE UNDER. JUST NEED A MINUTE TO CATCH MY BREATH AND--
I'M SORRY, G. THERE'S A CAGE IN YOUR HEAD I COULDN'T GET THROUGH. COULDN'T PICK THE LOCK.
CAGE? WHAT THE HELL ARE YOU TALKING ABOUT?
INSIDE YOUR HEAD. YOUR NOODLE. I COULDN'T GET PAST THE--
I NEED YOU TO STOP WORRYING ABOUT WHAT'S INSIDE MY DAMNED HEAD AND HELP ME FIGURE OUT HOW TO KILL THESE GUYS.
RIGHT. RIGHT. IN THE NOW. BE IN THE NOW.
CAN YOU GET IN THEIR HEADS FROM HERE AT ALL?
NOT--WELL, SORT OF? I CAN FEEL THE GUN--THE SHOOTER. FEEL HIS BRAIN SPIKE BEFORE HE SHOOTS. BUT TOO FAR AND TOO MUCH CHAOS TO CLIMB INSIDE.
TELL ME WHEN HE'S ABOUT TO RELOAD.
WHEN--OH. YES--FIND THE OPENING BETWEEN SHOTS--RIGHT--

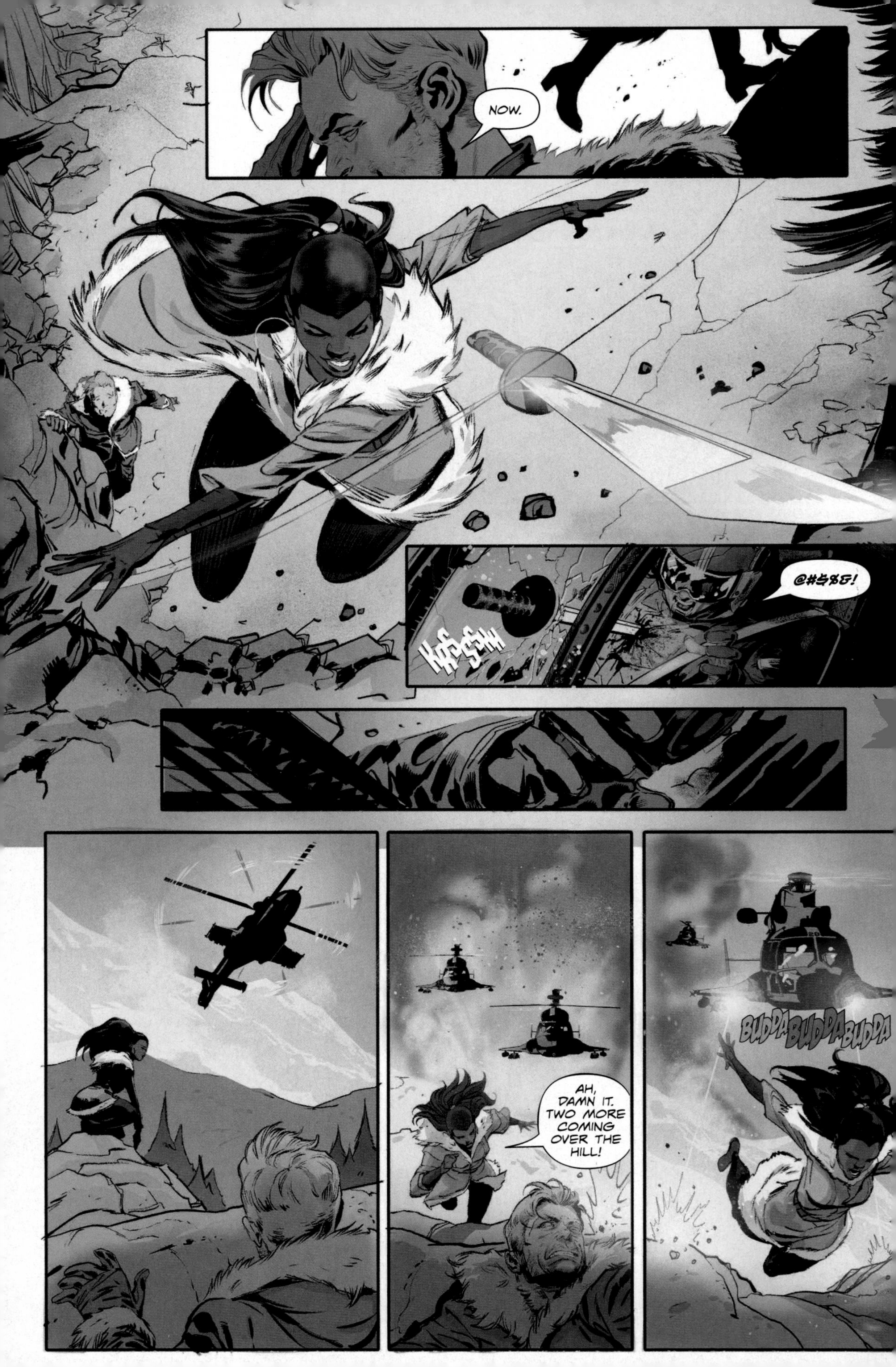

NOW.
@#$%&!
AH, DAMN IT. TWO MORE COMING OVER THE HILL!
BUDDA BUDDA BUDDA

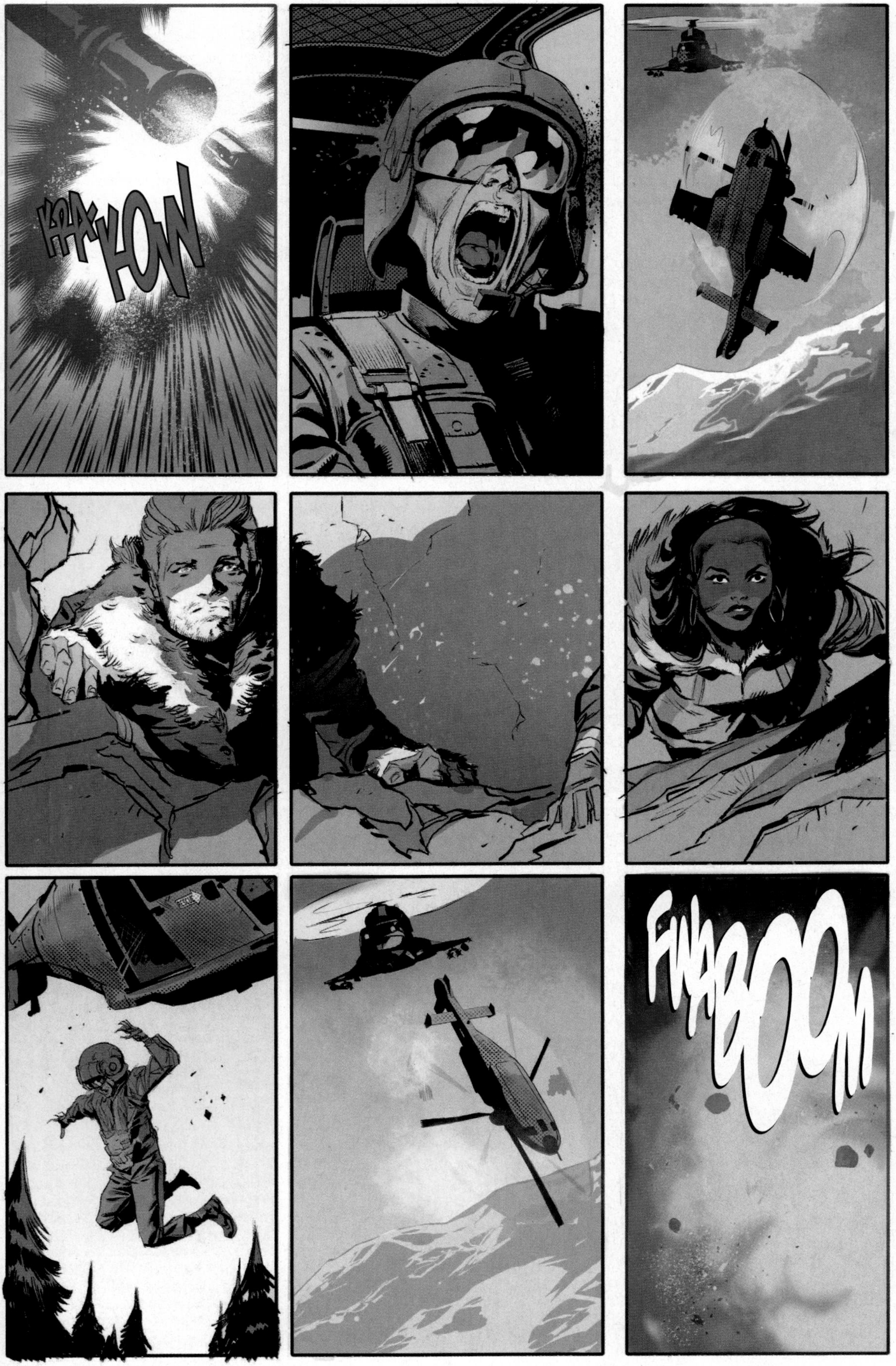
KRA-KOW
FWABOOM

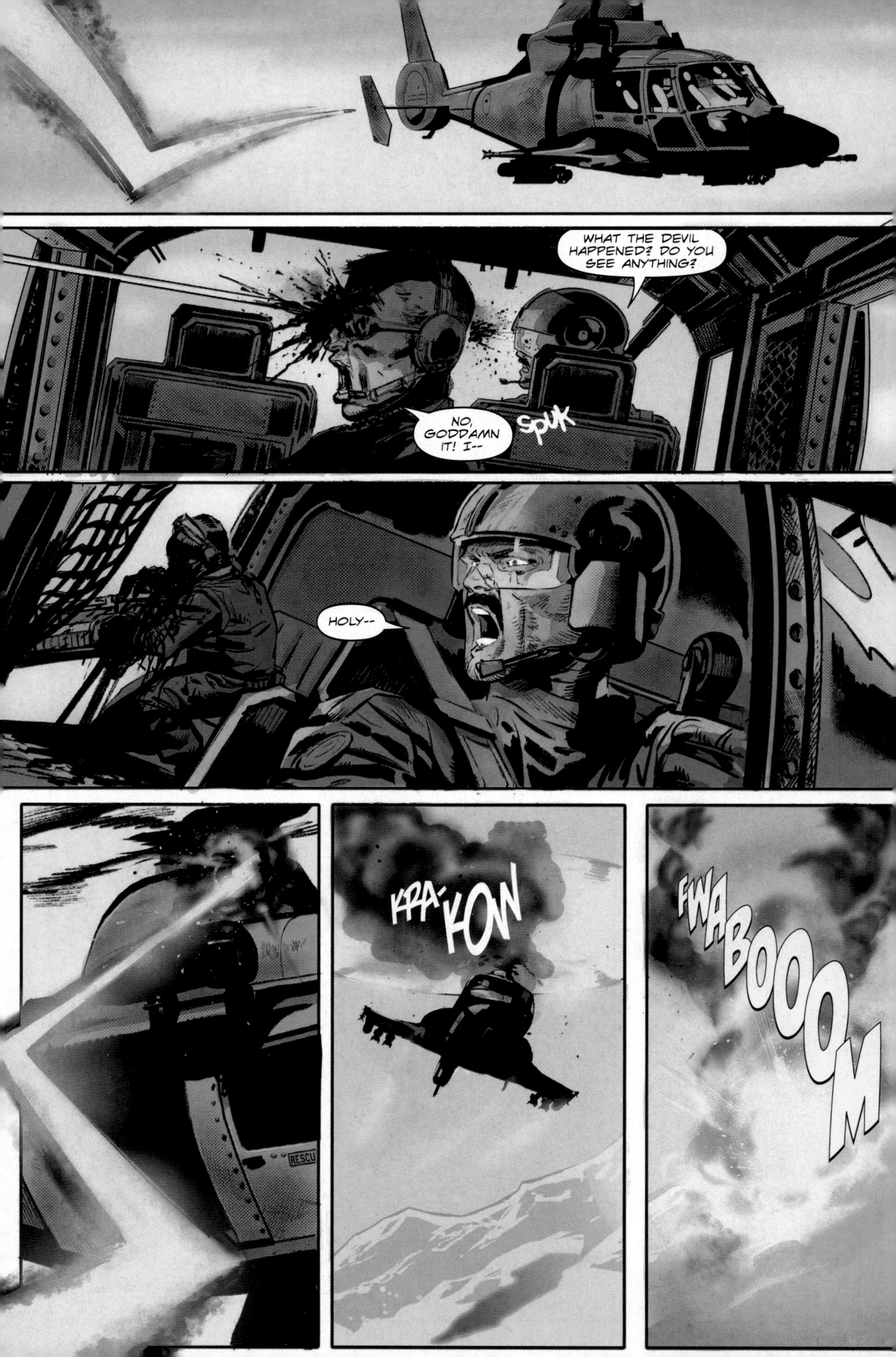
WHAT THE DEVIL HAPPENED? DO YOU SEE ANYTHING?
NO, GODDAMN IT! I--
SPUK
HOLY--
RESCU
KRA-KOW
FWABOOOOM

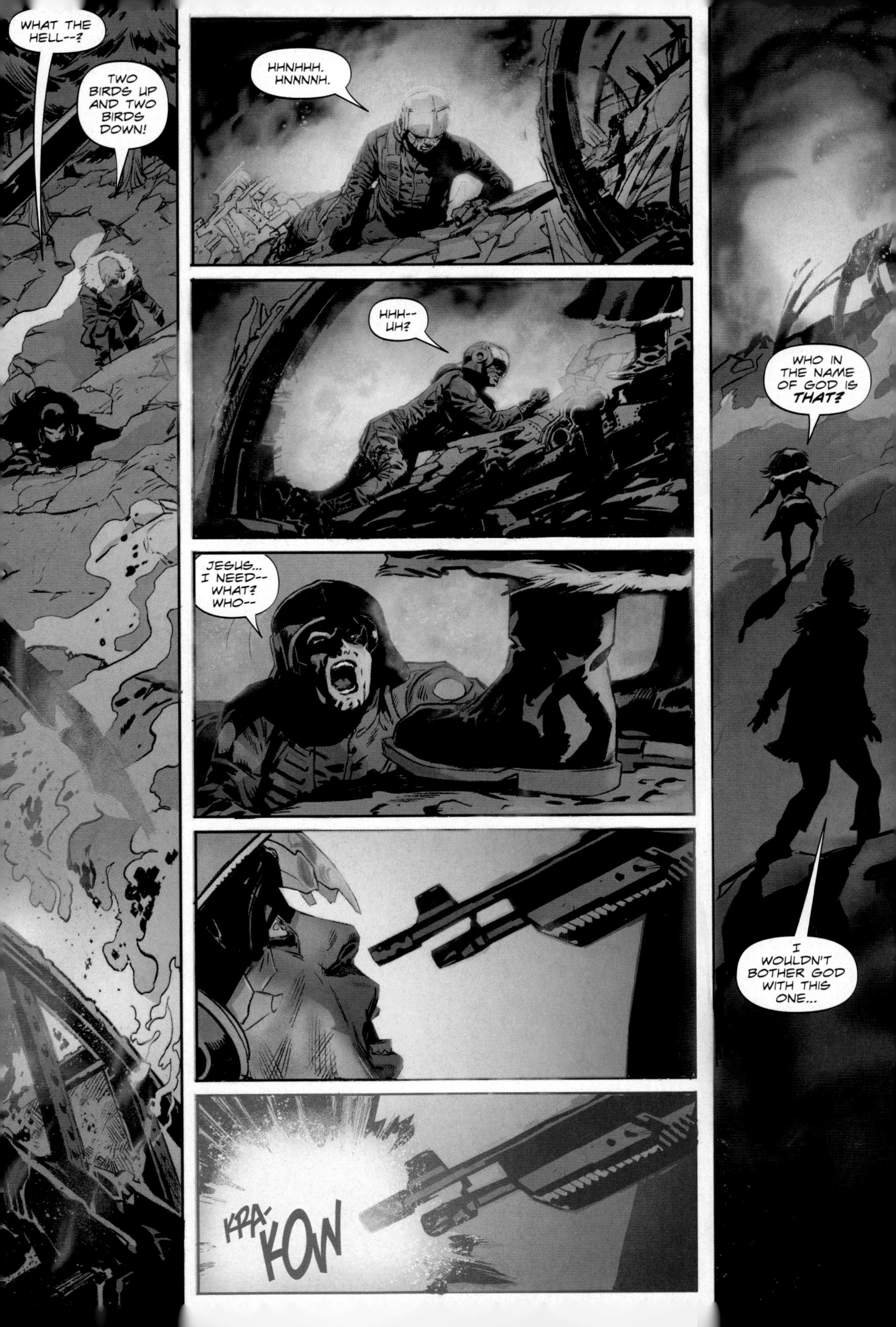
WHAT THE HELL--?
TWO BIRDS UP AND TWO BIRDS DOWN!
HHNHHH. HNNNNH.
HHH--UH?
JESUS... I NEED--WHAT? WHO--
KRA-KOW
WHO IN THE NAME OF GOD IS *THAT?*
I WOULDN'T BOTHER GOD WITH THIS ONE...

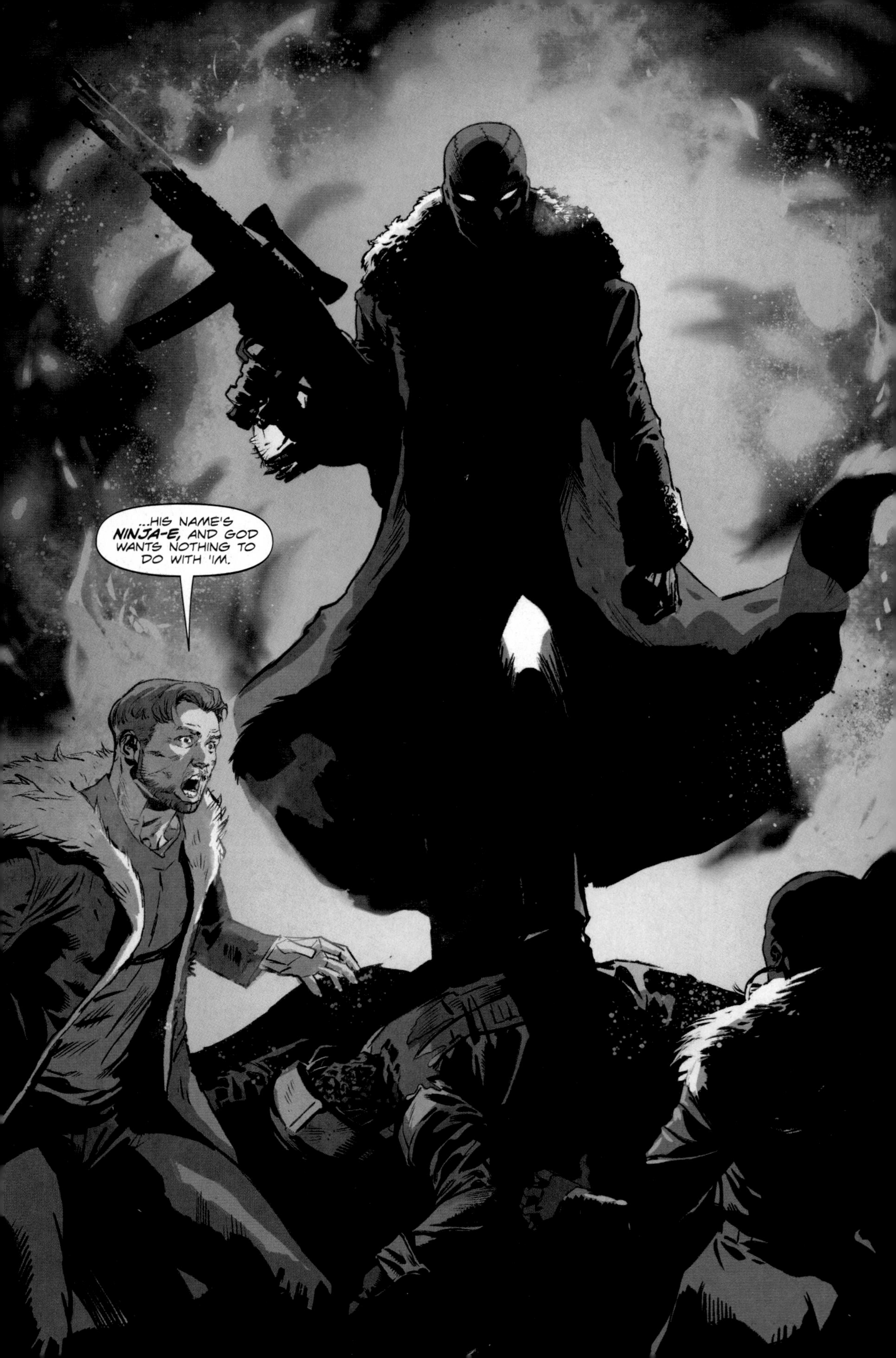
...HIS NAME'S NINJA-E, AND GOD WANTS NOTHING TO DO WITH 'IM.

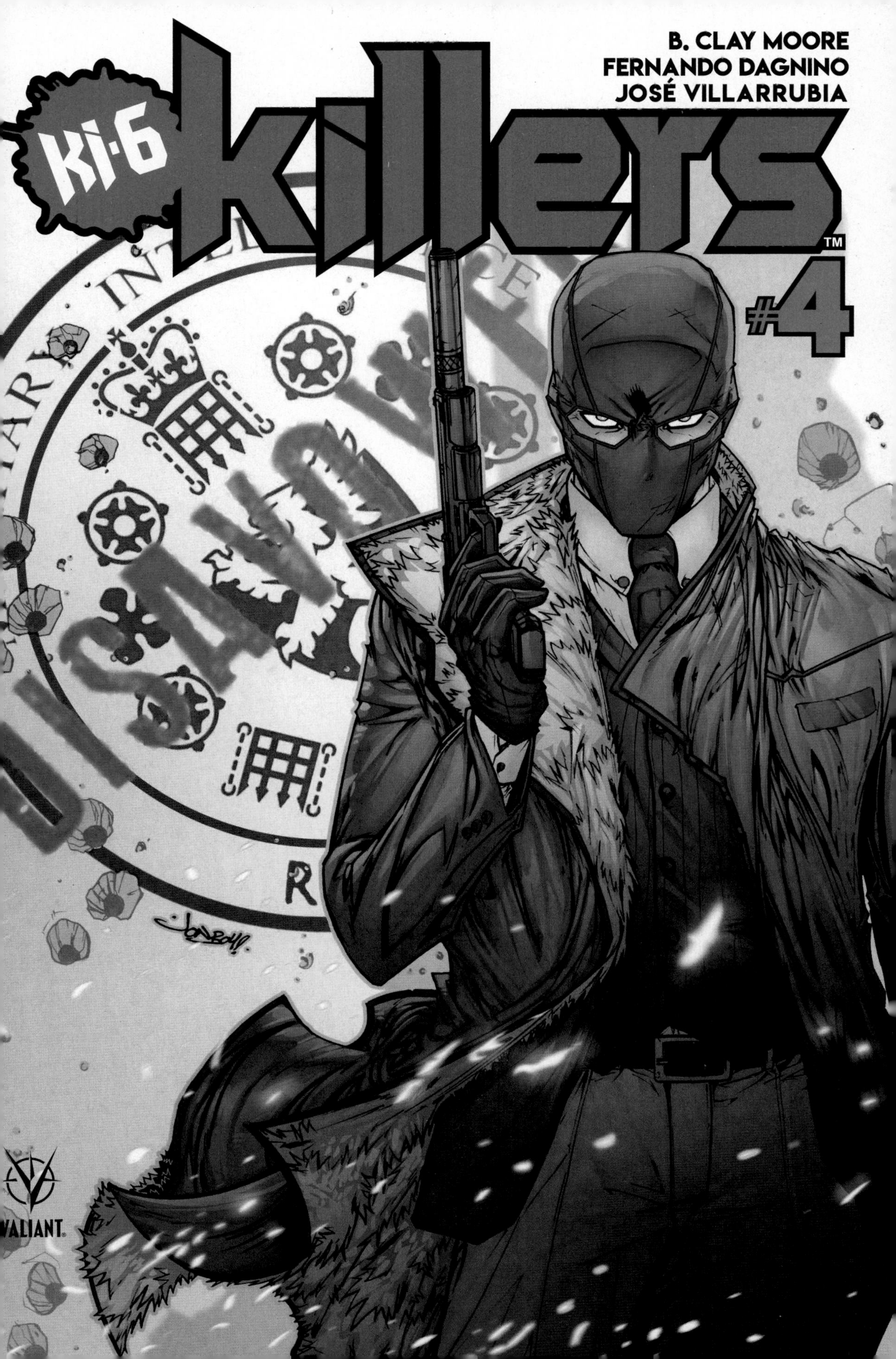
B. CLAY MOORE
FERNANDO DAGNINO
JOSÉ VILLARRUBIA
KI-6
killers™
#4
VALIANT

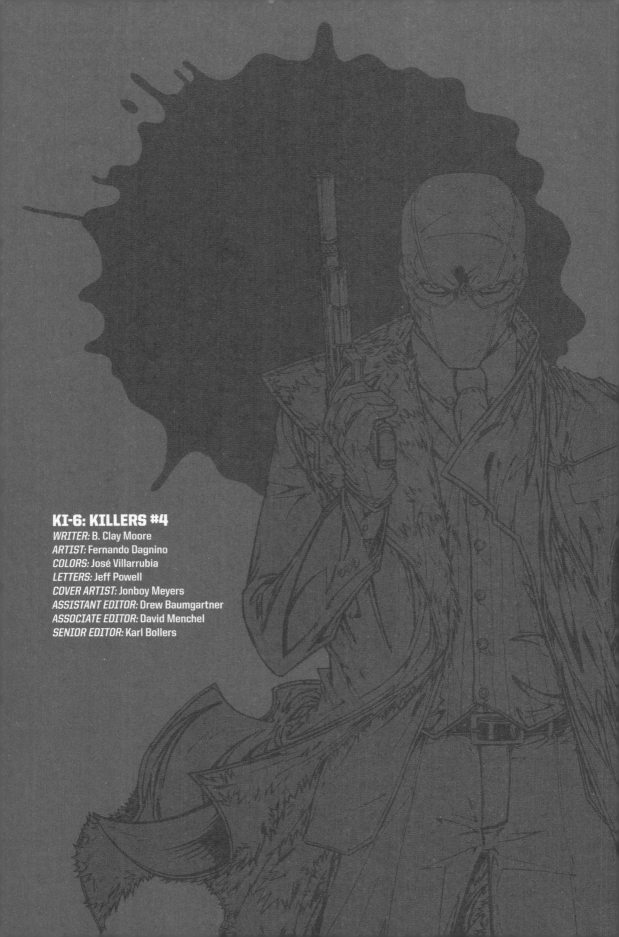

KI-6: KILLERS #4
WRITER: B. Clay Moore
ARTIST: Fernando Dagnino
COLORS: José Villarrubia
LETTERS: Jeff Powell
COVER ARTIST: Jonboy Meyers
ASSISTANT EDITOR: Drew Baumgartner
ASSOCIATE EDITOR: David Menchel
SENIOR EDITOR: Karl Bollers

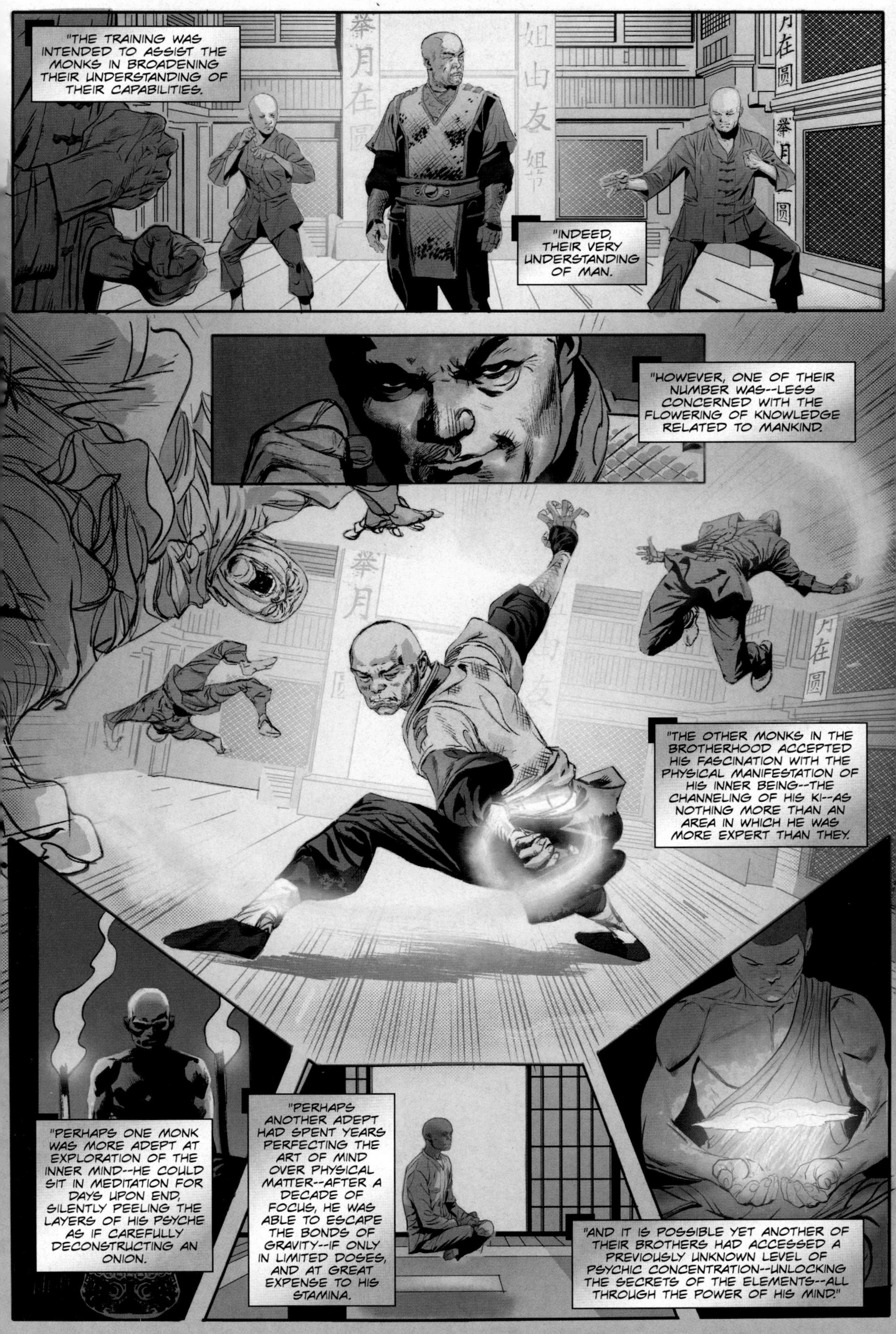
"THE TRAINING WAS INTENDED TO ASSIST THE MONKS IN BROADENING THEIR UNDERSTANDING OF THEIR CAPABILITIES.
"INDEED, THEIR VERY UNDERSTANDING OF MAN.
"HOWEVER, ONE OF THEIR NUMBER WAS--LESS CONCERNED WITH THE FLOWERING OF KNOWLEDGE RELATED TO MANKIND.
"THE OTHER MONKS IN THE BROTHERHOOD ACCEPTED HIS FASCINATION WITH THE PHYSICAL MANIFESTATION OF HIS INNER BEING--THE CHANNELING OF HIS KI--AS NOTHING MORE THAN AN AREA IN WHICH HE WAS MORE EXPERT THAN THEY.
"PERHAPS ONE MONK WAS MORE ADEPT AT EXPLORATION OF THE INNER MIND--HE COULD SIT IN MEDITATION FOR DAYS UPON END, SILENTLY PEELING THE LAYERS OF HIS PSYCHE AS IF CAREFULLY DECONSTRUCTING AN ONION.
"PERHAPS ANOTHER ADEPT HAD SPENT YEARS PERFECTING THE ART OF MIND OVER PHYSICAL MATTER--AFTER A DECADE OF FOCUS, HE WAS ABLE TO ESCAPE THE BONDS OF GRAVITY--IF ONLY IN LIMITED DOSES, AND AT GREAT EXPENSE TO HIS STAMINA.
"AND IT IS POSSIBLE YET ANOTHER OF THEIR BROTHERS HAD ACCESSED A PREVIOUSLY UNKNOWN LEVEL OF PSYCHIC CONCENTRATION--UNLOCKING THE SECRETS OF THE ELEMENTS--ALL THROUGH THE POWER OF HIS MIND."

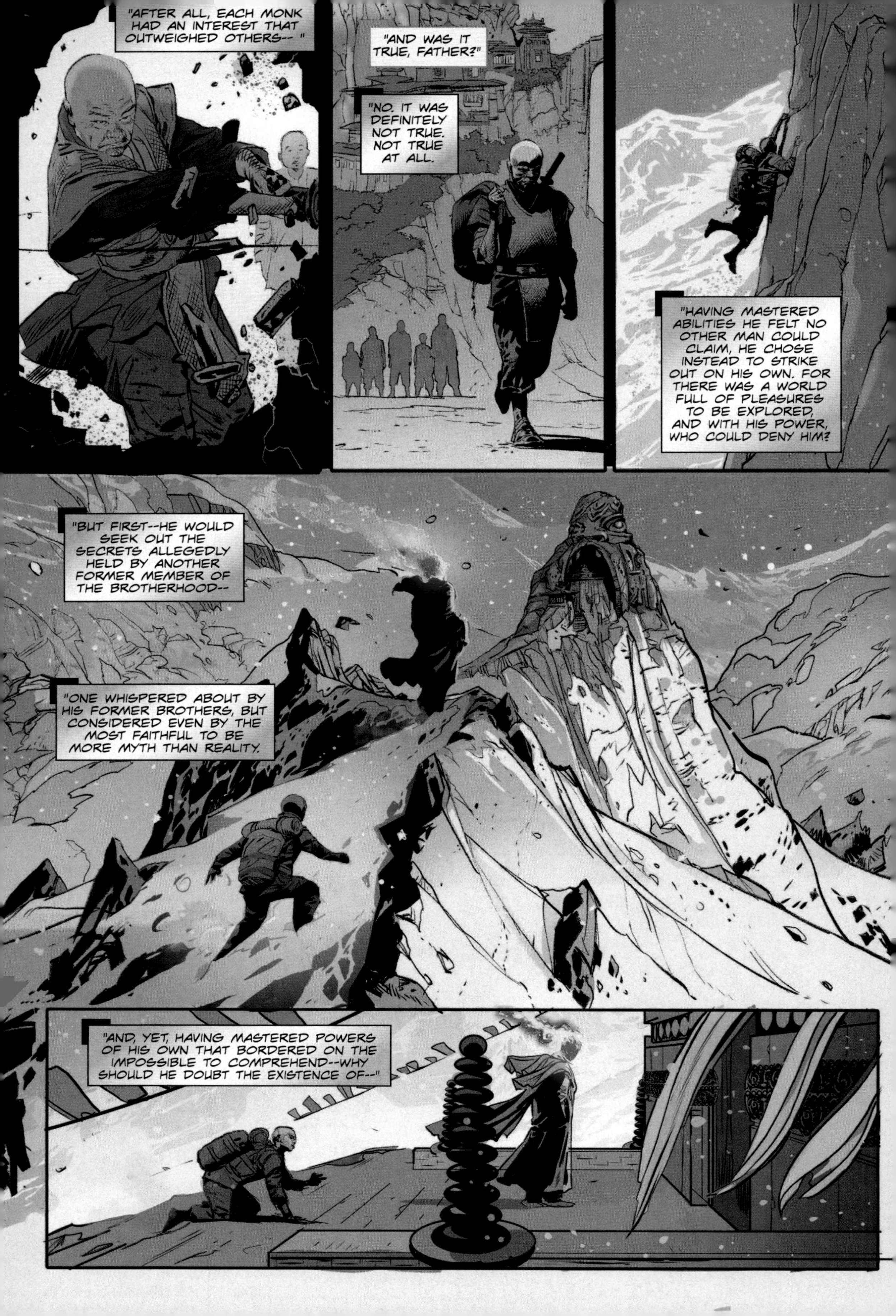
"AFTER ALL, EACH MONK HAD AN INTEREST THAT OUTWEIGHED OTHERS-- "
"AND WAS IT TRUE, FATHER?"
"NO. IT WAS DEFINITELY NOT TRUE. NOT TRUE AT ALL.
"HAVING MASTERED ABILITIES HE FELT NO OTHER MAN COULD CLAIM, HE CHOSE INSTEAD TO STRIKE OUT ON HIS OWN. FOR THERE WAS A WORLD FULL OF PLEASURES TO BE EXPLORED, AND WITH HIS POWER, WHO COULD DENY HIM?
"BUT FIRST--HE WOULD SEEK OUT THE SECRETS ALLEGEDLY HELD BY ANOTHER FORMER MEMBER OF THE BROTHERHOOD--
"ONE WHISPERED ABOUT BY HIS FORMER BROTHERS, BUT CONSIDERED EVEN BY THE MOST FAITHFUL TO BE MORE MYTH THAN REALITY.
"AND, YET, HAVING MASTERED POWERS OF HIS OWN THAT BORDERED ON THE IMPOSSIBLE TO COMPREHEND--WHY SHOULD HE DOUBT THE EXISTENCE OF--"

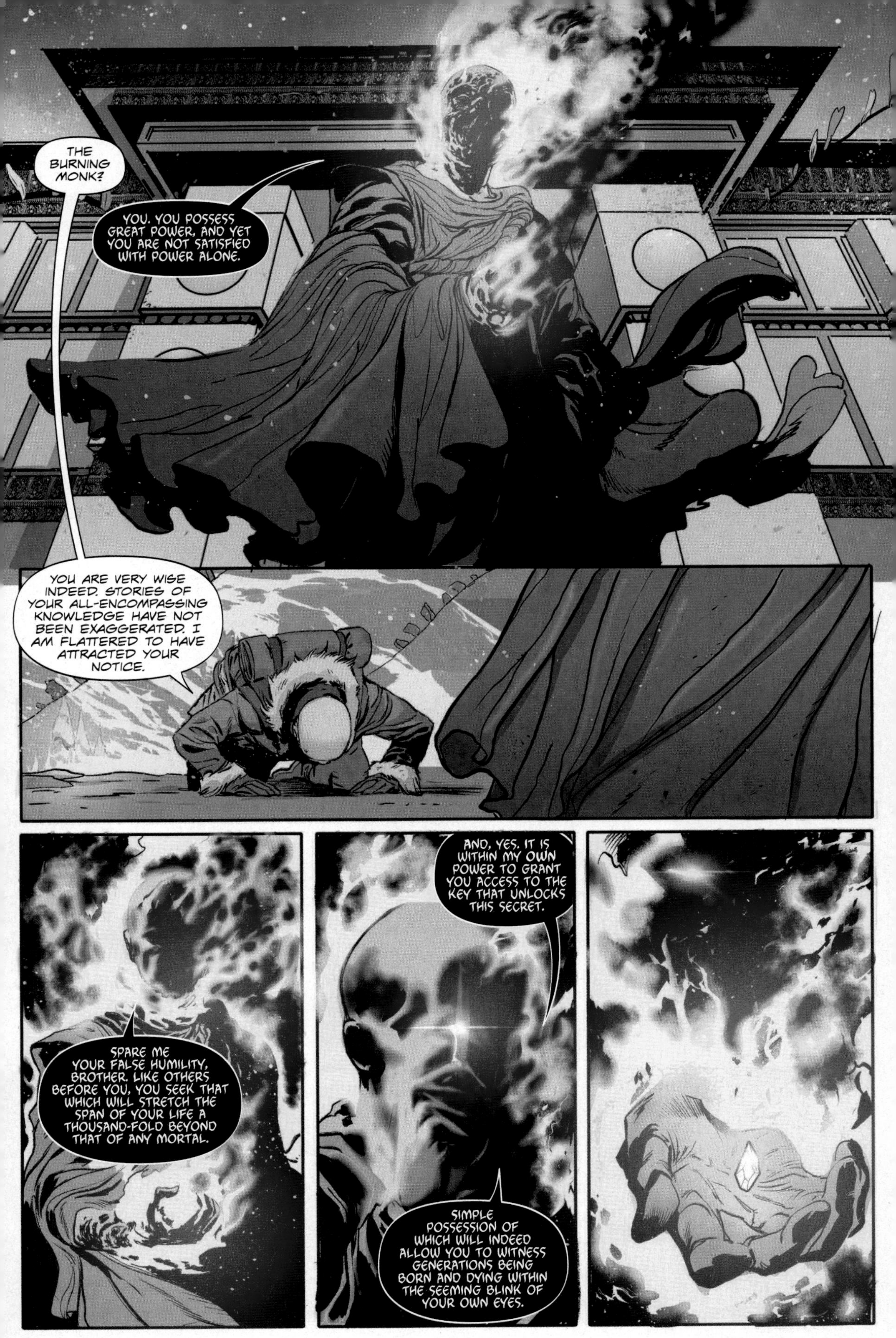
THE BURNING MONK?
YOU. YOU POSSESS GREAT POWER, AND YET YOU ARE NOT SATISFIED WITH POWER ALONE.
YOU ARE VERY WISE INDEED. STORIES OF YOUR ALL-ENCOMPASSING KNOWLEDGE HAVE NOT BEEN EXAGGERATED. I AM FLATTERED TO HAVE ATTRACTED YOUR NOTICE.
SPARE ME YOUR FALSE HUMILITY, BROTHER. LIKE OTHERS BEFORE YOU, YOU SEEK THAT WHICH WILL STRETCH THE SPAN OF YOUR LIFE A THOUSAND-FOLD BEYOND THAT OF ANY MORTAL.
AND, YES. IT IS WITHIN MY OWN POWER TO GRANT YOU ACCESS TO THE KEY THAT UNLOCKS THIS SECRET.
SIMPLE POSSESSION OF WHICH WILL INDEED ALLOW YOU TO WITNESS GENERATIONS BEING BORN AND DYING WITHIN THE SEEMING BLINK OF YOUR OWN EYES.

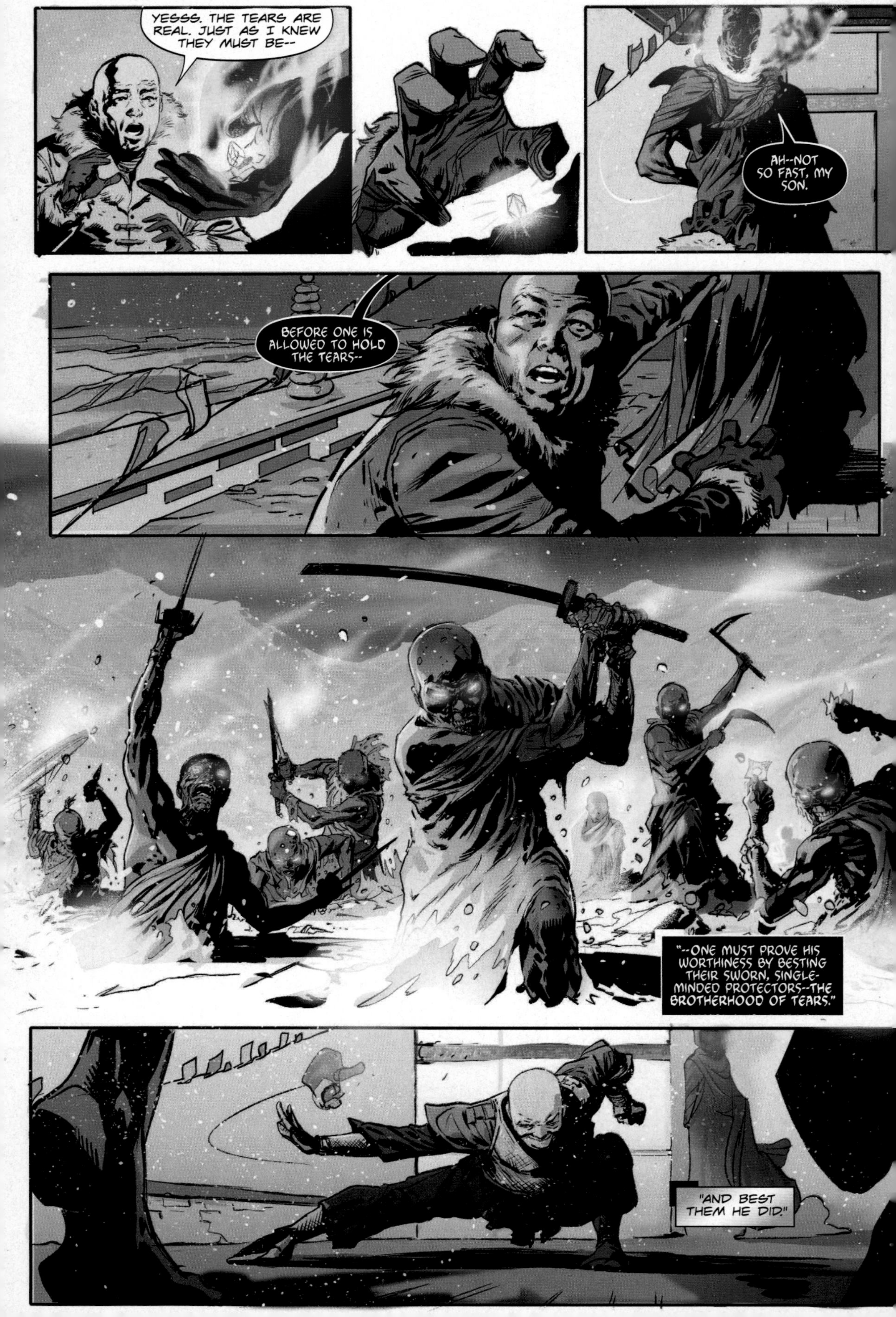
YESSS. THE TEARS ARE REAL. JUST AS I KNEW THEY MUST BE--
AH--NOT SO FAST, MY SON.
BEFORE ONE IS ALLOWED TO HOLD THE TEARS--
"--ONE MUST PROVE HIS WORTHINESS BY BESTING THEIR SWORN, SINGLE-MINDED PROTECTORS--THE BROTHERHOOD OF TEARS."
"AND BEST THEM HE DID."

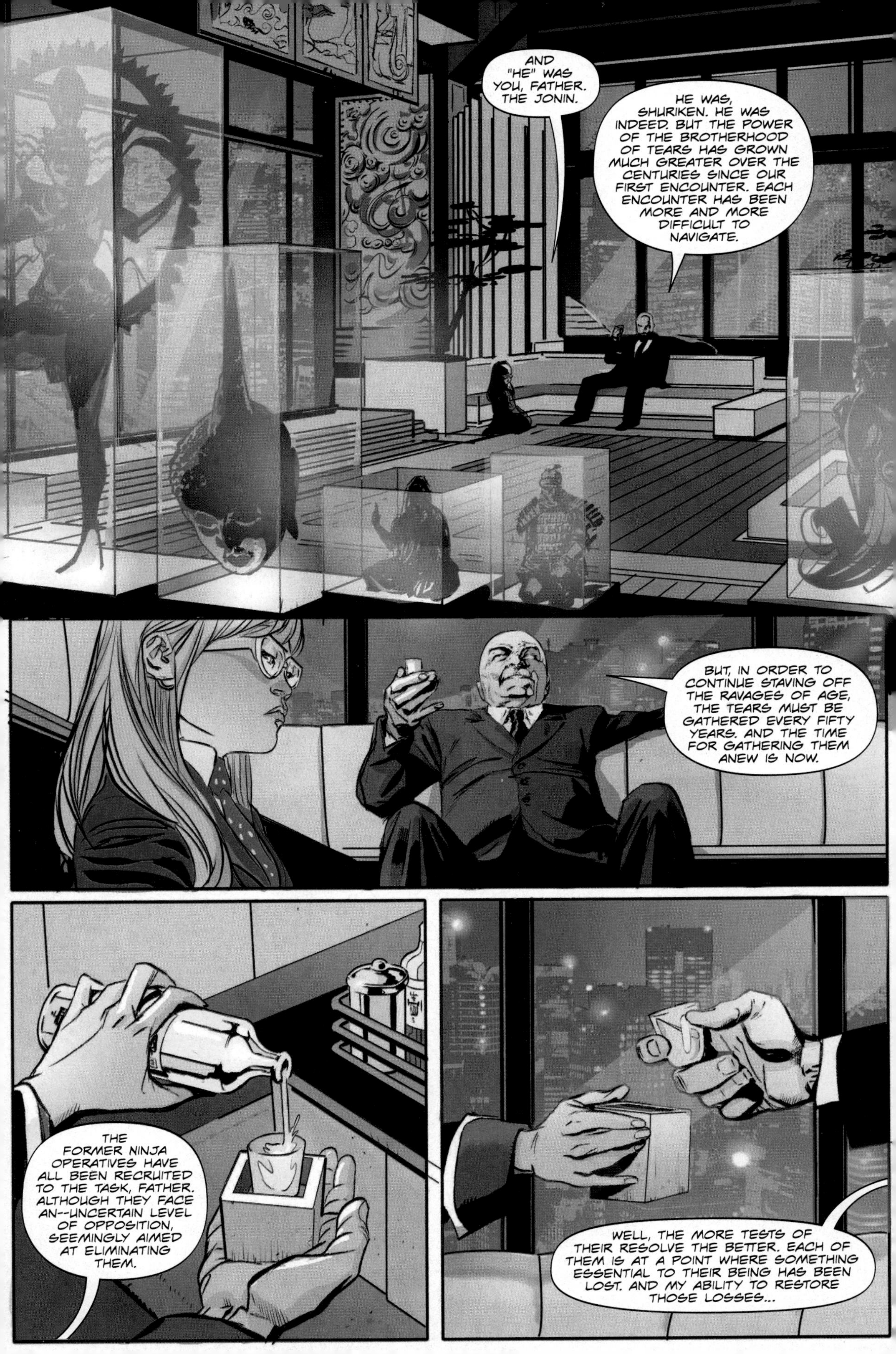
AND "HE" WAS YOU, FATHER. THE JONIN.
HE WAS, SHURIKEN. HE WAS INDEED. BUT THE POWER OF THE BROTHERHOOD OF TEARS HAS GROWN MUCH GREATER OVER THE CENTURIES SINCE OUR FIRST ENCOUNTER. EACH ENCOUNTER HAS BEEN MORE AND MORE DIFFICULT TO NAVIGATE.
BUT, IN ORDER TO CONTINUE STAVING OFF THE RAVAGES OF AGE, THE TEARS MUST BE GATHERED EVERY FIFTY YEARS. AND THE TIME FOR GATHERING THEM ANEW IS NOW.
THE FORMER NINJA OPERATIVES HAVE ALL BEEN RECRUITED TO THE TASK, FATHER. ALTHOUGH THEY FACE AN--UNCERTAIN LEVEL OF OPPOSITION, SEEMINGLY AIMED AT ELIMINATING THEM.
WELL, THE MORE TESTS OF THEIR RESOLVE THE BETTER. EACH OF THEM IS AT A POINT WHERE SOMETHING ESSENTIAL TO THEIR BEING HAS BEEN LOST. AND MY ABILITY TO RESTORE THOSE LOSSES...

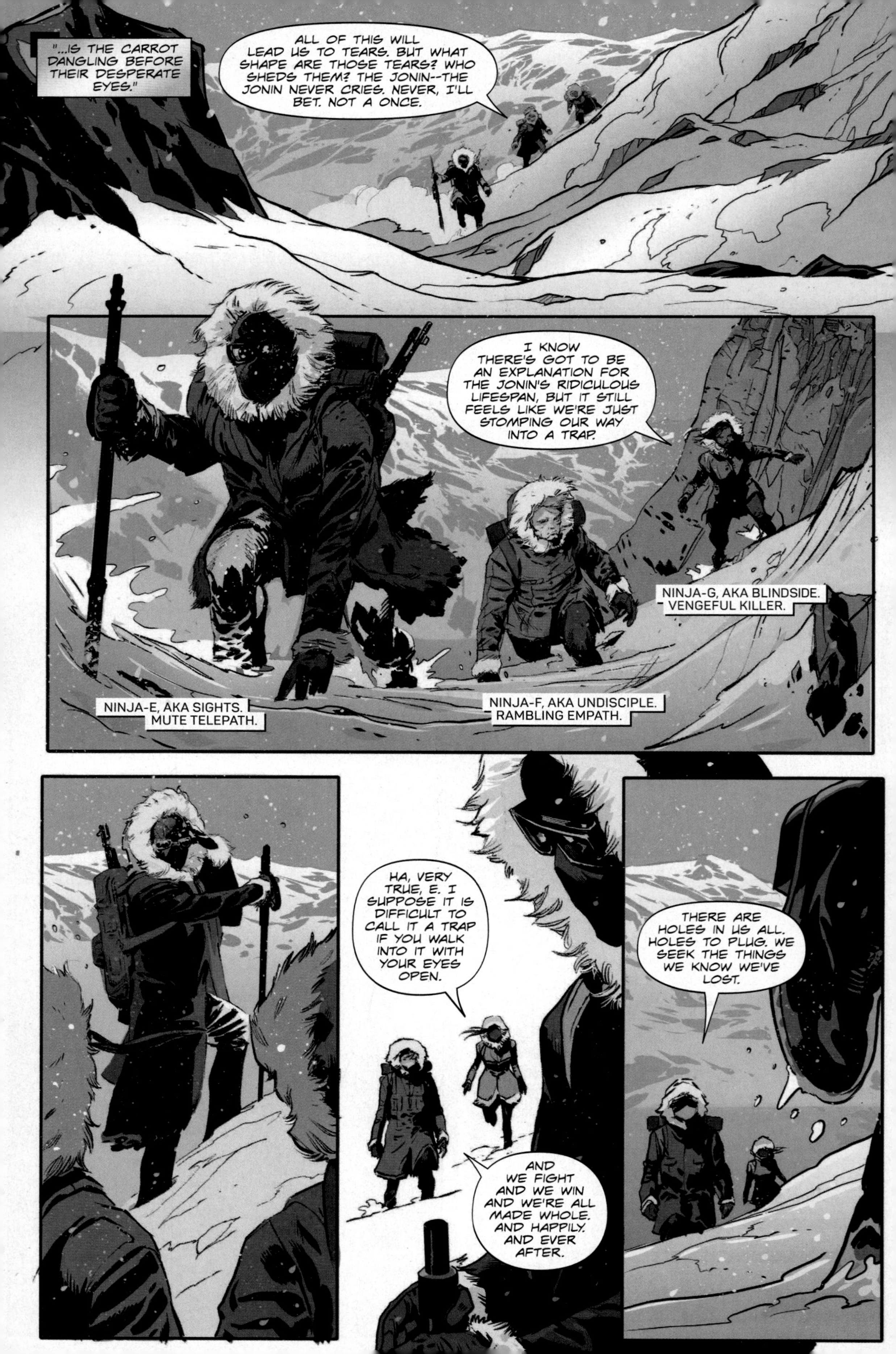
"...IS THE CARROT DANGLING BEFORE THEIR DESPERATE EYES."
ALL OF THIS WILL LEAD US TO TEARS. BUT WHAT SHAPE ARE THOSE TEARS? WHO SHEDS THEM? THE JONIN--THE JONIN NEVER CRIES. NEVER, I'LL BET. NOT A ONCE.
I KNOW THERE'S GOT TO BE AN EXPLANATION FOR THE JONIN'S RIDICULOUS LIFESPAN, BUT IT STILL FEELS LIKE WE'RE JUST STOMPING OUR WAY INTO A TRAP.
NINJA-G, AKA BLINDSIDE. VENGEFUL KILLER.
NINJA-E, AKA SIGHTS. MUTE TELEPATH.
NINJA-F, AKA UNDISCIPLE. RAMBLING EMPATH.
HA, VERY TRUE, E. I SUPPOSE IT IS DIFFICULT TO CALL IT A TRAP IF YOU WALK INTO IT WITH YOUR EYES OPEN.
AND WE FIGHT AND WE WIN AND WE'RE ALL MADE WHOLE. AND HAPPILY. AND EVER AFTER.
THERE ARE HOLES IN US ALL. HOLES TO PLUG. WE SEEK THE THINGS WE KNOW WE'VE LOST.

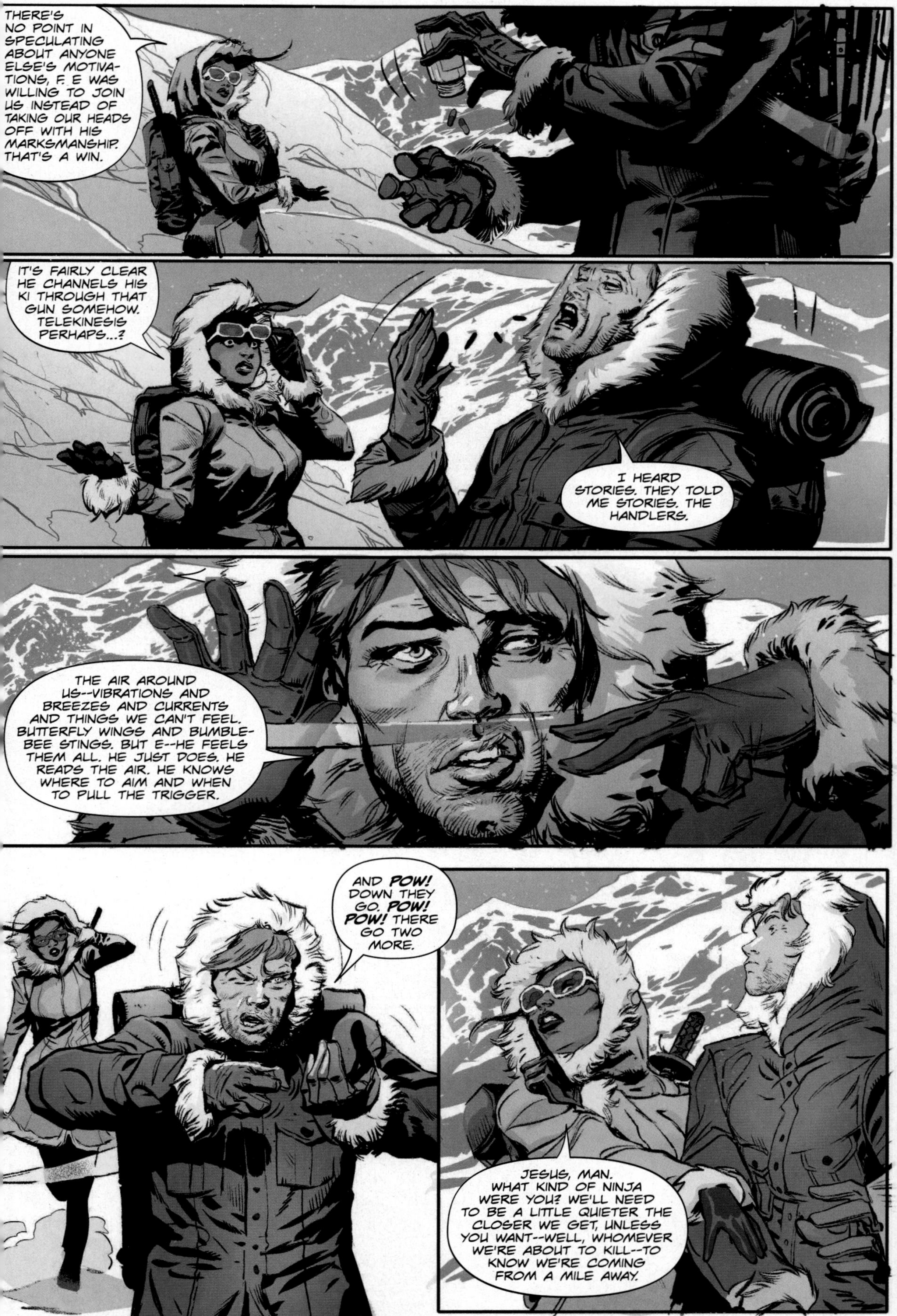
THERE'S NO POINT IN SPECULATING ABOUT ANYONE ELSE'S MOTIVATIONS, F. E WAS WILLING TO JOIN US INSTEAD OF TAKING OUR HEADS OFF WITH HIS MARKSMANSHIP. THAT'S A WIN.
IT'S FAIRLY CLEAR HE CHANNELS HIS KI THROUGH THAT GUN SOMEHOW. TELEKINESIS PERHAPS...?
I HEARD STORIES. THEY TOLD ME STORIES. THE HANDLERS.
THE AIR AROUND US--VIBRATIONS AND BREEZES AND CURRENTS AND THINGS WE CAN'T FEEL. BUTTERFLY WINGS AND BUMBLE-BEE STINGS. BUT E--HE FEELS THEM ALL. HE JUST DOES. HE READS THE AIR. HE KNOWS WHERE TO AIM AND WHEN TO PULL THE TRIGGER.
AND POW! DOWN THEY GO. POW! POW! THERE GO TWO MORE.
JESUS, MAN. WHAT KIND OF NINJA WERE YOU? WE'LL NEED TO BE A LITTLE QUIETER THE CLOSER WE GET, UNLESS YOU WANT--WELL, WHOMEVER WE'RE ABOUT TO KILL--TO KNOW WE'RE COMING FROM A MILE AWAY.

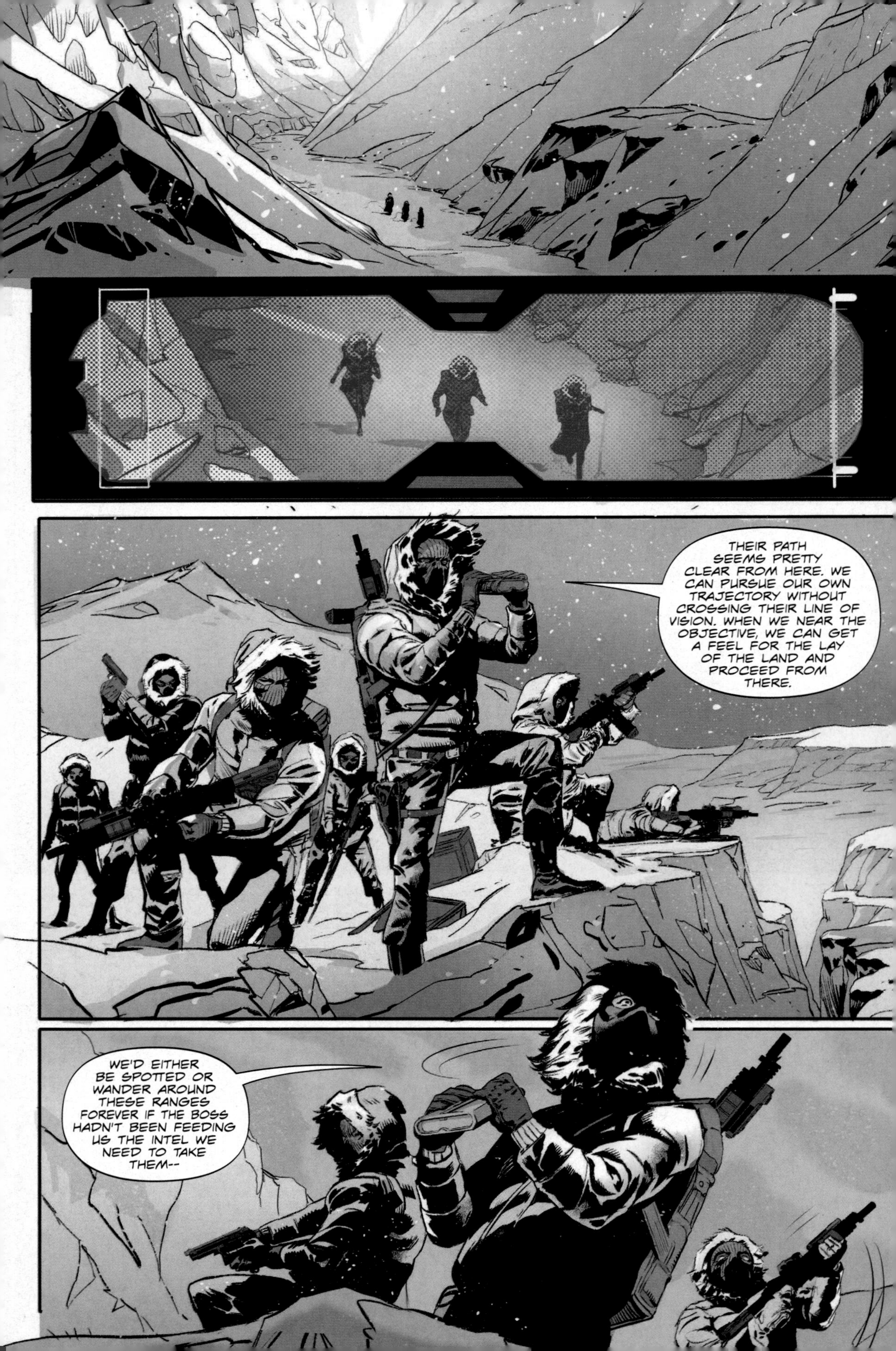
THEIR PATH SEEMS PRETTY CLEAR FROM HERE. WE CAN PURSUE OUR OWN TRAJECTORY WITHOUT CROSSING THEIR LINE OF VISION. WHEN WE NEAR THE OBJECTIVE, WE CAN GET A FEEL FOR THE LAY OF THE LAND AND PROCEED FROM THERE.
WE'D EITHER BE SPOTTED OR WANDER AROUND THESE RANGES FOREVER IF THE BOSS HADN'T BEEN FEEDING US THE INTEL WE NEED TO TAKE THEM--

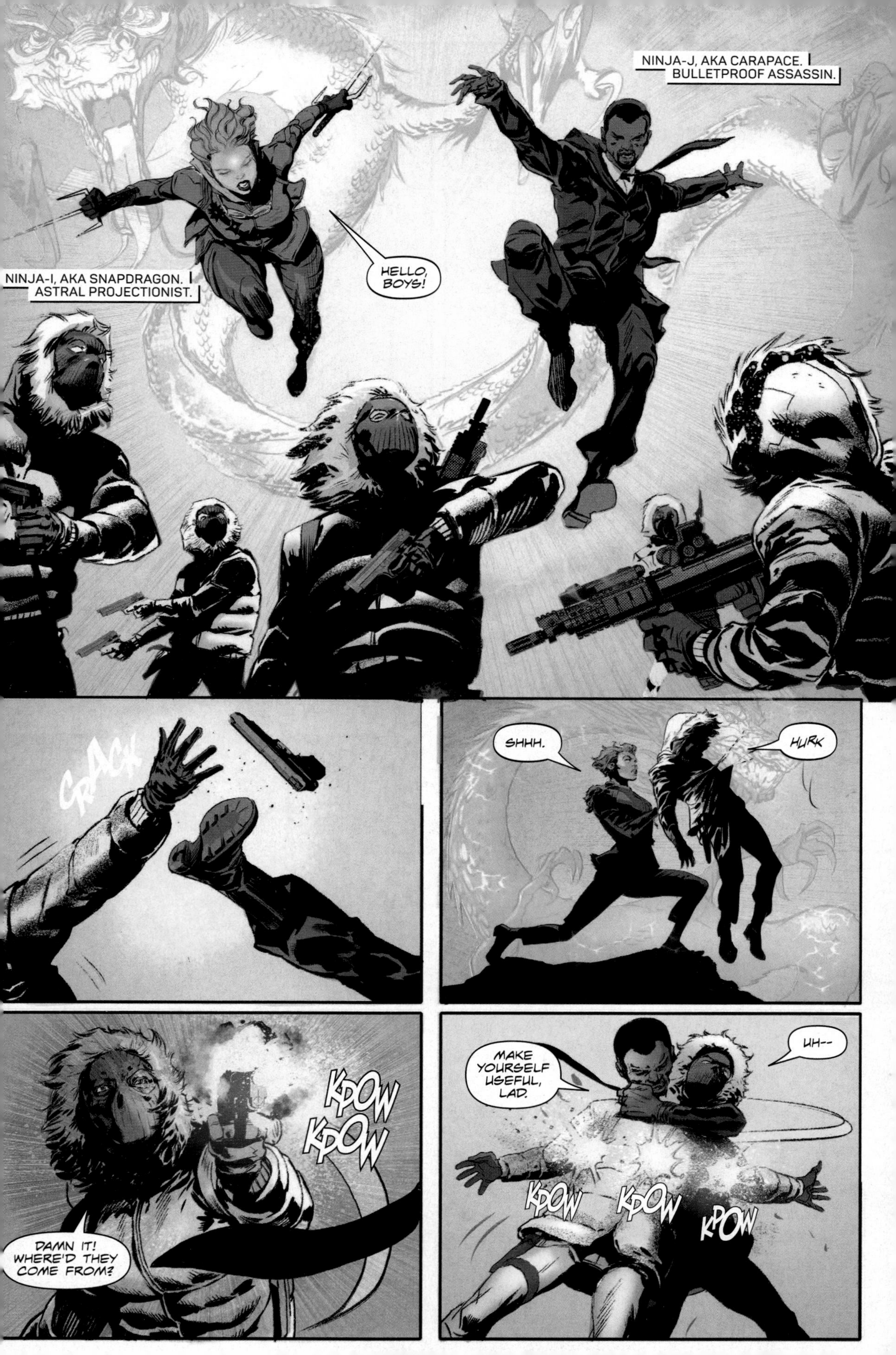
NINJA-J, AKA CARAPACE. BULLETPROOF ASSASSIN.
NINJA-I, AKA SNAPDRAGON. ASTRAL PROJECTIONIST.
HELLO, BOYS!
CRACK
SHHH.
HURK
KPOW KPOW
DAMN IT! WHERE'D THEY COME FROM?
MAKE YOURSELF USEFUL, LAD.
UH--
KPOW KPOW KPOW

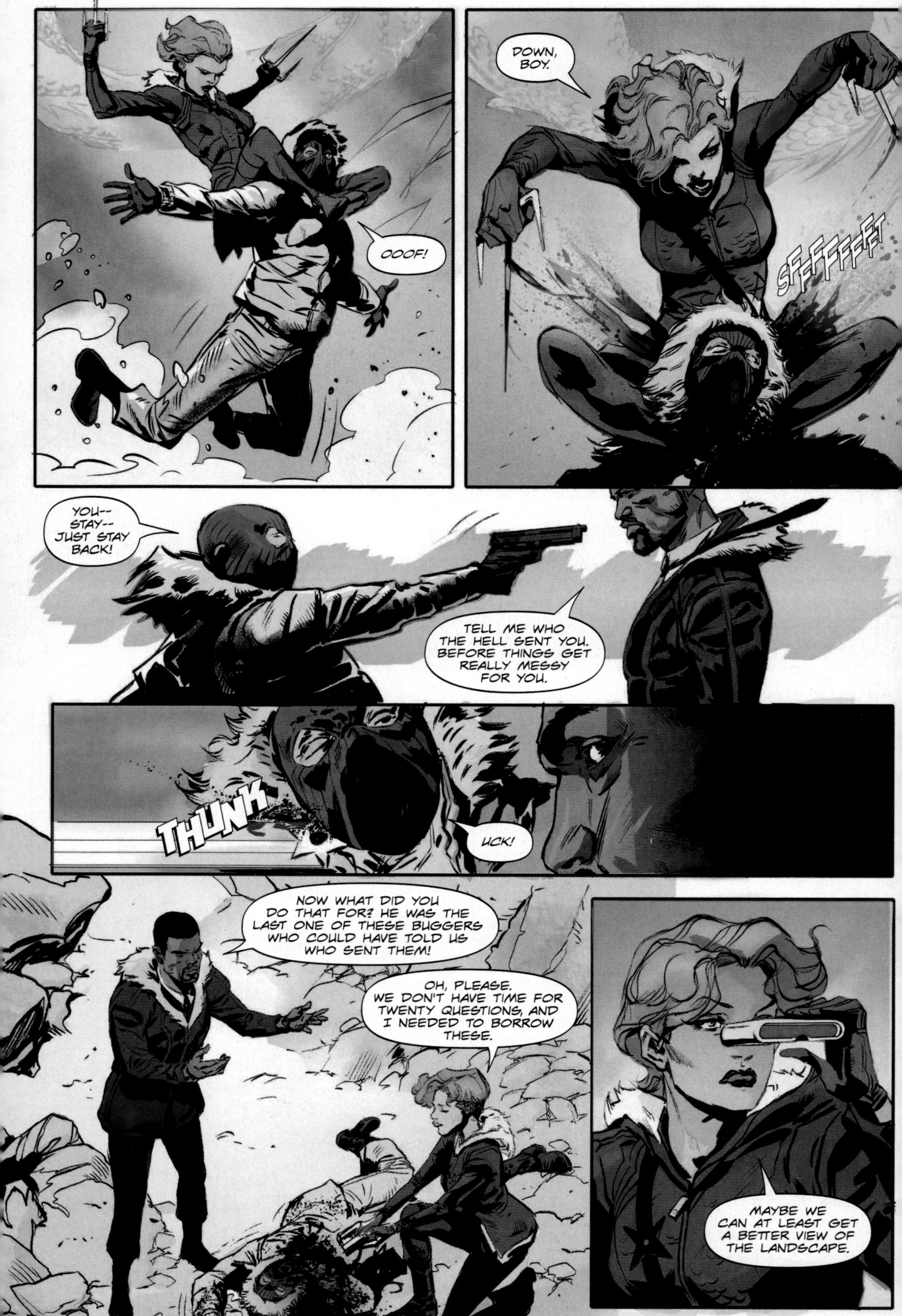
OOOF!
DOWN, BOY.
SFFFFFFFFT
YOU-- STAY-- JUST STAY BACK!
TELL ME WHO THE HELL SENT YOU. BEFORE THINGS GET REALLY MESSY FOR YOU.
THUNK
UCK!
NOW WHAT DID YOU DO THAT FOR? HE WAS THE LAST ONE OF THESE BUGGERS WHO COULD HAVE TOLD US WHO SENT THEM!
OH, PLEASE. WE DON'T HAVE TIME FOR TWENTY QUESTIONS, AND I NEEDED TO BORROW THESE.
MAYBE WE CAN AT LEAST GET A BETTER VIEW OF THE LANDSCAPE.

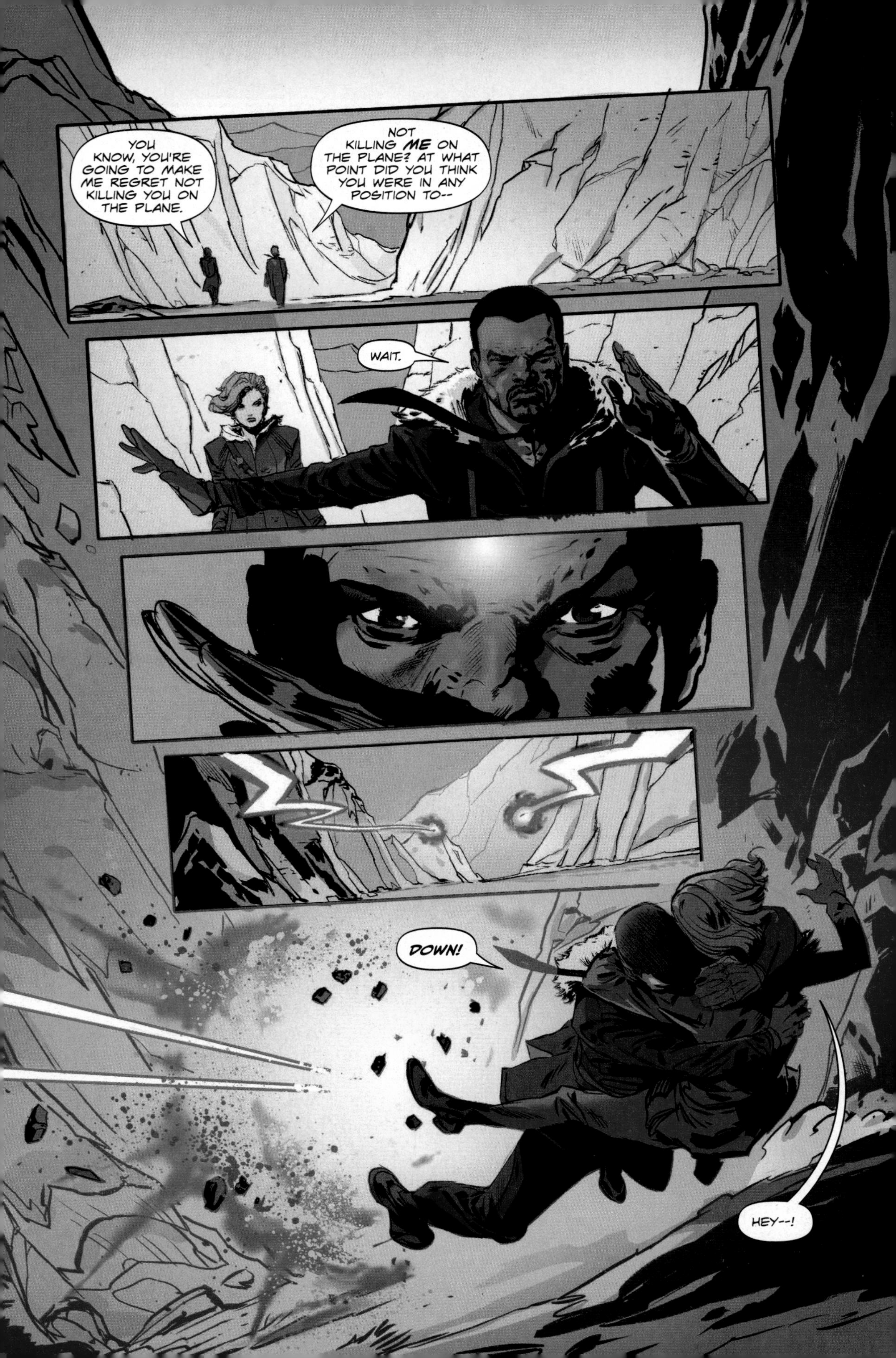
YOU KNOW, YOU'RE GOING TO MAKE ME REGRET NOT KILLING YOU ON THE PLANE.
NOT KILLING ME ON THE PLANE? AT WHAT POINT DID YOU THINK YOU WERE IN ANY POSITION TO--
WAIT.
DOWN!
HEY--!

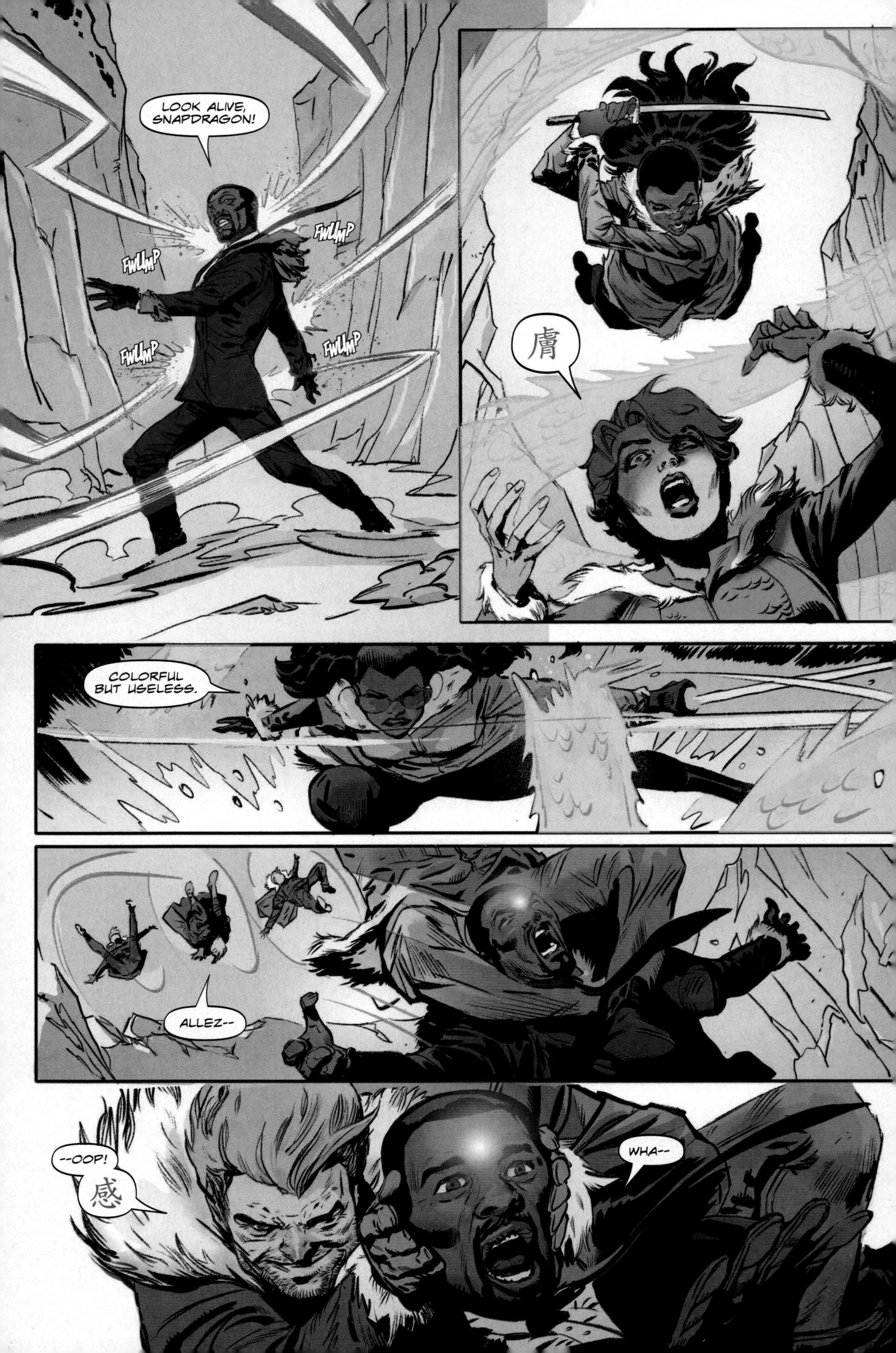
LOOK ALIVE, SNAPDRAGON!
FWUMP
FWUMP
FWUMP
FWUMP
虜
COLORFUL BUT USELESS.
ALLEZ--
--OOP!
感
WHA--

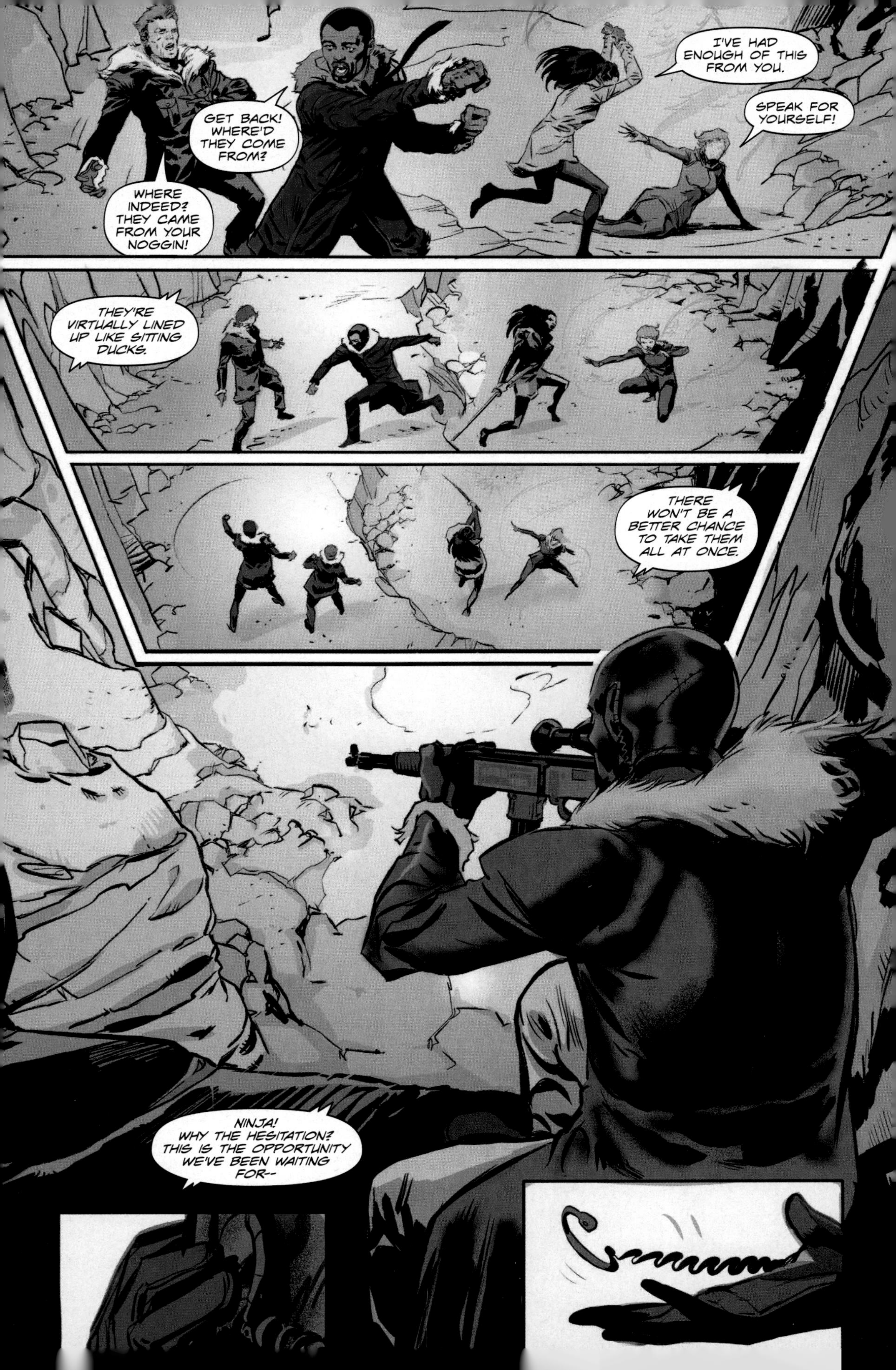
GET BACK! WHERE'D THEY COME FROM?
WHERE INDEED? THEY CAME FROM YOUR NOGGIN!
I'VE HAD ENOUGH OF THIS FROM YOU.
SPEAK FOR YOURSELF!
THEY'RE VIRTUALLY LINED UP LIKE SITTING DUCKS.
THERE WON'T BE A BETTER CHANCE TO TAKE THEM ALL AT ONCE.
NINJA! WHY THE HESITATION? THIS IS THE OPPORTUNITY WE'VE BEEN WAITING FOR--

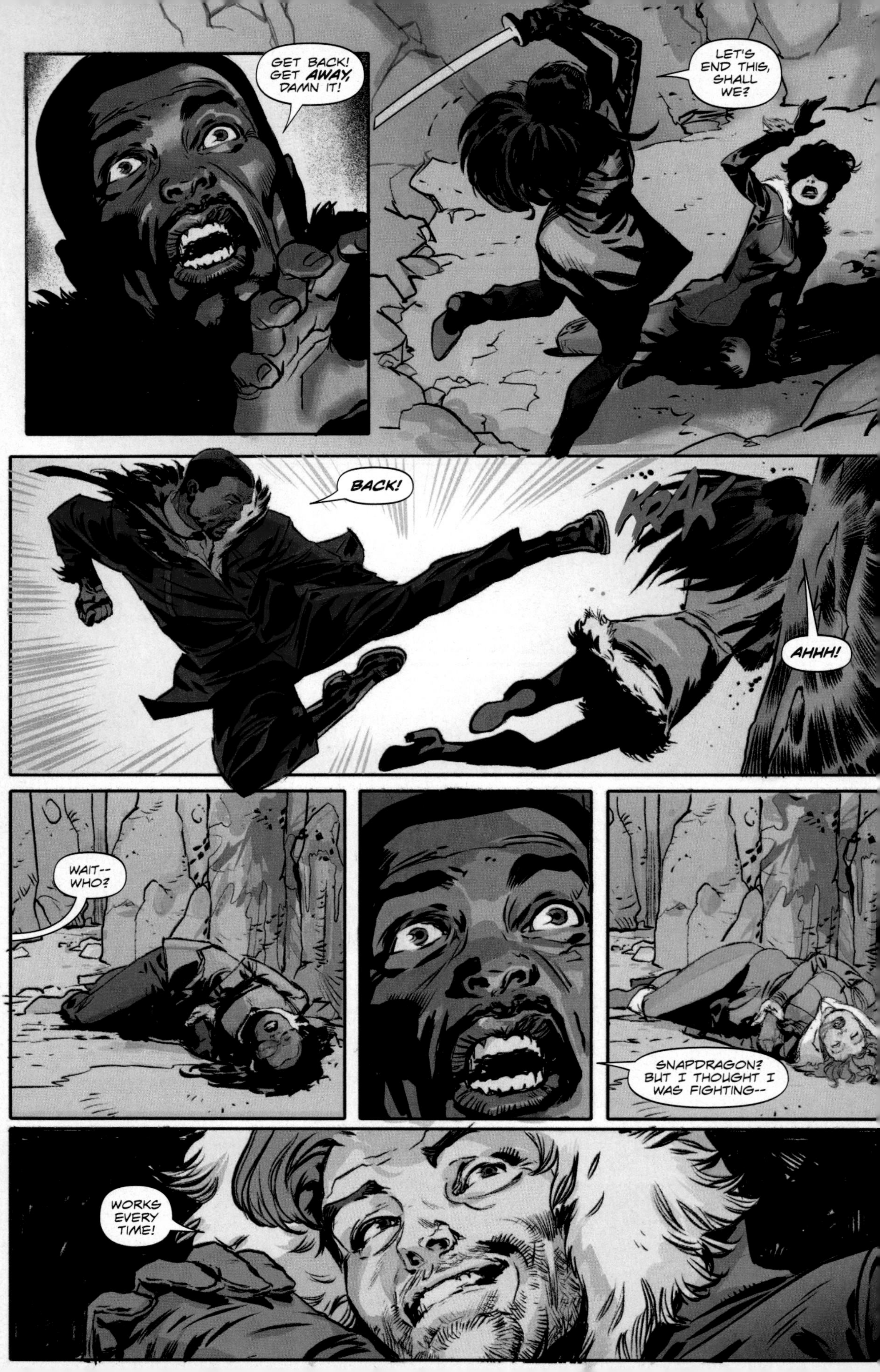
GET BACK! GET **AWAY,** DAMN IT!
LET'S END THIS, SHALL WE?
BACK!
KRAK
AHHH!
WAIT-- WHO?
SNAPDRAGON? BUT I THOUGHT I WAS FIGHTING--
WORKS EVERY TIME!

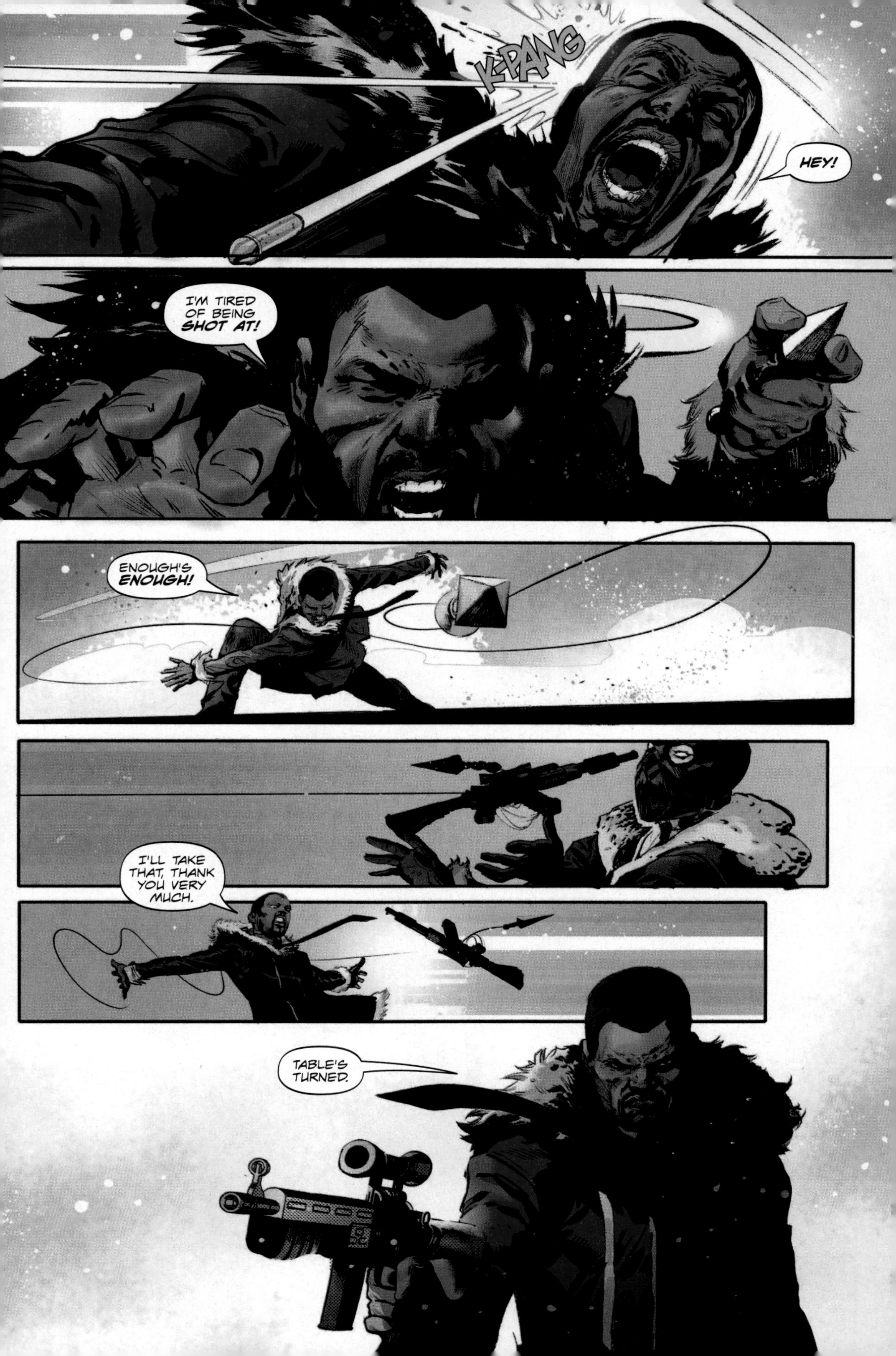
K-PANG
HEY!
I'M TIRED OF BEING SHOT AT!
ENOUGH'S ENOUGH!
I'LL TAKE THAT, THANK YOU VERY MUCH.
TABLE'S TURNED.

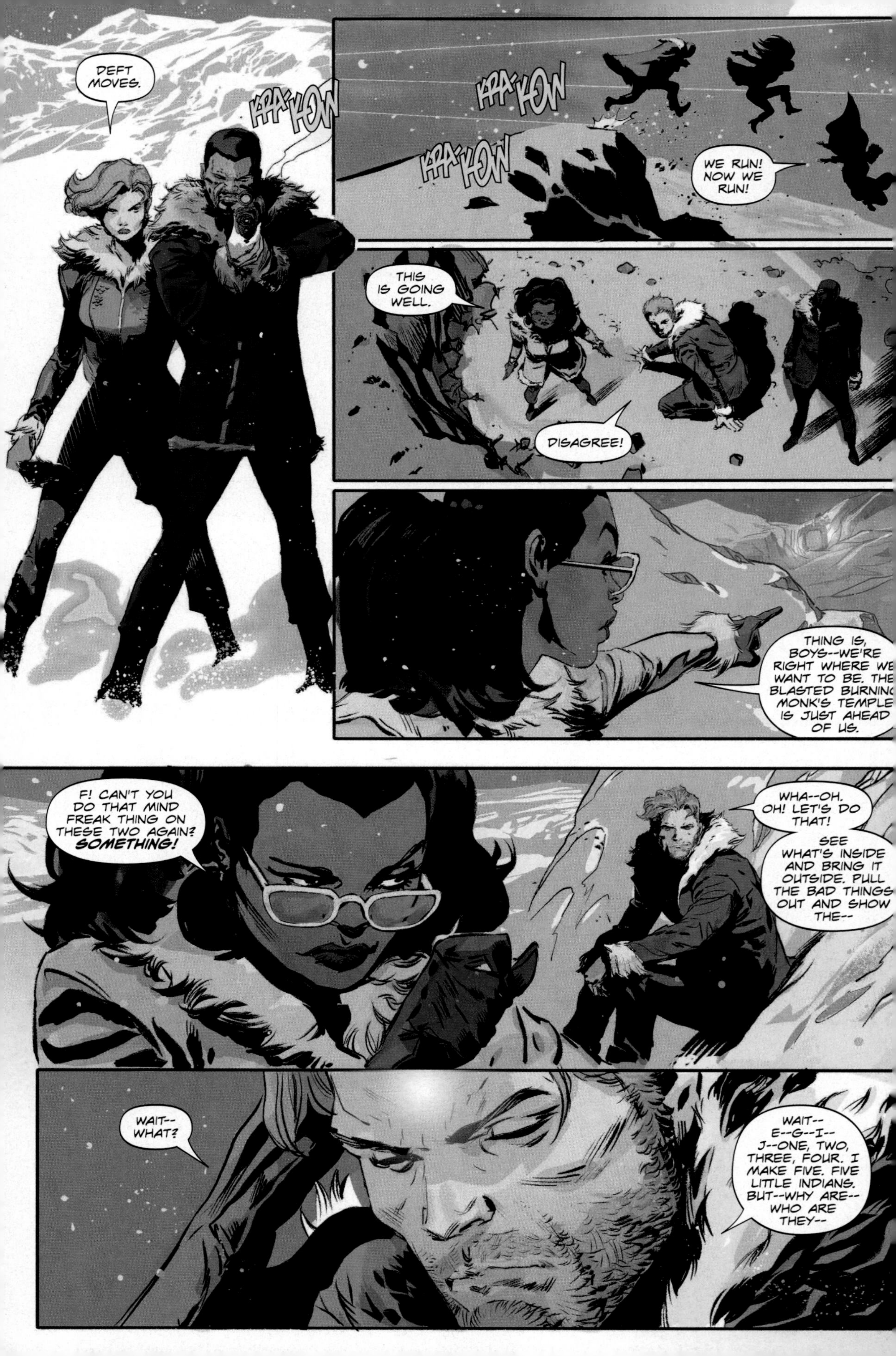
DEFT MOVES.
KRA-KOW
KRA-KOW
KRA-KOW
WE RUN! NOW WE RUN!
THIS IS GOING WELL.
DISAGREE!
THING IS, BOYS--WE'RE RIGHT WHERE WE WANT TO BE. THE BLASTED BURNING MONK'S TEMPLE IS JUST AHEAD OF US.
F! CAN'T YOU DO THAT MIND FREAK THING ON THESE TWO AGAIN? SOMETHING!
WHA--OH. OH! LET'S DO THAT!
SEE WHAT'S INSIDE AND BRING IT OUTSIDE. PULL THE BAD THINGS OUT AND SHOW THE--
WAIT--WHAT?
WAIT--E--G--I--J--ONE, TWO, THREE, FOUR. I MAKE FIVE. FIVE LITTLE INDIANS. BUT--WHY ARE--WHO ARE THEY--

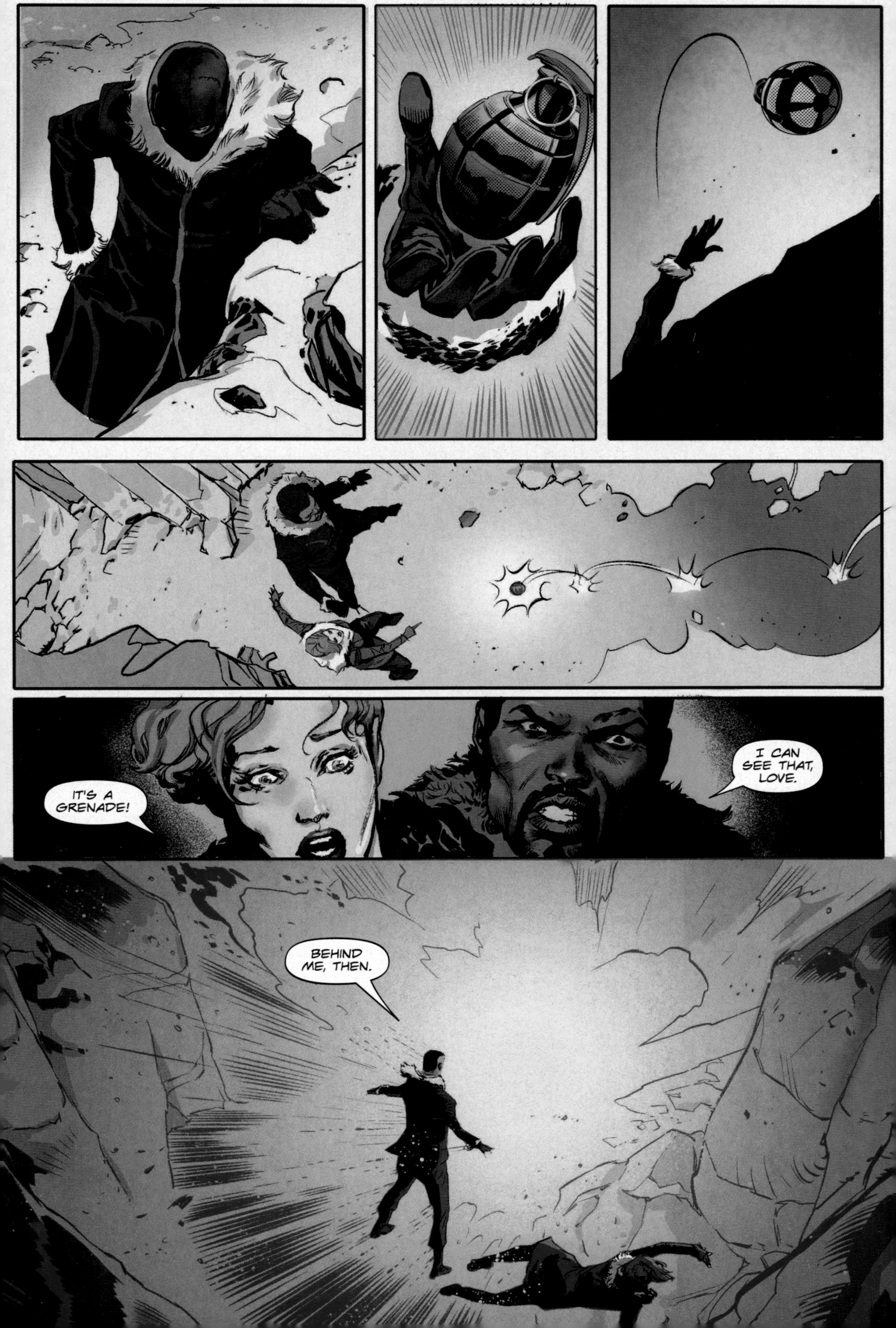
IT'S A GRENADE!
I CAN SEE THAT, LOVE.
BEHIND ME, THEN.

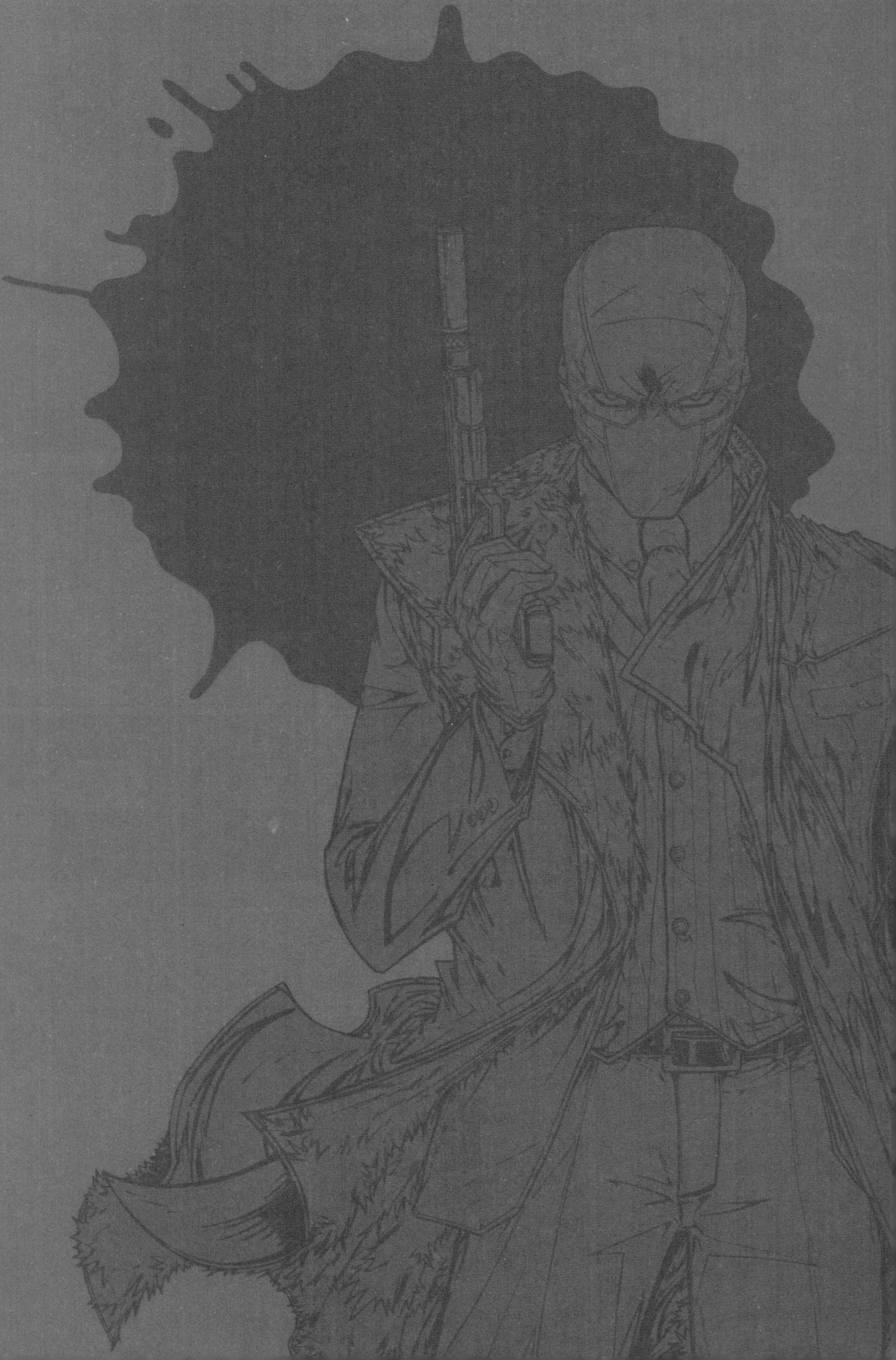

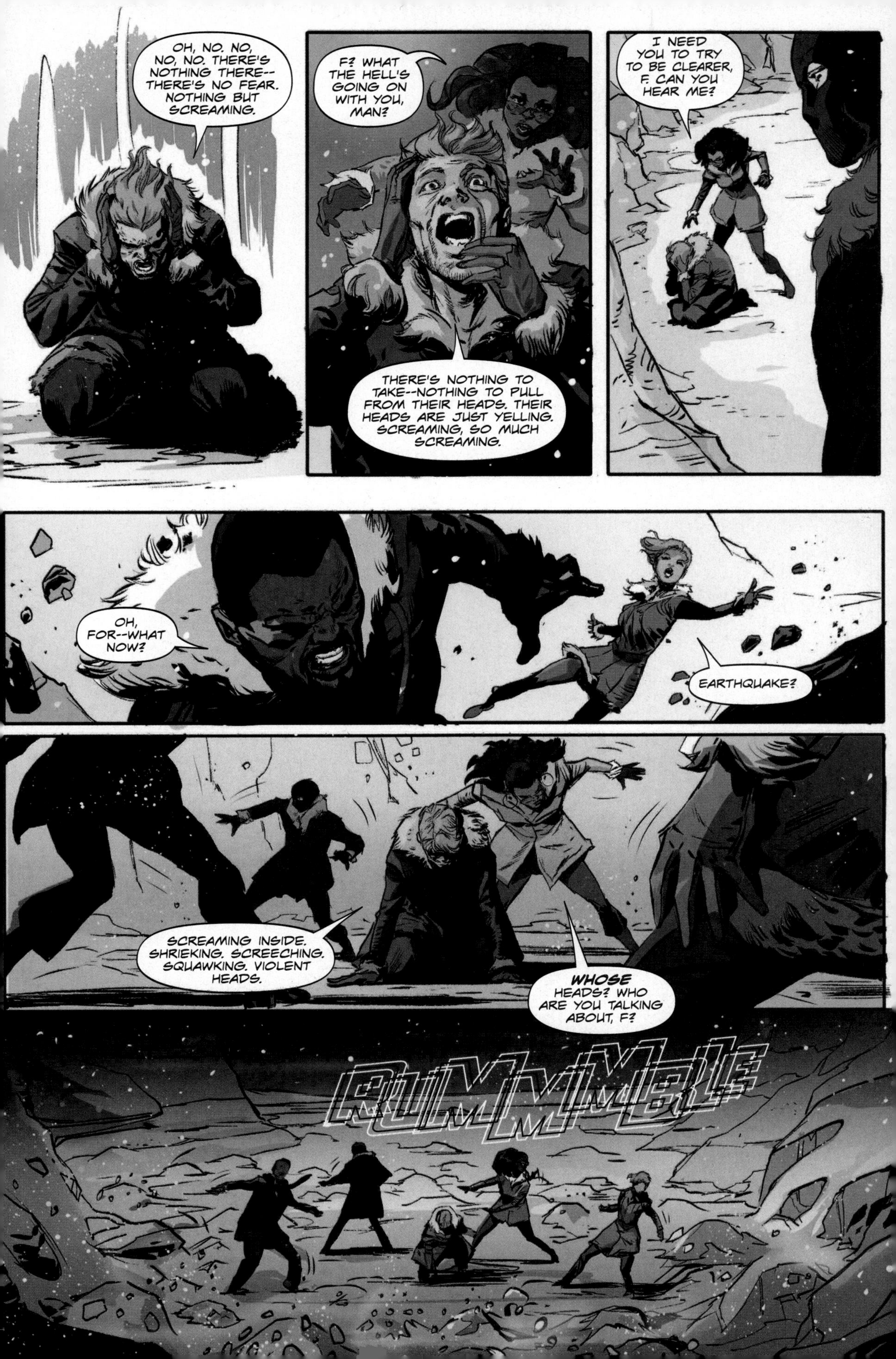
OH, NO. NO, NO, NO. THERE'S NOTHING THERE-- THERE'S NO FEAR. NOTHING BUT SCREAMING.
F? WHAT THE HELL'S GOING ON WITH YOU, MAN?
THERE'S NOTHING TO TAKE--NOTHING TO PULL FROM THEIR HEADS. THEIR HEADS ARE JUST YELLING. SCREAMING, SO MUCH SCREAMING.
I NEED YOU TO TRY TO BE CLEARER, F. CAN YOU HEAR ME?
OH, FOR--WHAT NOW?
EARTHQUAKE?
SCREAMING INSIDE. SHRIEKING. SCREECHING. SQUAWKING. VIOLENT HEADS.
WHOSE HEADS? WHO ARE YOU TALKING ABOUT, F?
RUMMMBLE

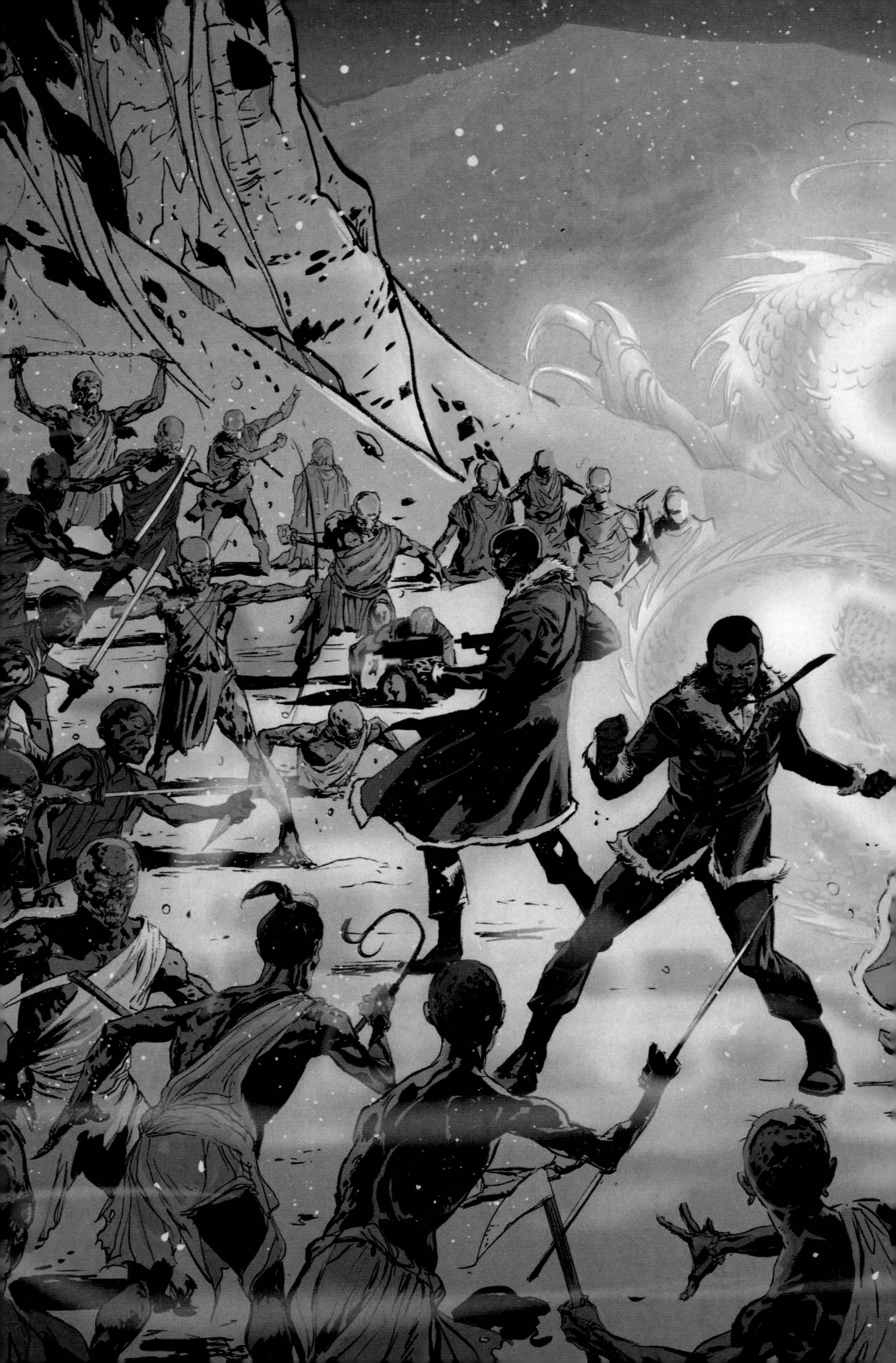

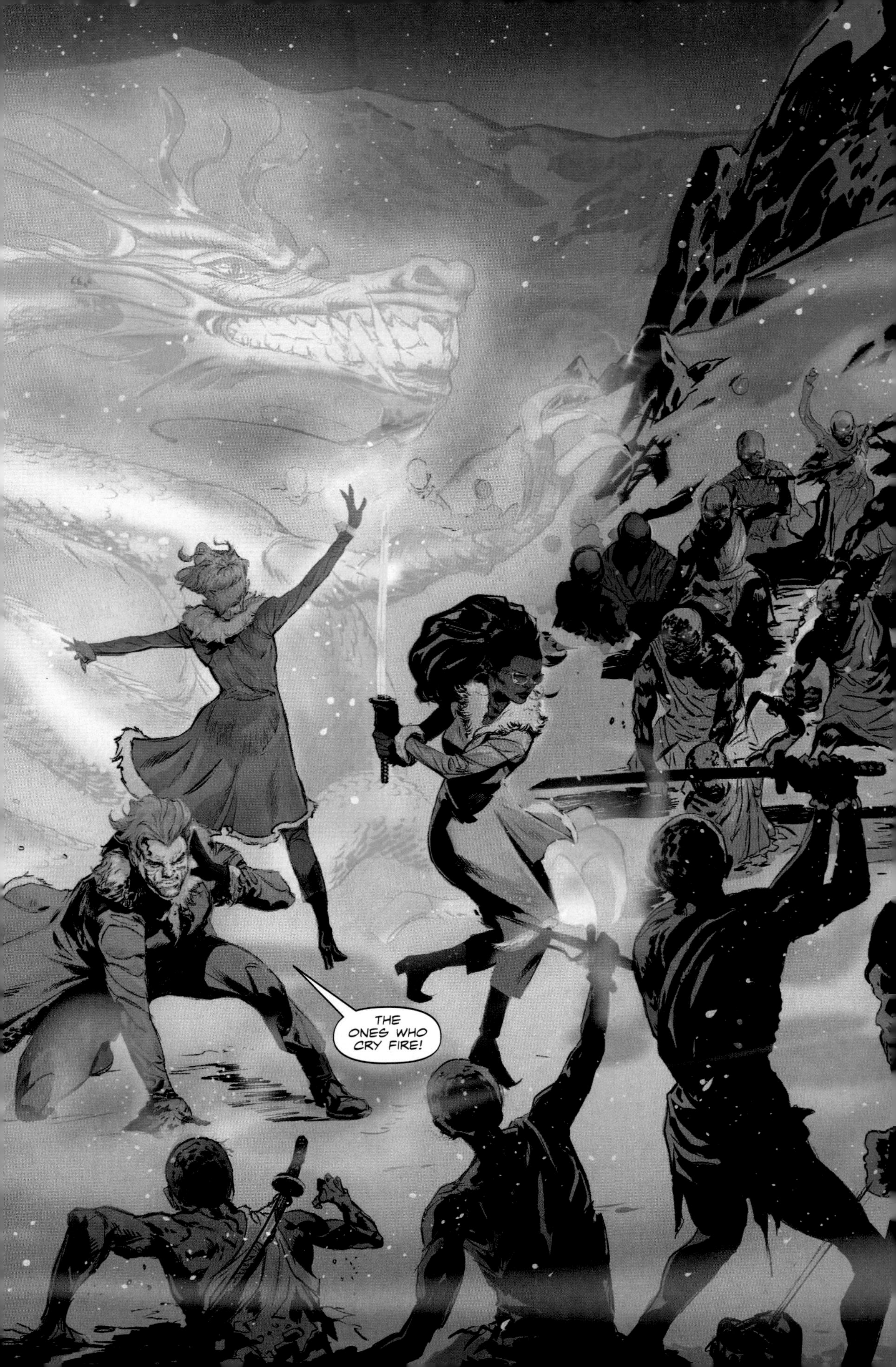
THE ONES WHO CRY FIRE!

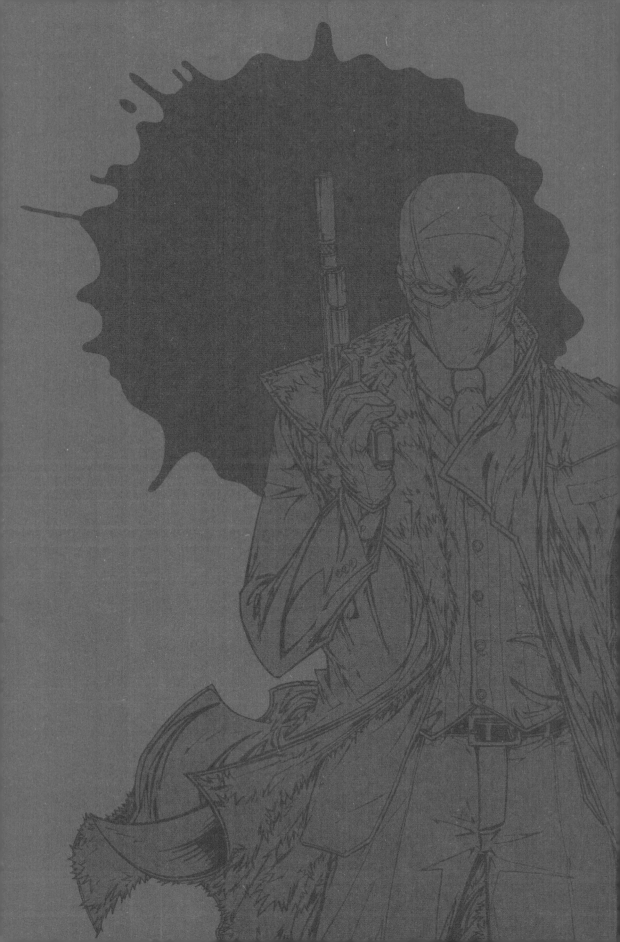

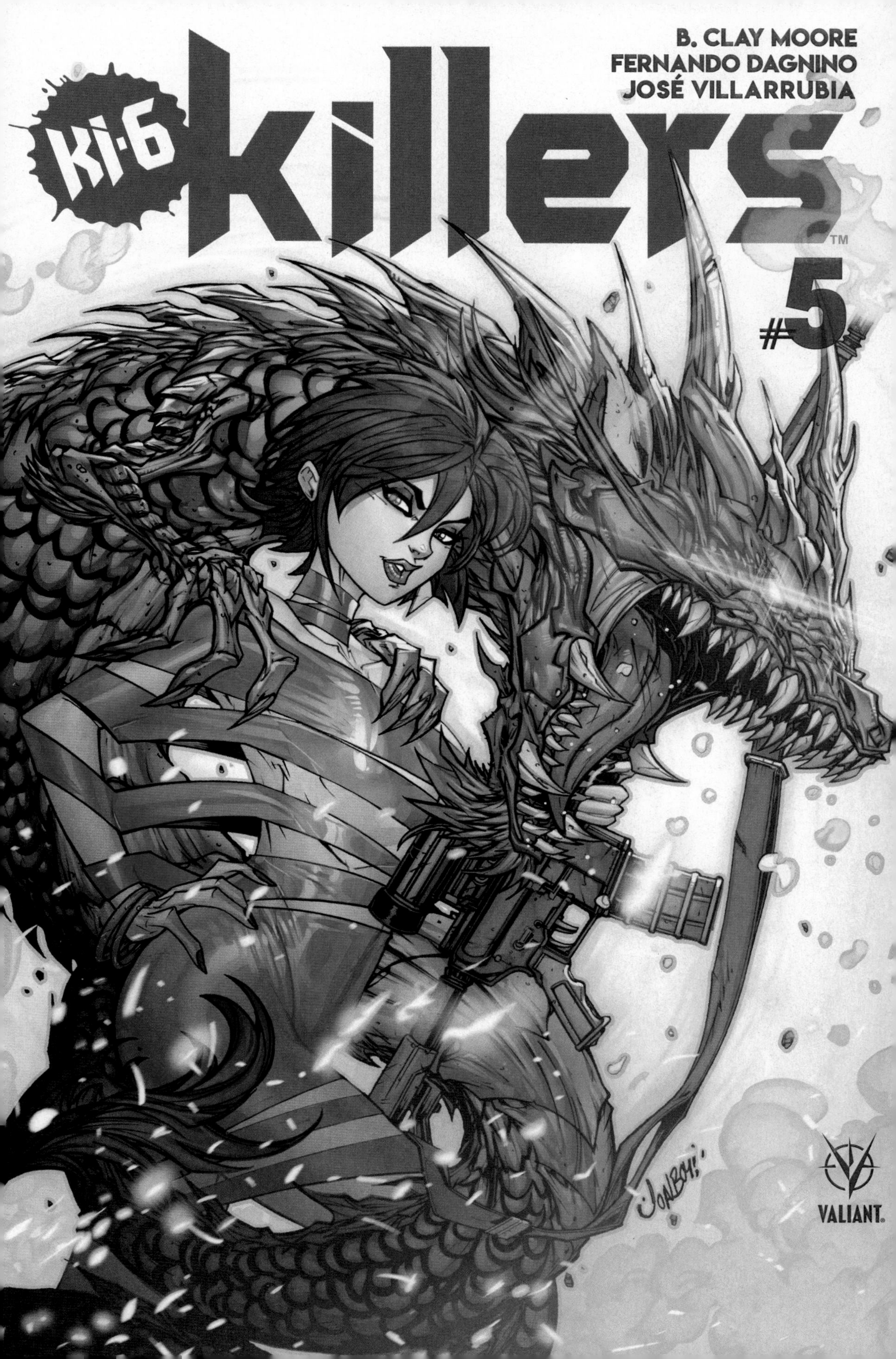
B. CLAY MOORE
FERNANDO DAGNINO
JOSÉ VILLARRUBIA
KI-6
killers™
#5
VALIANT

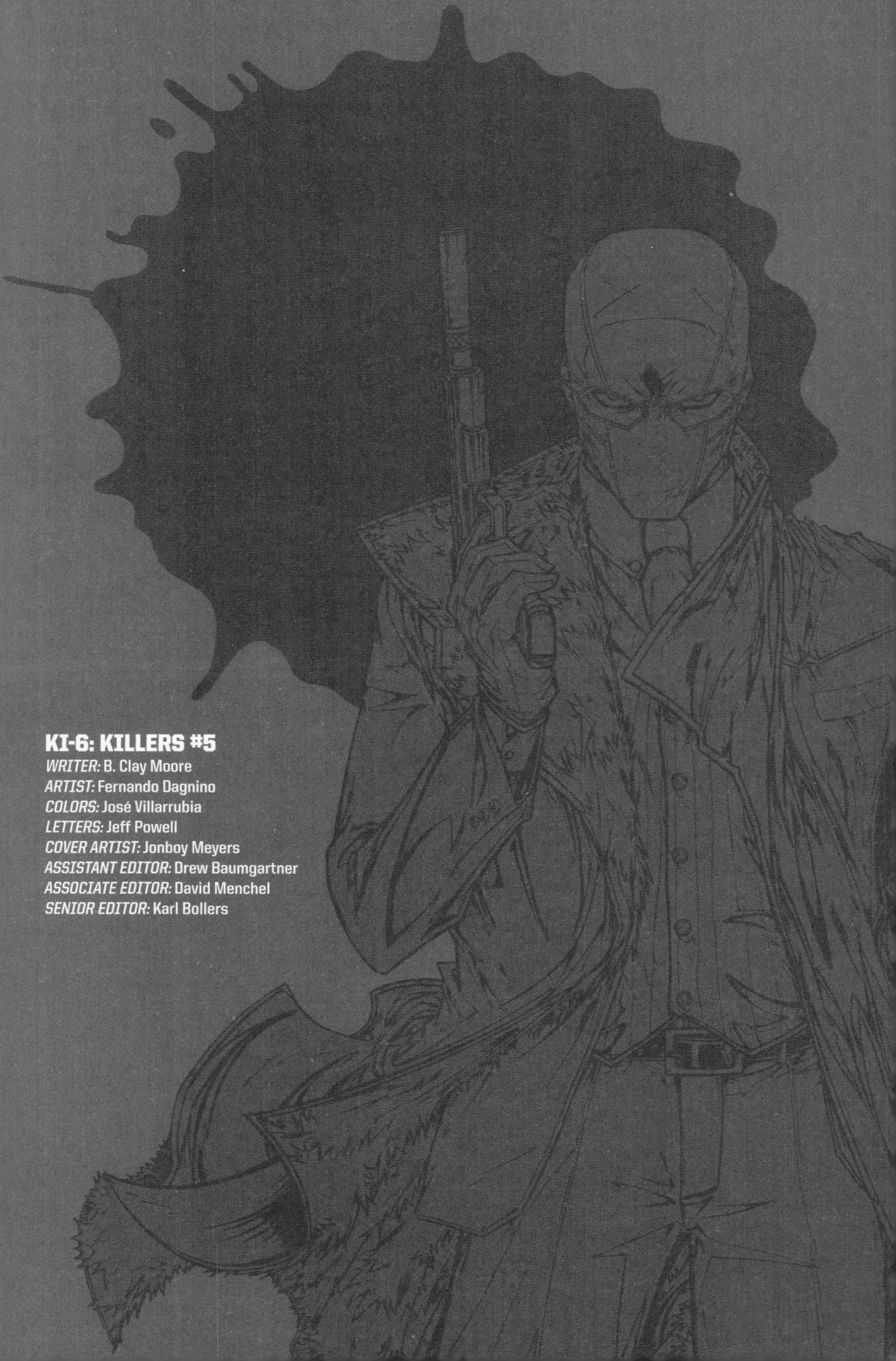

KI-6: KILLERS #5

WRITER: B. Clay Moore
ARTIST: Fernando Dagnino
COLORS: José Villarrubia
LETTERS: Jeff Powell
COVER ARTIST: Jonboy Meyers
ASSISTANT EDITOR: Drew Baumgartner
ASSOCIATE EDITOR: David Menchel
SENIOR EDITOR: Karl Bollers

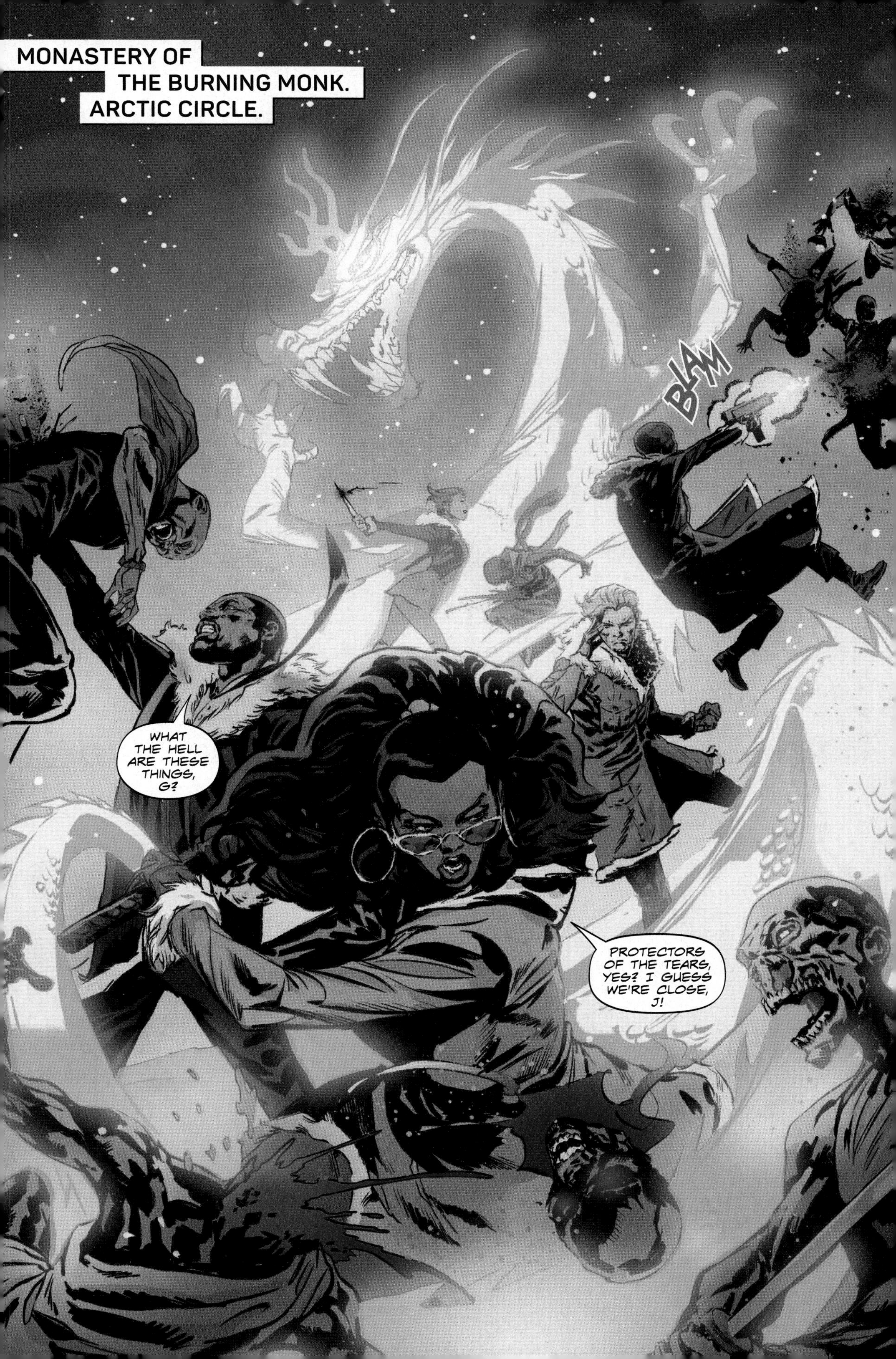
MONASTERY OF THE BURNING MONK. ARCTIC CIRCLE.
BLAM
WHAT THE HELL ARE THESE THINGS, G?
PROTECTORS OF THE TEARS, YES? I GUESS WE'RE CLOSE, J!

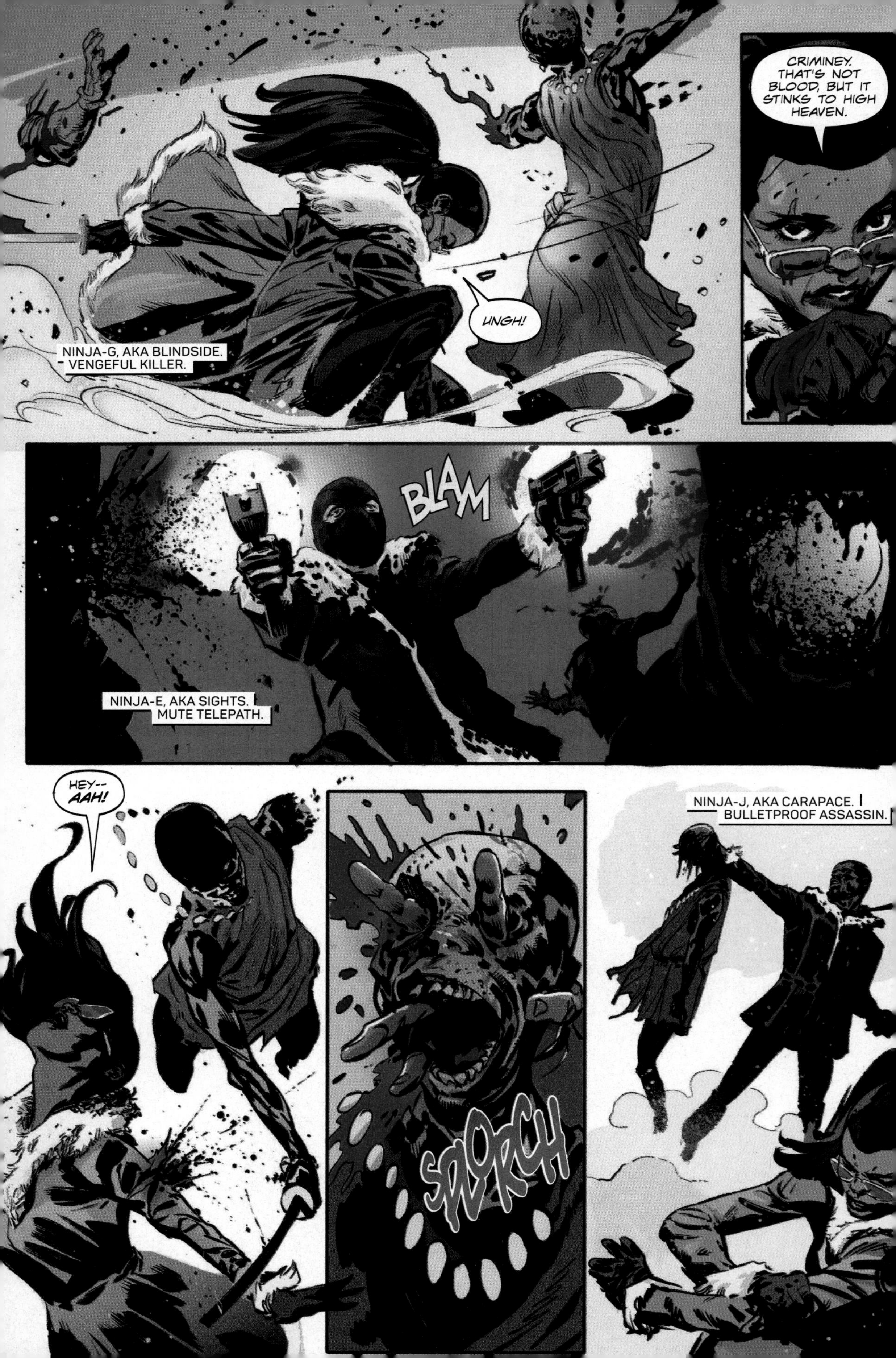
CRIMINEY. THAT'S NOT BLOOD, BUT IT STINKS TO HIGH HEAVEN.
UNGH!
NINJA-G, AKA BLINDSIDE. VENGEFUL KILLER.
BLAM
NINJA-E, AKA SIGHTS. MUTE TELEPATH.
HEY-- AAH!
SPLORCH
NINJA-J, AKA CARAPACE. BULLETPROOF ASSASSIN.

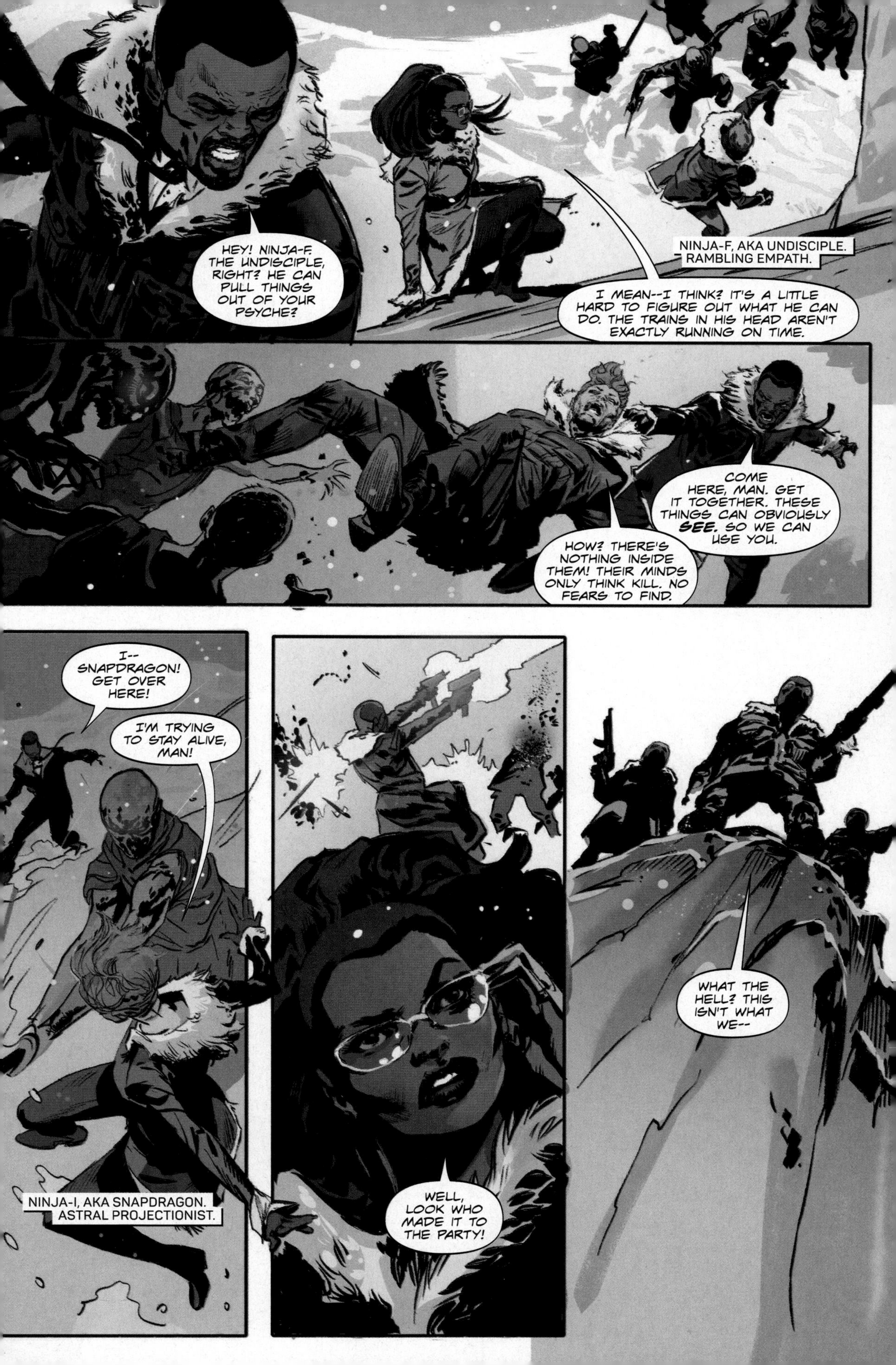
HEY! NINJA-F. THE UNDISCIPLE, RIGHT? HE CAN PULL THINGS OUT OF YOUR PSYCHE?
NINJA-F, AKA UNDISCIPLE. RAMBLING EMPATH.
I MEAN--I THINK? IT'S A LITTLE HARD TO FIGURE OUT WHAT HE CAN DO. THE TRAINS IN HIS HEAD AREN'T EXACTLY RUNNING ON TIME.
COME HERE, MAN. GET IT TOGETHER. THESE THINGS CAN OBVIOUSLY SEE. SO WE CAN USE YOU.
HOW? THERE'S NOTHING INSIDE THEM! THEIR MINDS ONLY THINK KILL. NO FEARS TO FIND.
I-- SNAPDRAGON! GET OVER HERE!
I'M TRYING TO STAY ALIVE, MAN!
NINJA-I, AKA SNAPDRAGON. ASTRAL PROJECTIONIST.
WELL, LOOK WHO MADE IT TO THE PARTY!
WHAT THE HELL? THIS ISN'T WHAT WE--

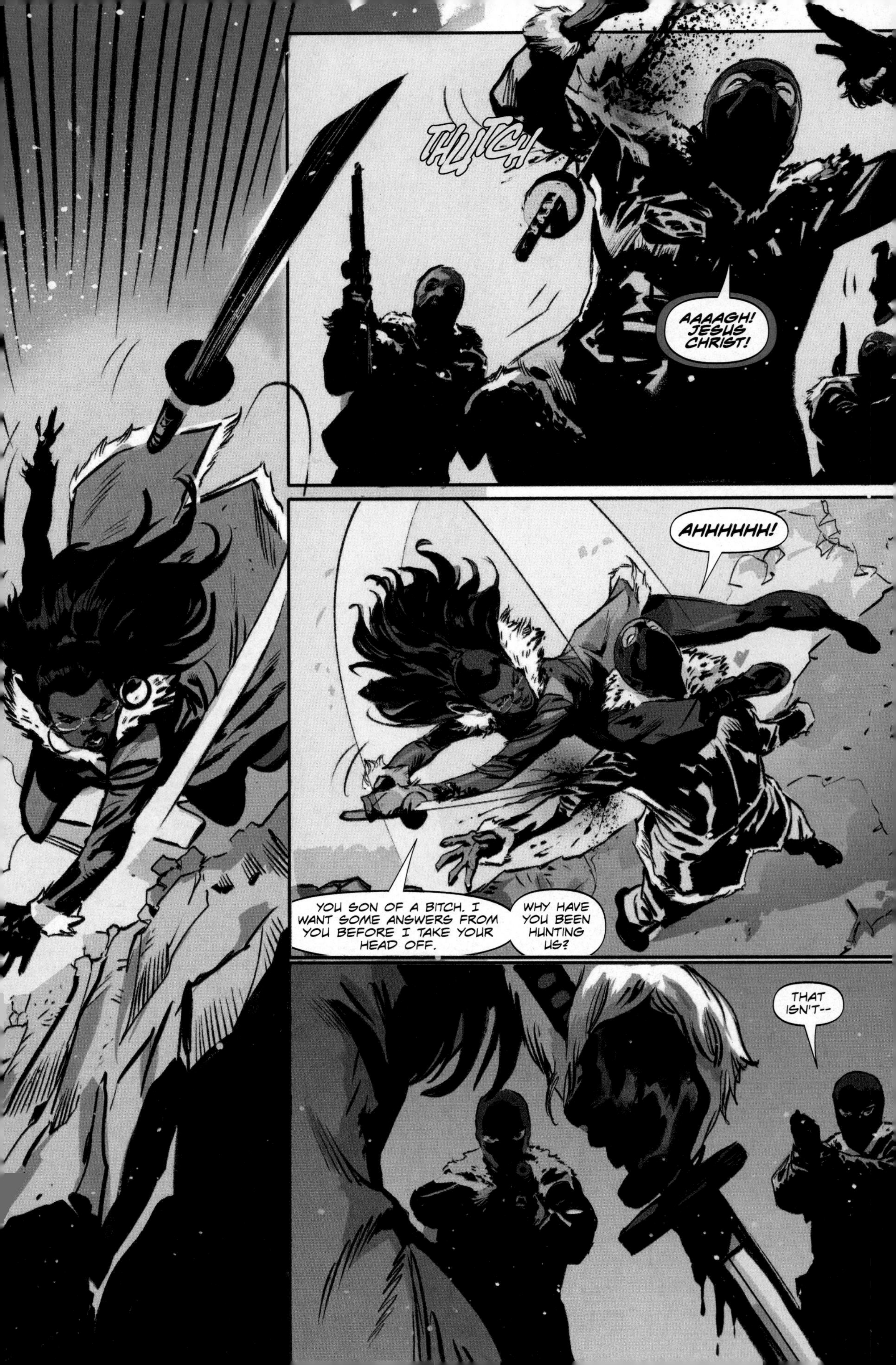

THUTCH
AAAAGH! JESUS CHRIST!
AHHHHHH!
YOU SON OF A BITCH. I WANT SOME ANSWERS FROM YOU BEFORE I TAKE YOUR HEAD OFF.
WHY HAVE YOU BEEN HUNTING US?
THAT ISN'T--

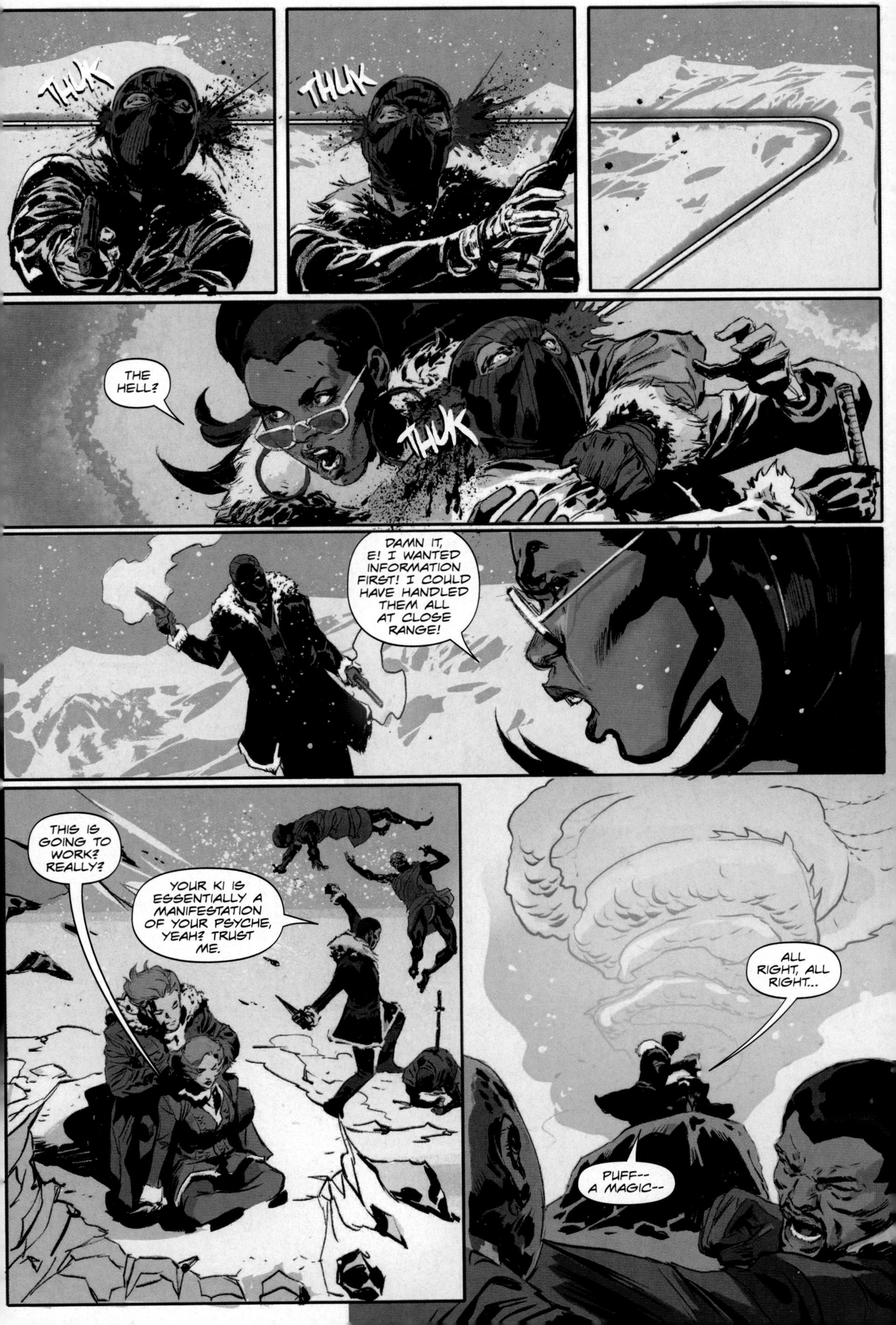
THUK
THUK
THE HELL?
THUK
DAMN IT, E! I WANTED INFORMATION FIRST! I COULD HAVE HANDLED THEM ALL AT CLOSE RANGE!
THIS IS GOING TO WORK? REALLY?
YOUR KI IS ESSENTIALLY A MANIFESTATION OF YOUR PSYCHE, YEAH? TRUST ME.
ALL RIGHT, ALL RIGHT...
PUFF-- A MAGIC--

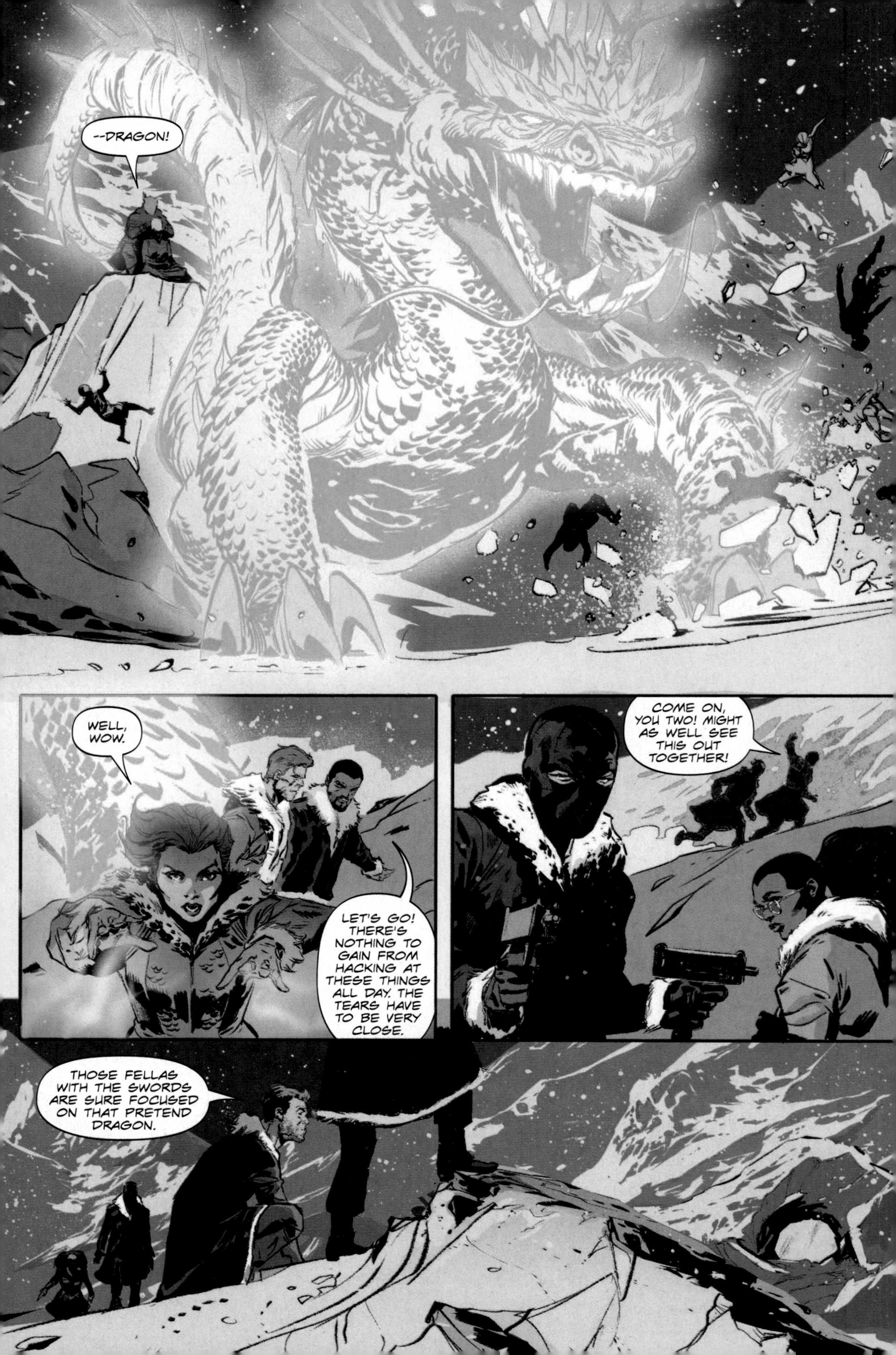
--DRAGON!
WELL, WOW.
LET'S GO! THERE'S NOTHING TO GAIN FROM HACKING AT THESE THINGS ALL DAY. THE TEARS HAVE TO BE VERY CLOSE.
COME ON, YOU TWO! MIGHT AS WELL SEE THIS OUT TOGETHER!
THOSE FELLAS WITH THE SWORDS ARE SURE FOCUSED ON THAT PRETEND DRAGON.

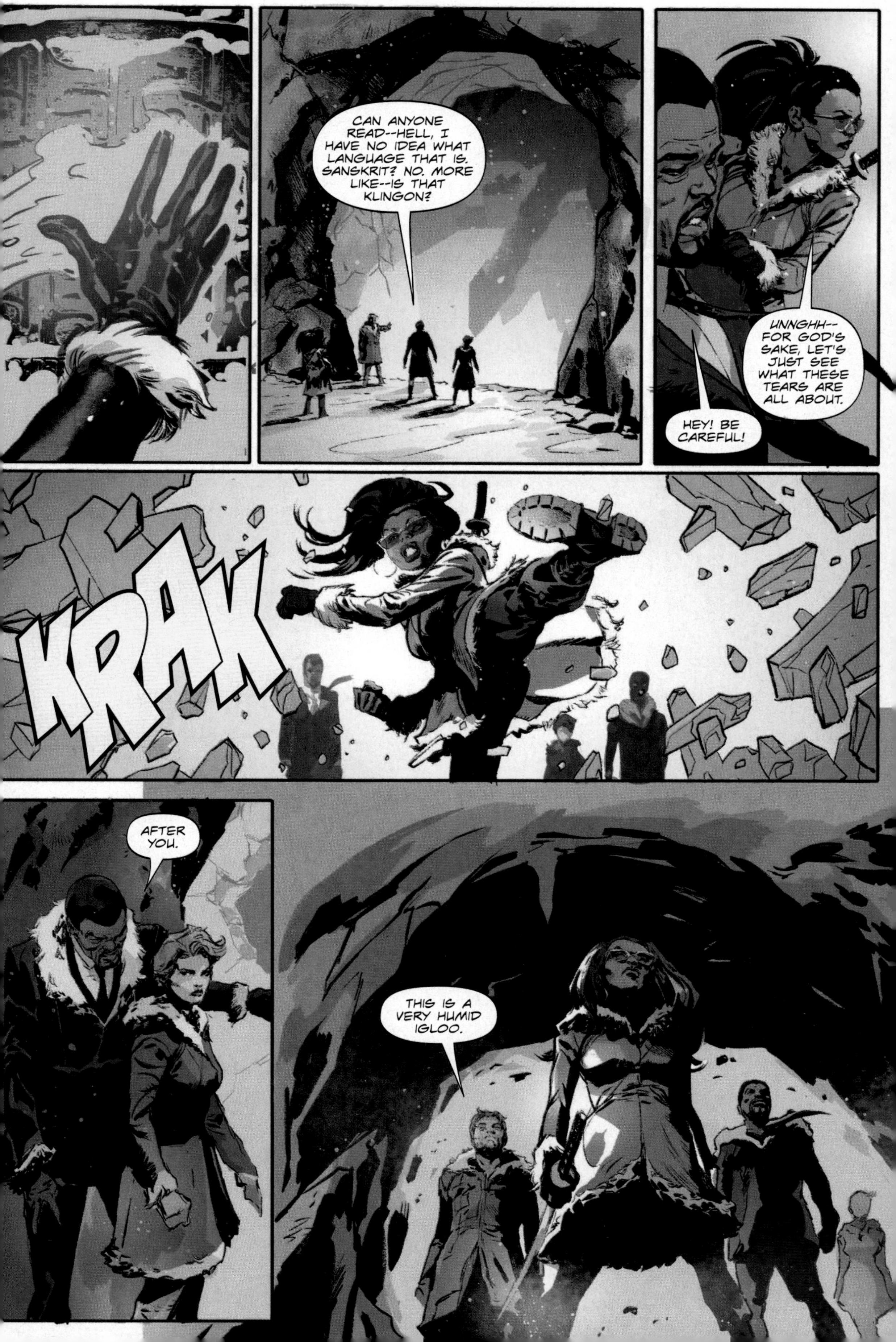
CAN ANYONE READ--HELL, I HAVE NO IDEA WHAT LANGUAGE THAT IS. SANSKRIT? NO. MORE LIKE--IS THAT KLINGON?
UNNGHH-- FOR GOD'S SAKE, LET'S JUST SEE WHAT THESE TEARS ARE ALL ABOUT.
HEY! BE CAREFUL!
KRAK
AFTER YOU.
THIS IS A VERY HUMID IGLOO.

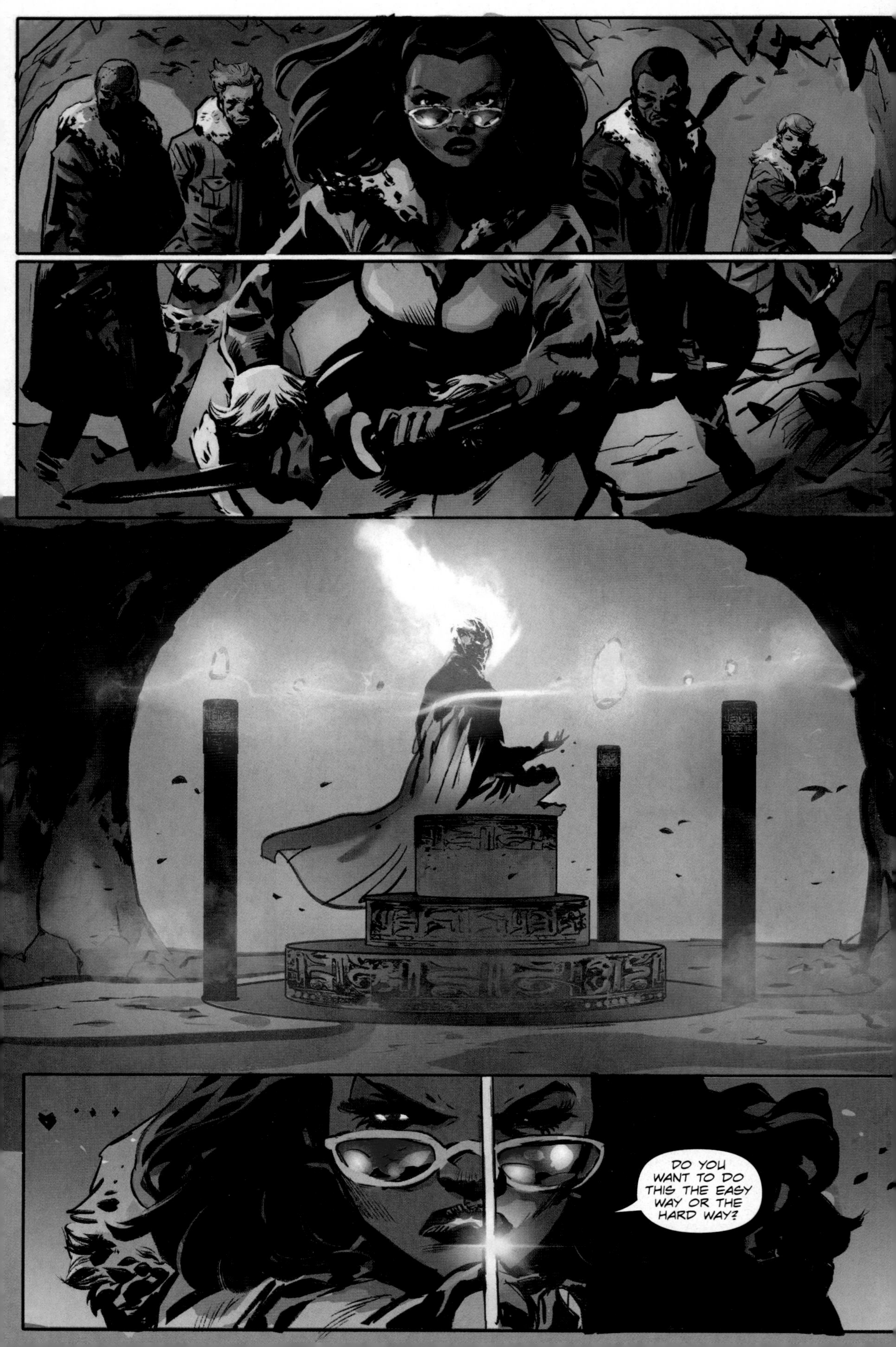
DO YOU WANT TO DO THIS THE EASY WAY OR THE HARD WAY?

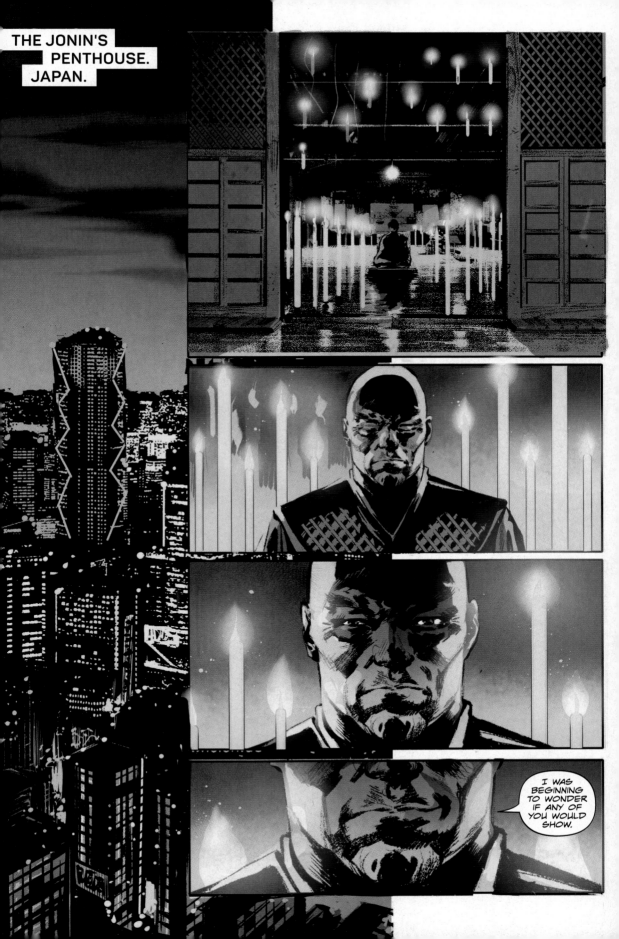

THE JONIN'S
PENTHOUSE.
JAPAN.

I WAS
BEGINNING
TO WONDER
IF ANY OF
YOU WOULD
SHOW.

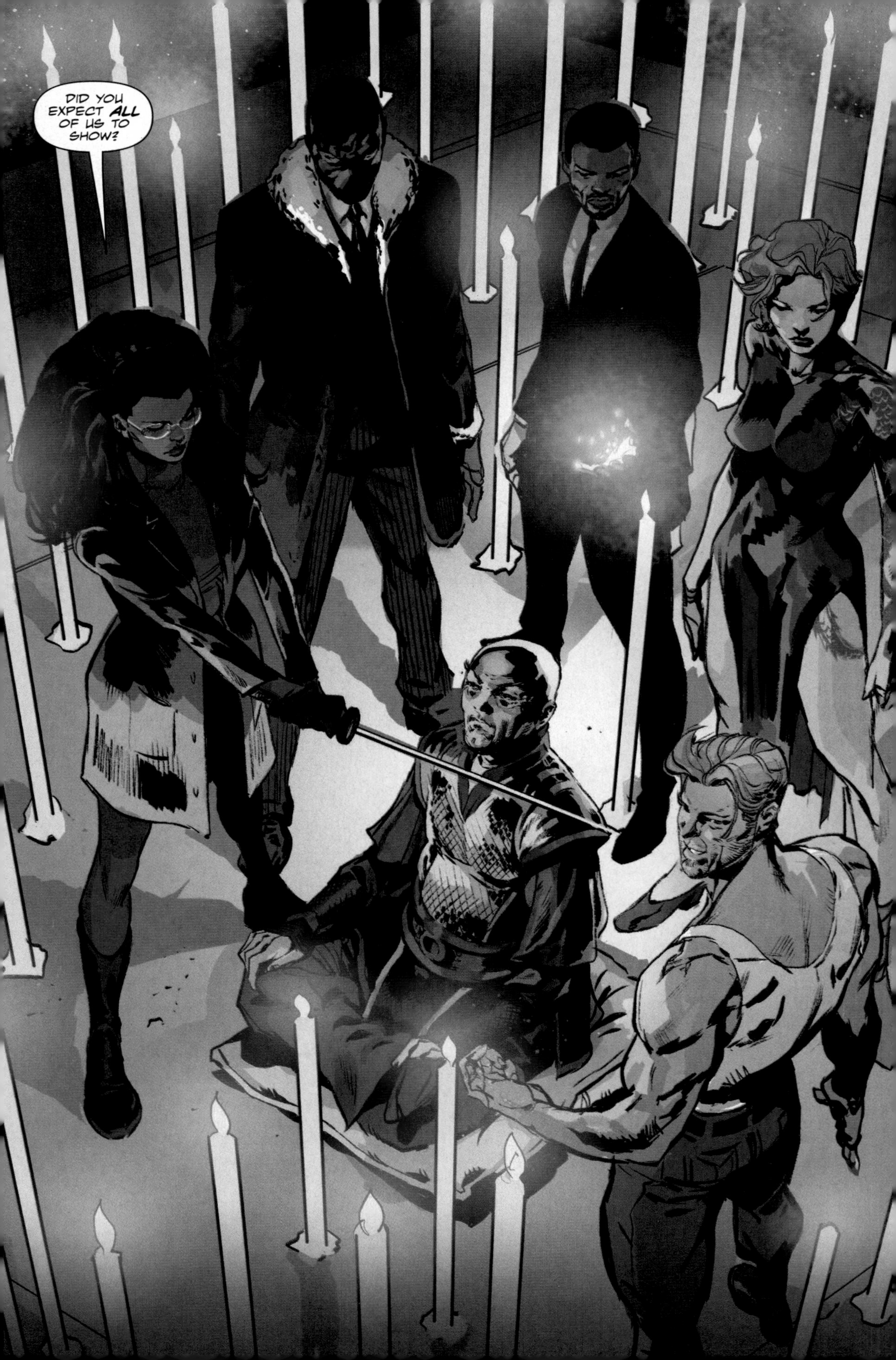
DID YOU EXPECT ALL OF US TO SHOW?

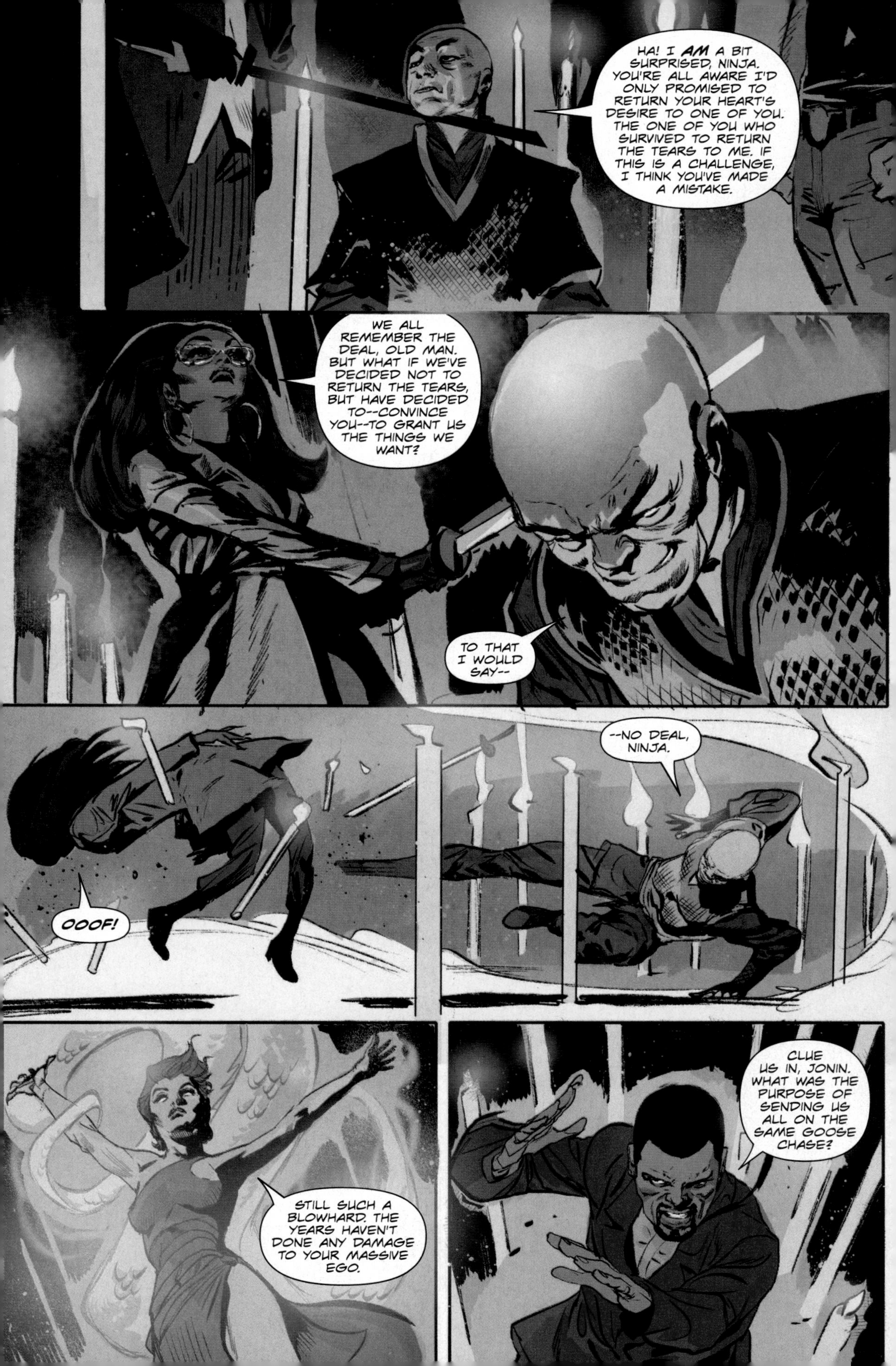
HA! I AM A BIT SURPRISED, NINJA. YOU'RE ALL AWARE I'D ONLY PROMISED TO RETURN YOUR HEART'S DESIRE TO ONE OF YOU. THE ONE OF YOU WHO SURVIVED TO RETURN THE TEARS TO ME. IF THIS IS A CHALLENGE, I THINK YOU'VE MADE A MISTAKE.
WE ALL REMEMBER THE DEAL, OLD MAN. BUT WHAT IF WE'VE DECIDED NOT TO RETURN THE TEARS, BUT HAVE DECIDED TO--CONVINCE YOU--TO GRANT US THE THINGS WE WANT?
TO THAT I WOULD SAY--
--NO DEAL, NINJA.
OOOF!
STILL SUCH A BLOWHARD. THE YEARS HAVEN'T DONE ANY DAMAGE TO YOUR MASSIVE EGO.
CLUE US IN, JONIN. WHAT WAS THE PURPOSE OF SENDING US ALL ON THE SAME GOOSE CHASE?

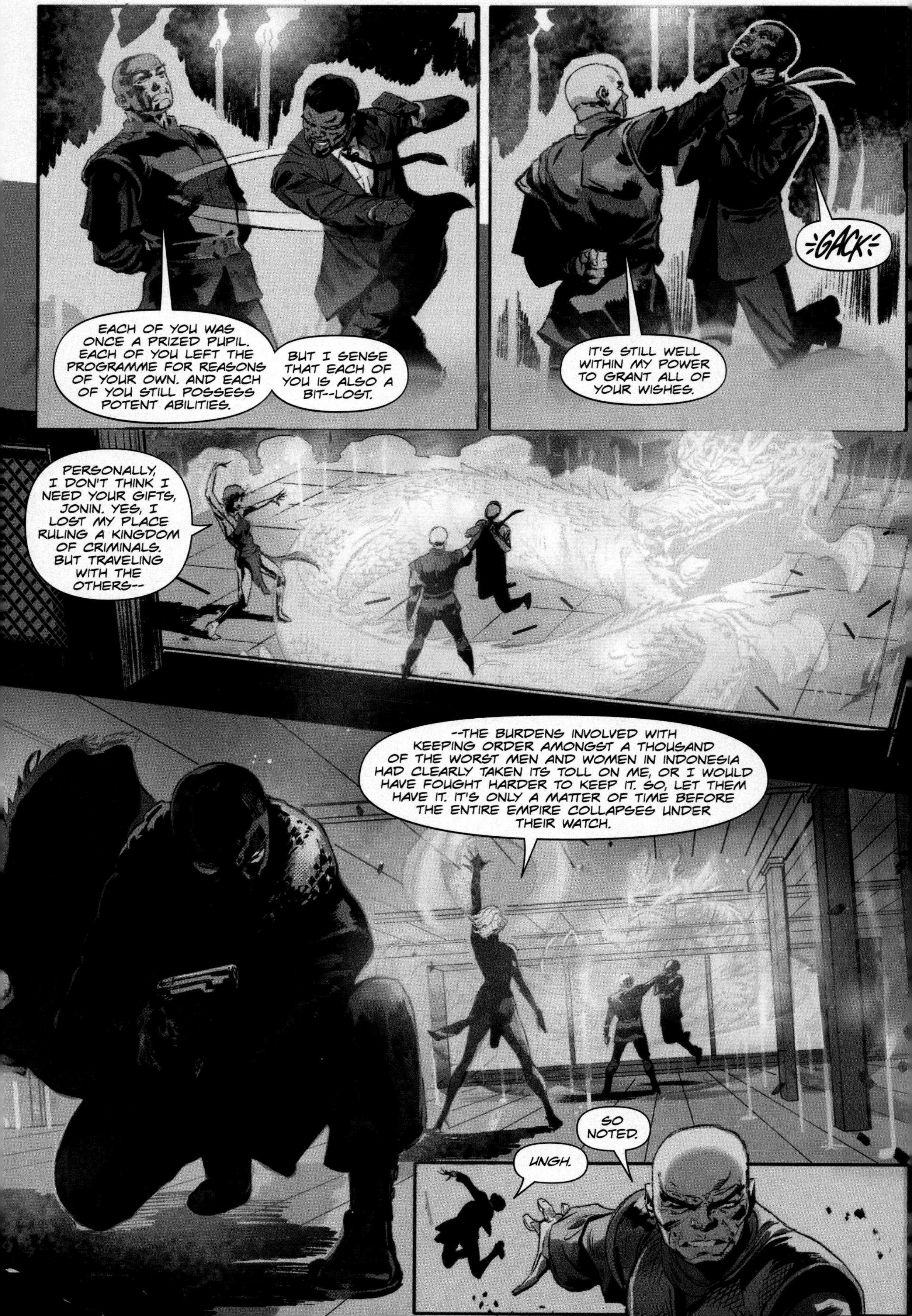
EACH OF YOU WAS ONCE A PRIZED PUPIL. EACH OF YOU LEFT THE PROGRAMME FOR REASONS OF YOUR OWN. AND EACH OF YOU STILL POSSESS POTENT ABILITIES.
BUT I SENSE THAT EACH OF YOU IS ALSO A BIT--LOST.
GACK
IT'S STILL WELL WITHIN MY POWER TO GRANT ALL OF YOUR WISHES.
PERSONALLY, I DON'T THINK I NEED YOUR GIFTS, JONIN. YES, I LOST MY PLACE RULING A KINGDOM OF CRIMINALS. BUT TRAVELING WITH THE OTHERS--
--THE BURDENS INVOLVED WITH KEEPING ORDER AMONGST A THOUSAND OF THE WORST MEN AND WOMEN IN INDONESIA HAD CLEARLY TAKEN ITS TOLL ON ME, OR I WOULD HAVE FOUGHT HARDER TO KEEP IT. SO, LET THEM HAVE IT. IT'S ONLY A MATTER OF TIME BEFORE THE ENTIRE EMPIRE COLLAPSES UNDER THEIR WATCH.
SO NOTED.
UNGH.

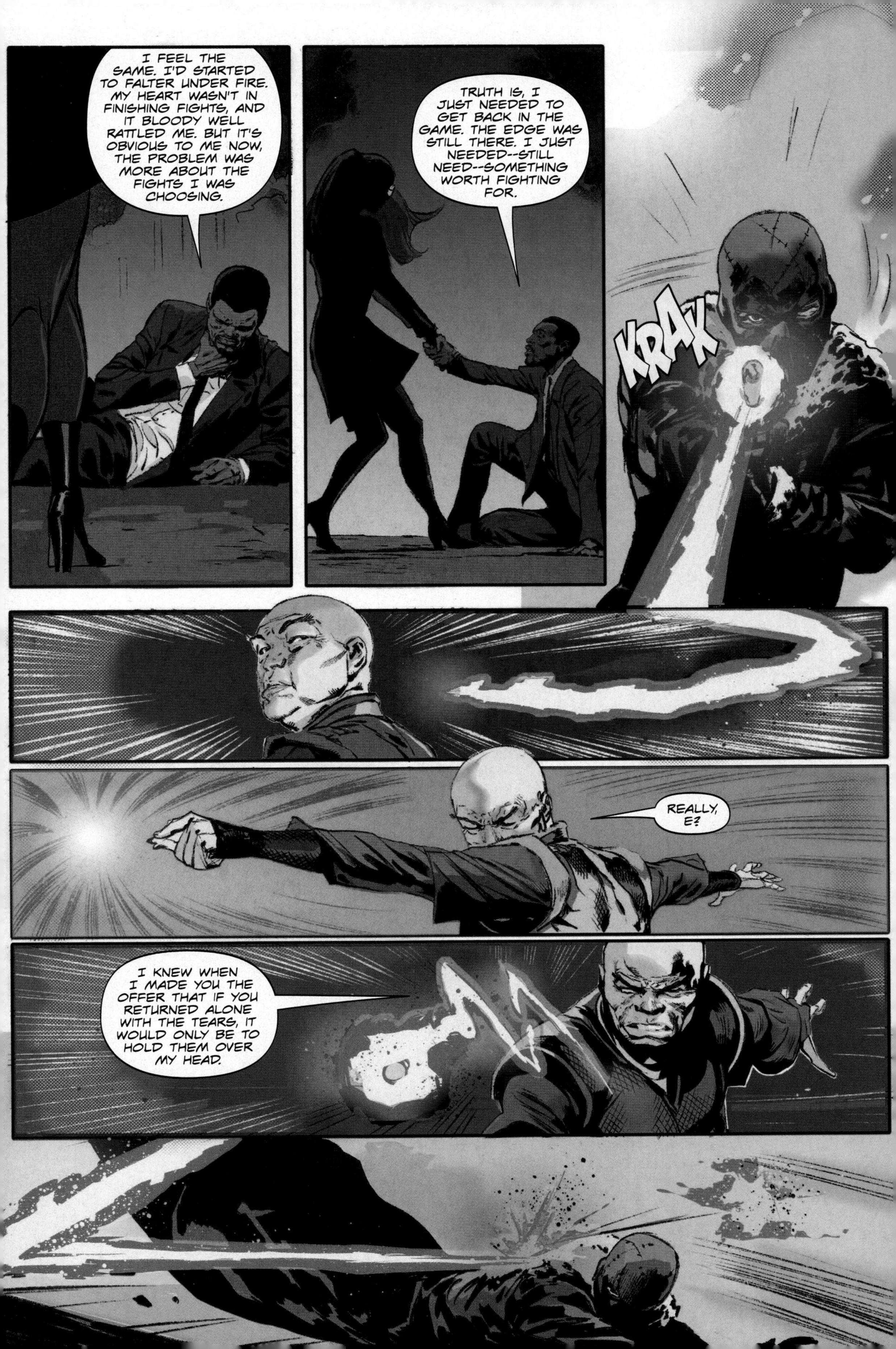
I FEEL THE SAME. I'D STARTED TO FALTER UNDER FIRE. MY HEART WASN'T IN FINISHING FIGHTS, AND IT BLOODY WELL RATTLED ME. BUT IT'S OBVIOUS TO ME NOW, THE PROBLEM WAS MORE ABOUT THE FIGHTS I WAS CHOOSING.
TRUTH IS, I JUST NEEDED TO GET BACK IN THE GAME. THE EDGE WAS STILL THERE. I JUST NEEDED--STILL NEED--SOMETHING WORTH FIGHTING FOR.
KRAK
REALLY, E?
I KNEW WHEN I MADE YOU THE OFFER THAT IF YOU RETURNED ALONE WITH THE TEARS, IT WOULD ONLY BE TO HOLD THEM OVER MY HEAD.

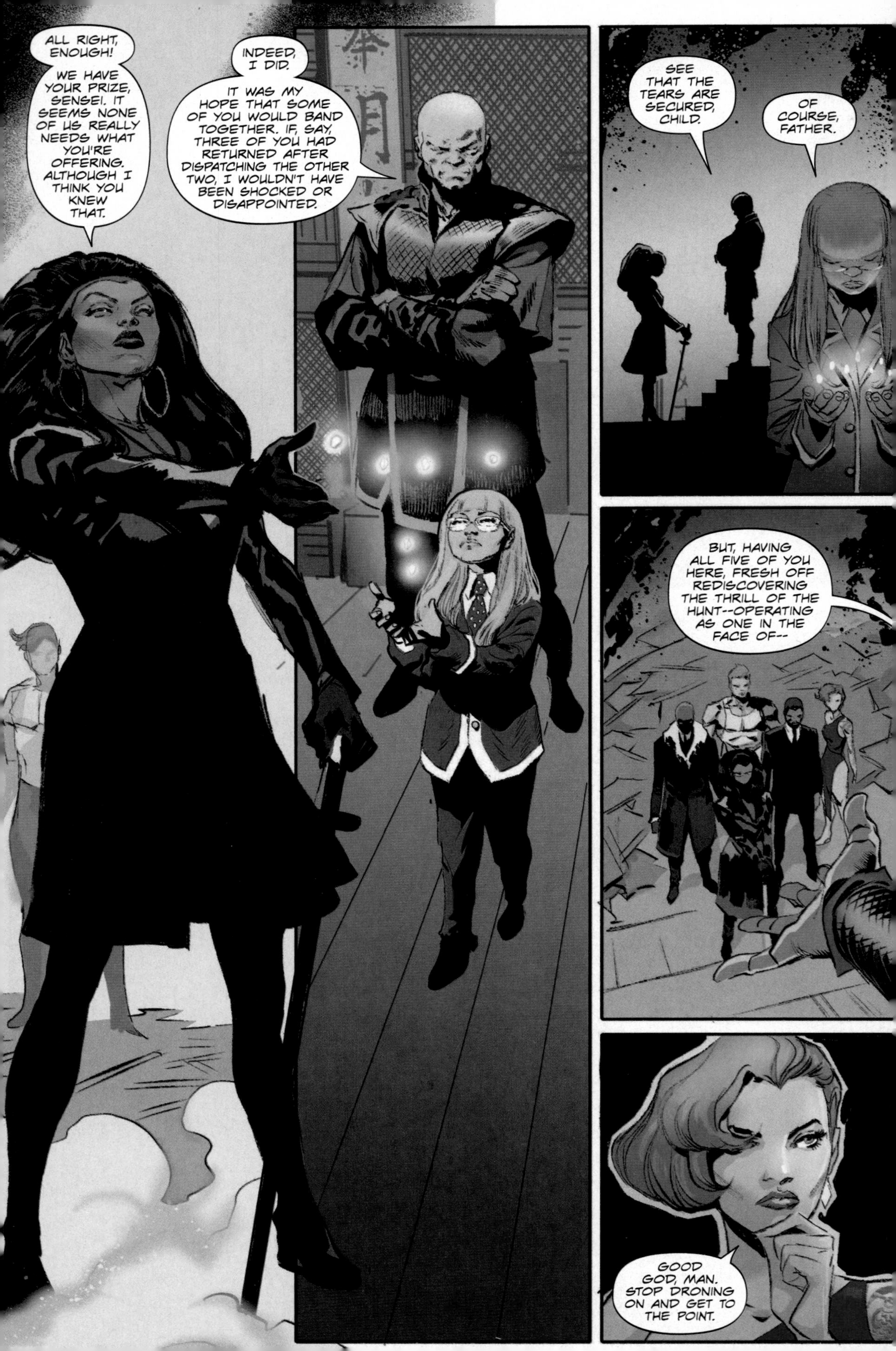
ALL RIGHT, ENOUGH!
WE HAVE YOUR PRIZE, SENSEI. IT SEEMS NONE OF US REALLY NEEDS WHAT YOU'RE OFFERING. ALTHOUGH I THINK YOU KNEW THAT.
INDEED, I DID.
IT WAS MY HOPE THAT SOME OF YOU WOULD BAND TOGETHER. IF, SAY, THREE OF YOU HAD RETURNED AFTER DISPATCHING THE OTHER TWO, I WOULDN'T HAVE BEEN SHOCKED OR DISAPPOINTED.
SEE THAT THE TEARS ARE SECURED, CHILD.
OF COURSE, FATHER.
BUT, HAVING ALL FIVE OF YOU HERE, FRESH OFF REDISCOVERING THE THRILL OF THE HUNT--OPERATING AS ONE IN THE FACE OF--
GOOD GOD, MAN. STOP DRONING ON AND GET TO THE POINT.

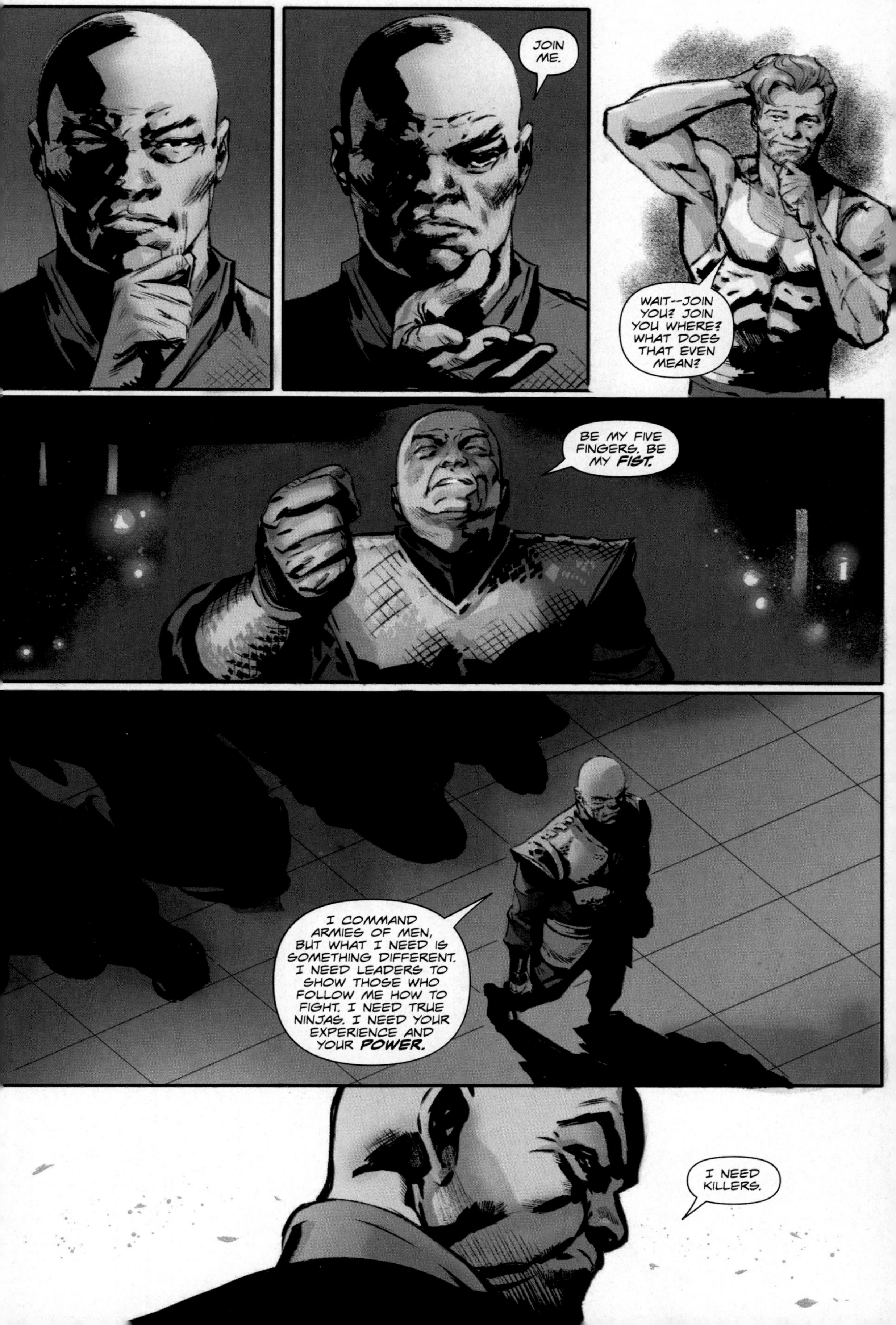
JOIN ME.
WAIT--JOIN YOU? JOIN YOU WHERE? WHAT DOES THAT EVEN MEAN?
BE MY FIVE FINGERS. BE MY FIST.
I COMMAND ARMIES OF MEN, BUT WHAT I NEED IS SOMETHING DIFFERENT. I NEED LEADERS TO SHOW THOSE WHO FOLLOW ME HOW TO FIGHT. I NEED TRUE NINJAS. I NEED YOUR EXPERIENCE AND YOUR POWER.
I NEED KILLERS.

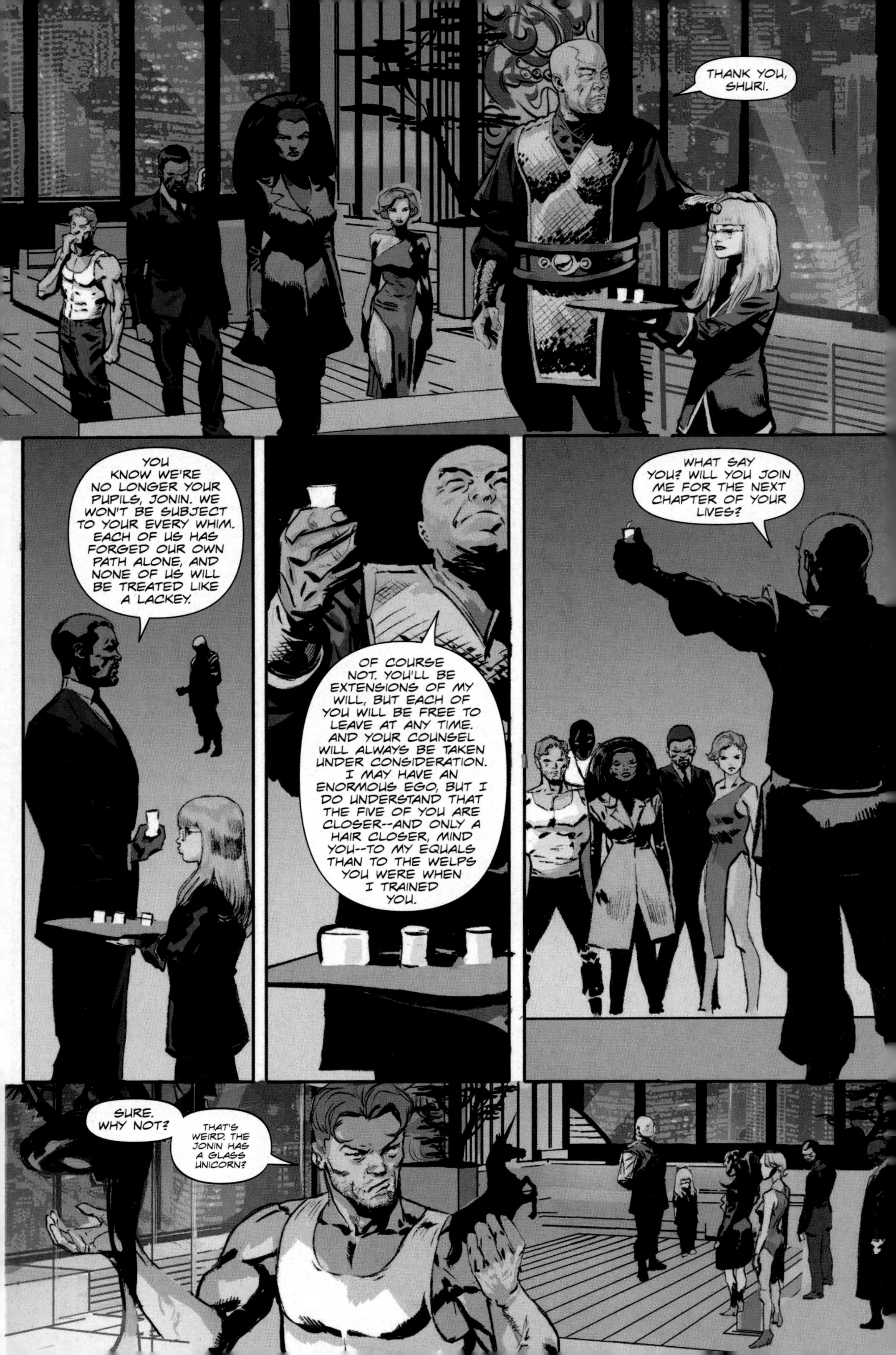

THANK YOU, SHURI.
YOU KNOW WE'RE NO LONGER YOUR PUPILS, JONIN. WE WON'T BE SUBJECT TO YOUR EVERY WHIM. EACH OF US HAS FORGED OUR OWN PATH ALONE, AND NONE OF US WILL BE TREATED LIKE A LACKEY.
OF COURSE NOT. YOU'LL BE EXTENSIONS OF MY WILL, BUT EACH OF YOU WILL BE FREE TO LEAVE AT ANY TIME. AND YOUR COUNSEL WILL ALWAYS BE TAKEN UNDER CONSIDERATION. I MAY HAVE AN ENORMOUS EGO, BUT I DO UNDERSTAND THAT THE FIVE OF YOU ARE CLOSER--AND ONLY A HAIR CLOSER, MIND YOU--TO MY EQUALS THAN TO THE WELPS YOU WERE WHEN I TRAINED YOU.
WHAT SAY YOU? WILL YOU JOIN ME FOR THE NEXT CHAPTER OF YOUR LIVES?
SURE. WHY NOT?
THAT'S WEIRD. THE JONIN HAS A GLASS UNICORN?

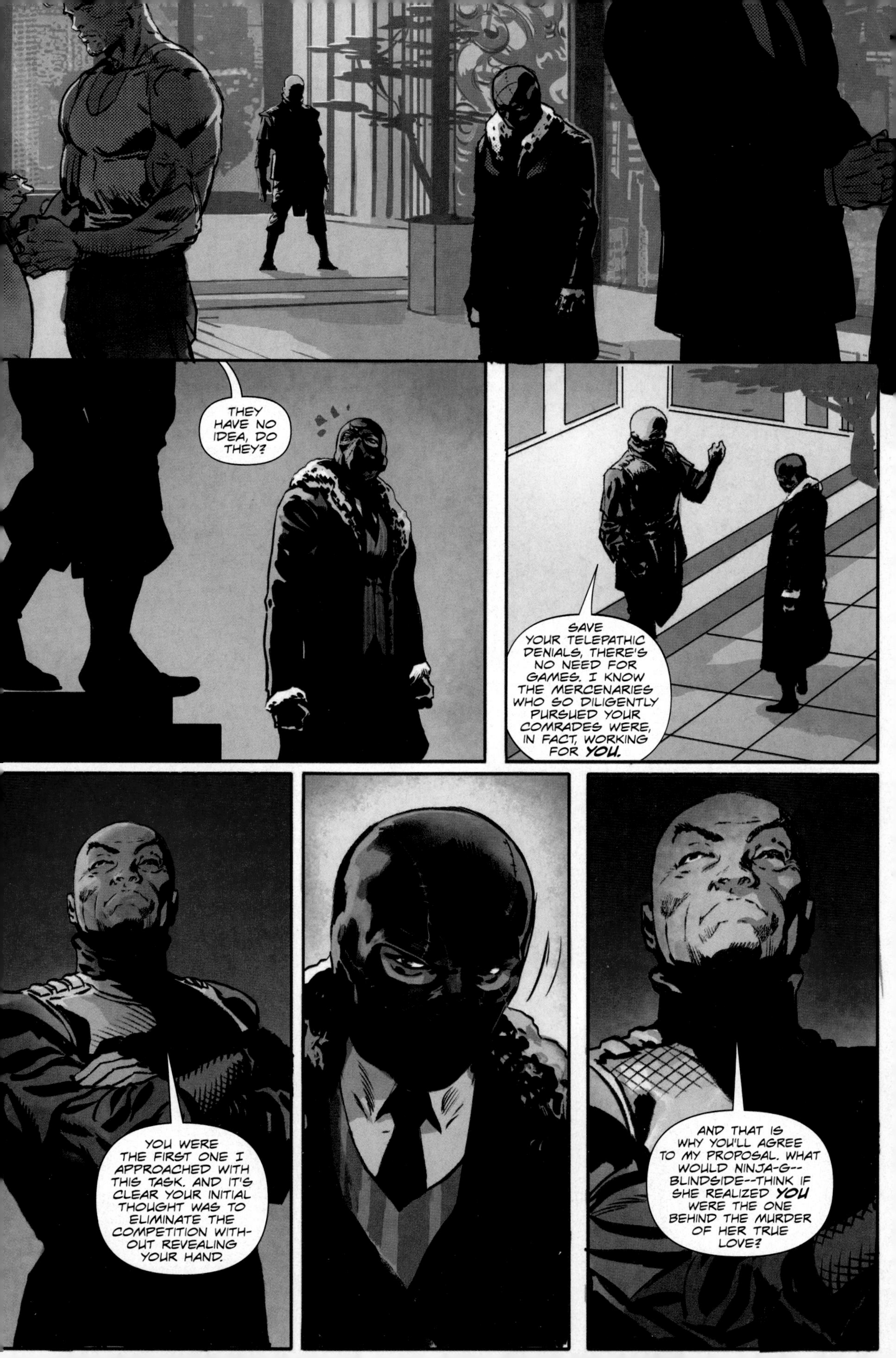
THEY HAVE NO IDEA, DO THEY?
SAVE YOUR TELEPATHIC DENIALS, THERE'S NO NEED FOR GAMES. I KNOW THE MERCENARIES WHO SO DILIGENTLY PURSUED YOUR COMRADES WERE, IN FACT, WORKING FOR YOU.
YOU WERE THE FIRST ONE I APPROACHED WITH THIS TASK. AND IT'S CLEAR YOUR INITIAL THOUGHT WAS TO ELIMINATE THE COMPETITION WITHOUT REVEALING YOUR HAND.
AND THAT IS WHY YOU'LL AGREE TO MY PROPOSAL. WHAT WOULD NINJA-G--BLINDSIDE--THINK IF SHE REALIZED YOU WERE THE ONE BEHIND THE MURDER OF HER TRUE LOVE?

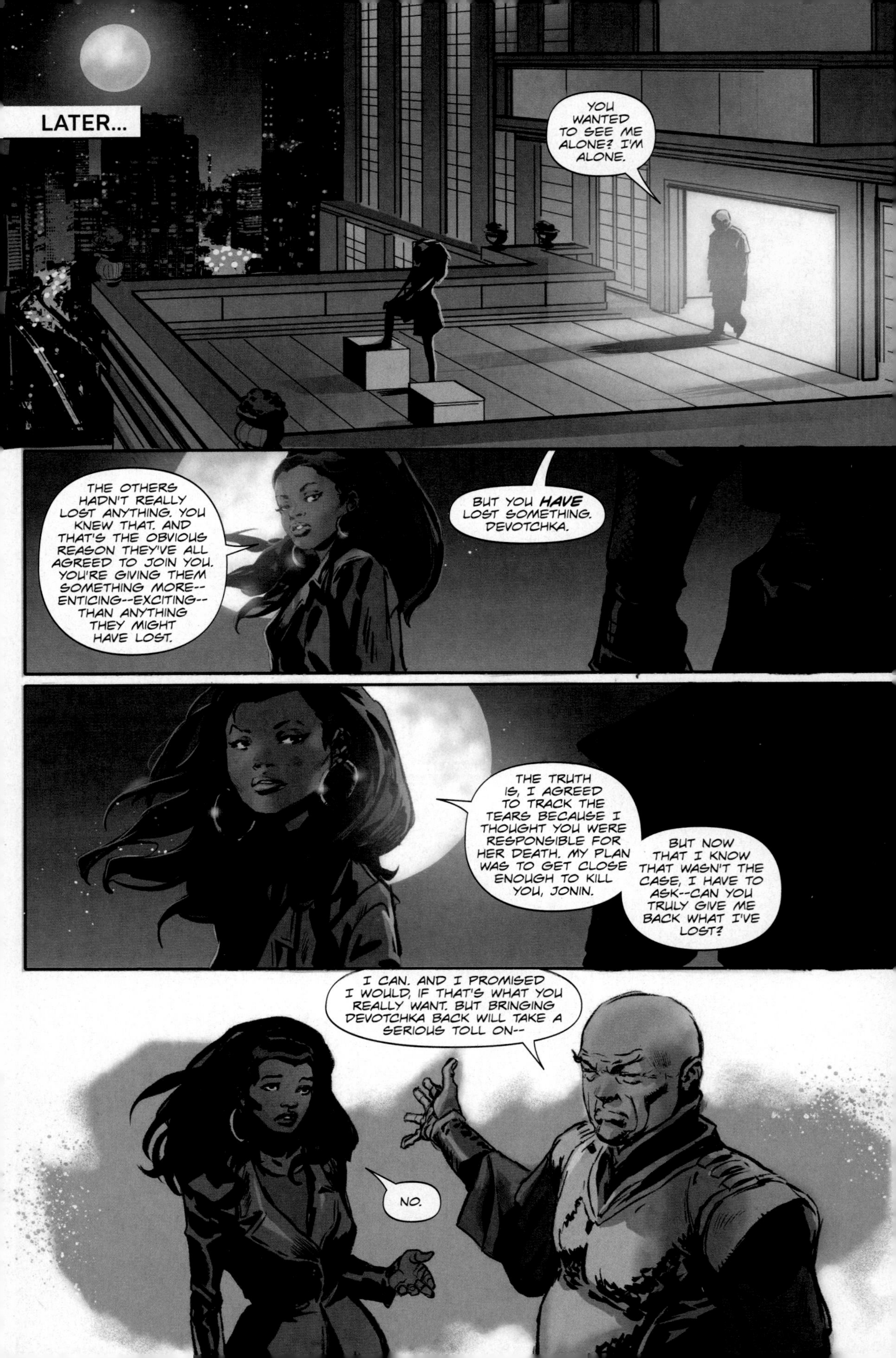
LATER...
YOU WANTED TO SEE ME ALONE? I'M ALONE.
THE OTHERS HADN'T REALLY LOST ANYTHING. YOU KNEW THAT. AND THAT'S THE OBVIOUS REASON THEY'VE ALL AGREED TO JOIN YOU. YOU'RE GIVING THEM SOMETHING MORE--ENTICING--EXCITING--THAN ANYTHING THEY MIGHT HAVE LOST.
BUT YOU HAVE LOST SOMETHING. DEVOTCHKA.
THE TRUTH IS, I AGREED TO TRACK THE TEARS BECAUSE I THOUGHT YOU WERE RESPONSIBLE FOR HER DEATH. MY PLAN WAS TO GET CLOSE ENOUGH TO KILL YOU, JONIN.
BUT NOW THAT I KNOW THAT WASN'T THE CASE, I HAVE TO ASK--CAN YOU TRULY GIVE ME BACK WHAT I'VE LOST?
I CAN. AND I PROMISED I WOULD, IF THAT'S WHAT YOU REALLY WANT. BUT BRINGING DEVOTCHKA BACK WILL TAKE A SERIOUS TOLL ON--
NO.

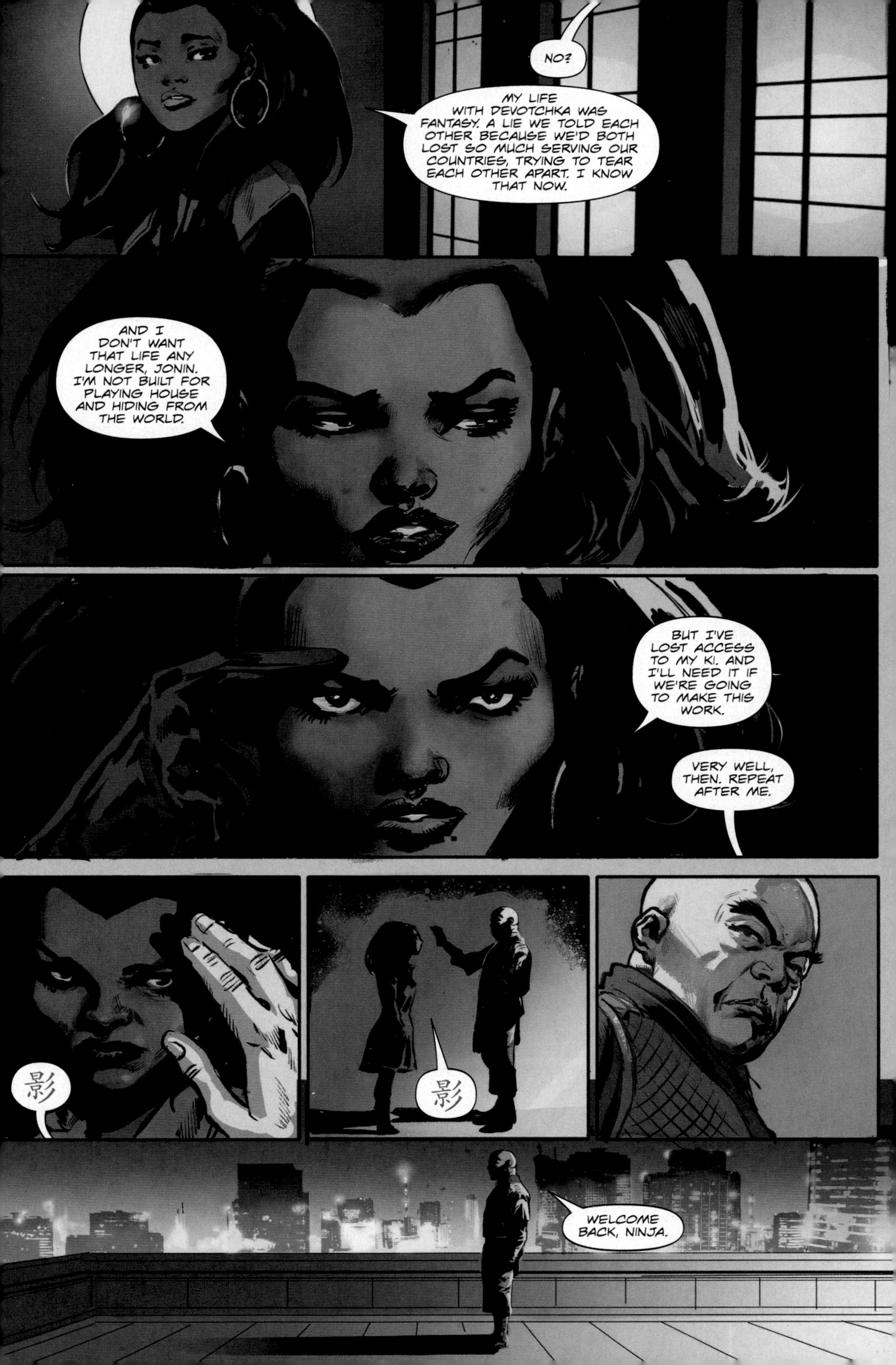
NO?
MY LIFE WITH DEVOTCHKA WAS FANTASY. A LIE WE TOLD EACH OTHER BECAUSE WE'D BOTH LOST SO MUCH SERVING OUR COUNTRIES, TRYING TO TEAR EACH OTHER APART. I KNOW THAT NOW.
AND I DON'T WANT THAT LIFE ANY LONGER, JONIN. I'M NOT BUILT FOR PLAYING HOUSE AND HIDING FROM THE WORLD.
BUT I'VE LOST ACCESS TO MY KI. AND I'LL NEED IT IF WE'RE GOING TO MAKE THIS WORK.
VERY WELL, THEN. REPEAT AFTER ME.
影
影
WELCOME BACK, NINJA.

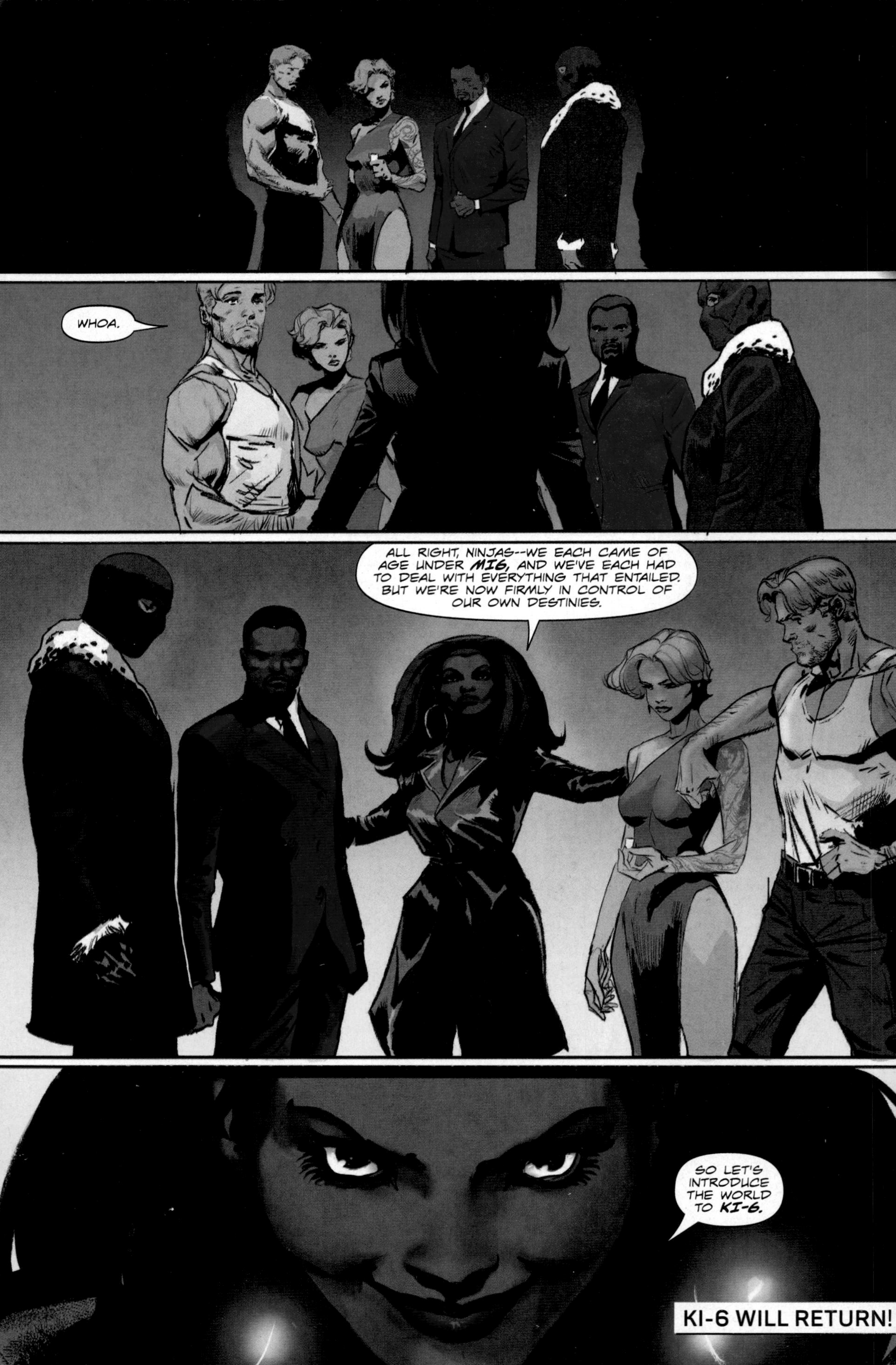
WHOA.
ALL RIGHT, NINJAS--WE EACH CAME OF AGE UNDER MI6, AND WE'VE EACH HAD TO DEAL WITH EVERYTHING THAT ENTAILED. BUT WE'RE NOW FIRMLY IN CONTROL OF OUR OWN DESTINIES.
SO LET'S INTRODUCE THE WORLD TO KI-6.
KI-6 WILL RETURN!

GALLERY

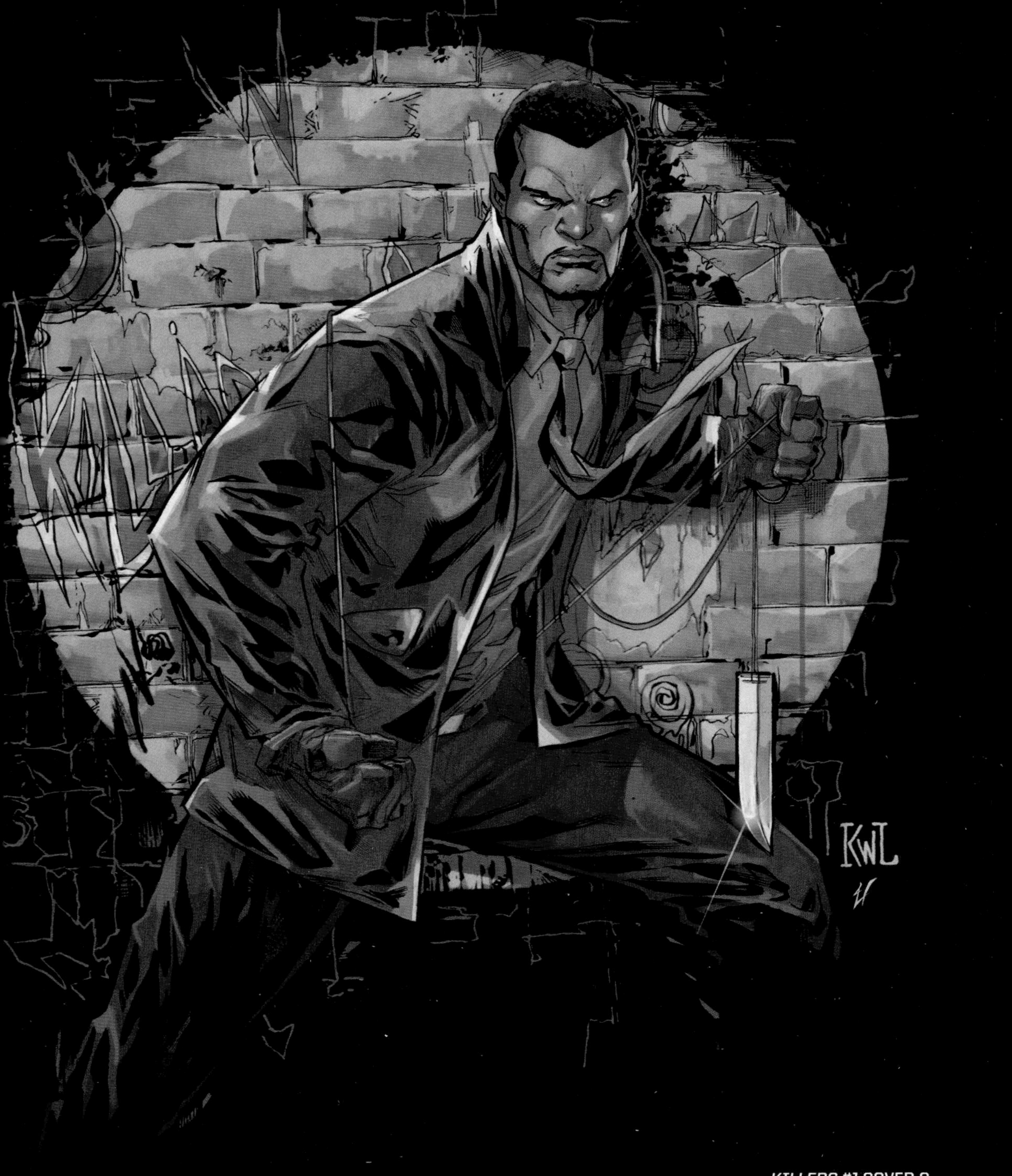

KILLERS #1 COVER C
Art by KEN LASHLEY with ULISES ARREOLA

KILLERS #2 COVER B
Art by SANFORD GREENE

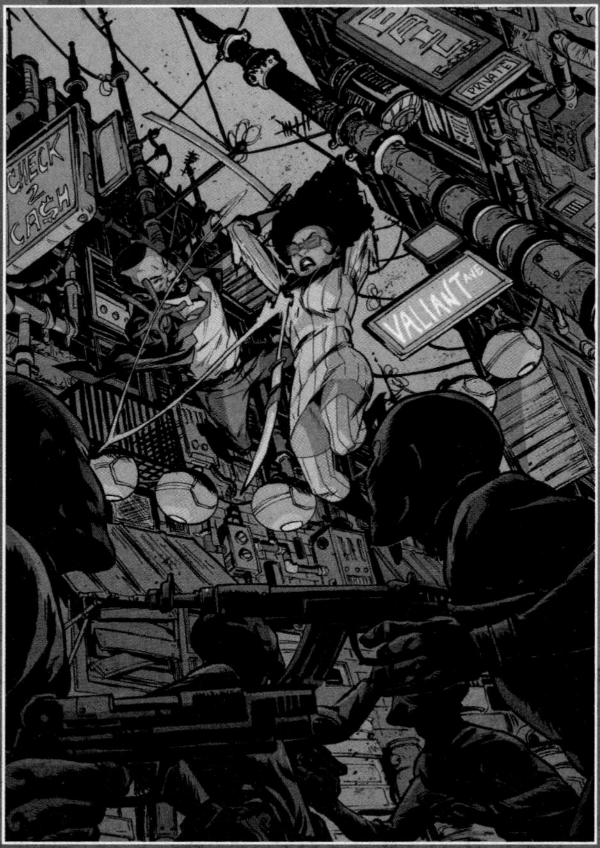
PRIVATE
CHECK 2 CASH
VALIANT AVE

KILLERS #3 COVER C
Art by YANNICK CORBOZ

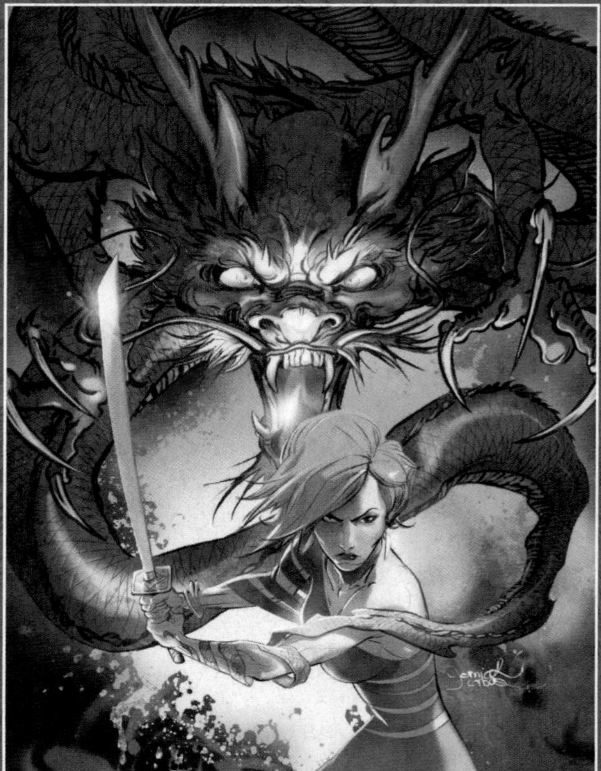

KILLERS #3 COVER B (facing)
Art by LARRY STROMAN with
ROB STULL and ULISES ARREOLA

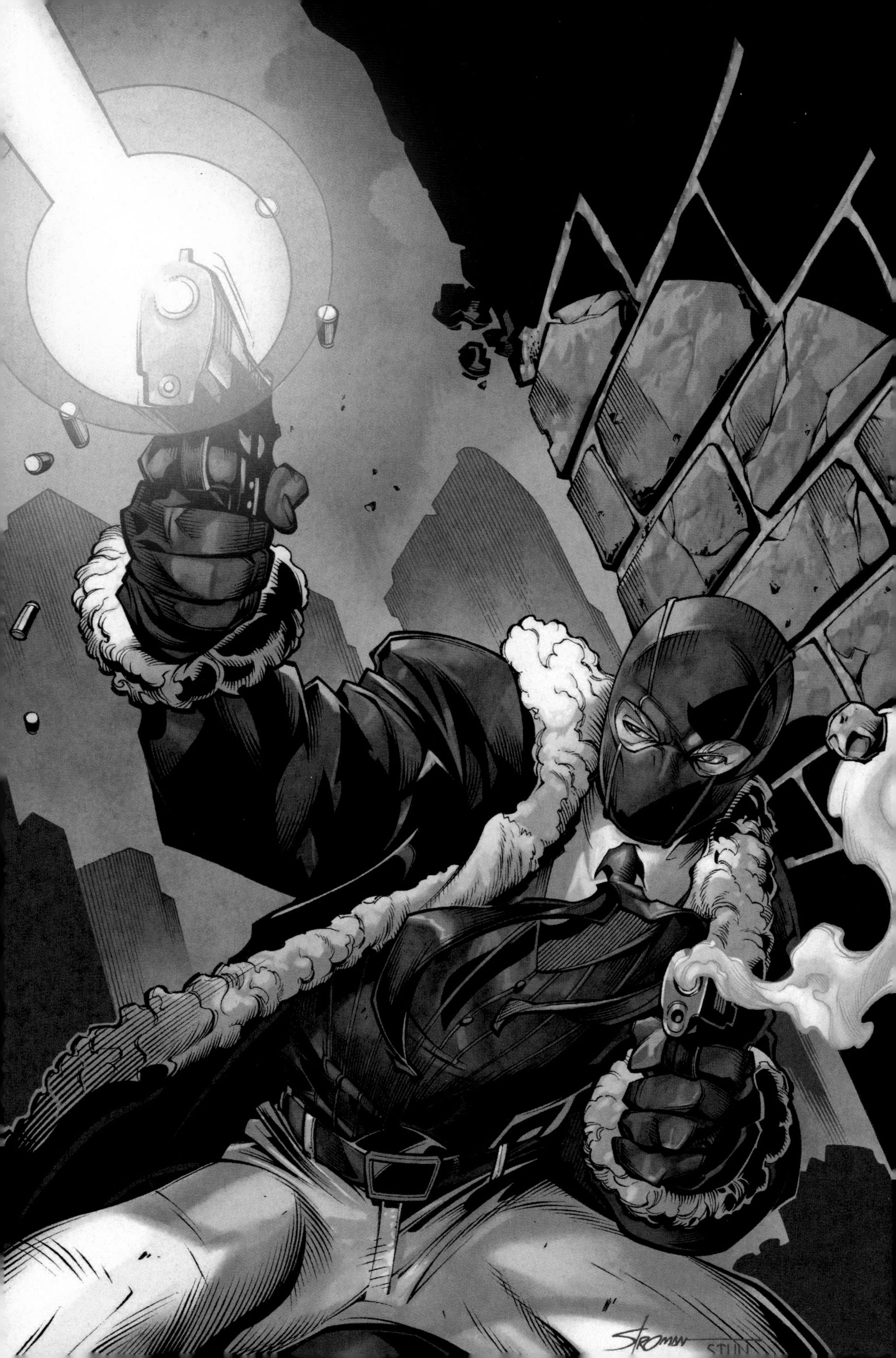
STROMAN

KI-6: KILLERS #4 COVER D
Art by VERONICA FISH with ANDY FISH

KI-6: KILLERS #5 COVER C
Art by JASON MASTERS

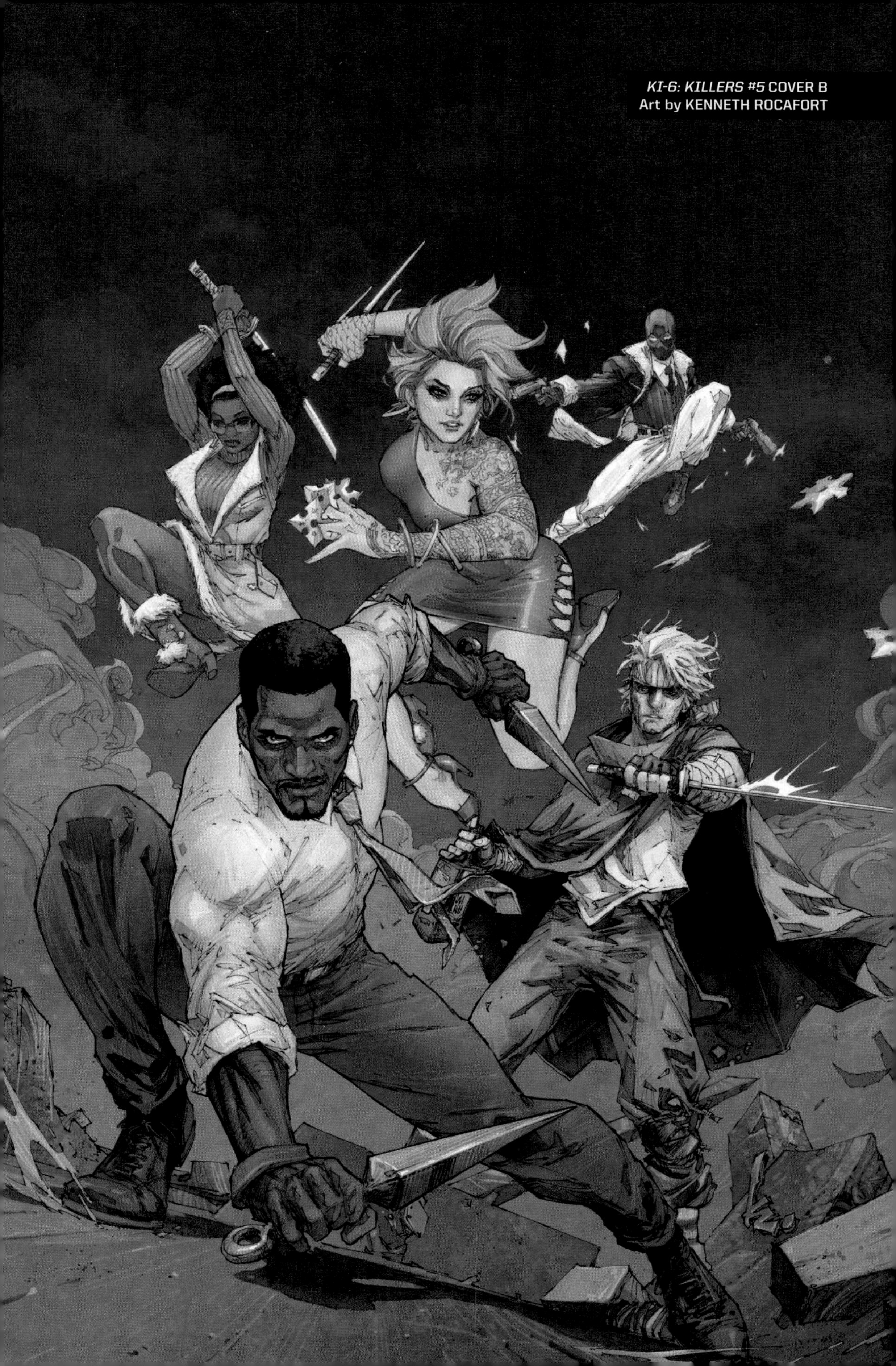

KI-6: KILLERS #5 COVER B
Art by KENNETH ROCAFORT

KILLERS #2, pages 12, 13, and (facing) 14
Art by FERNANDO DAGNINO

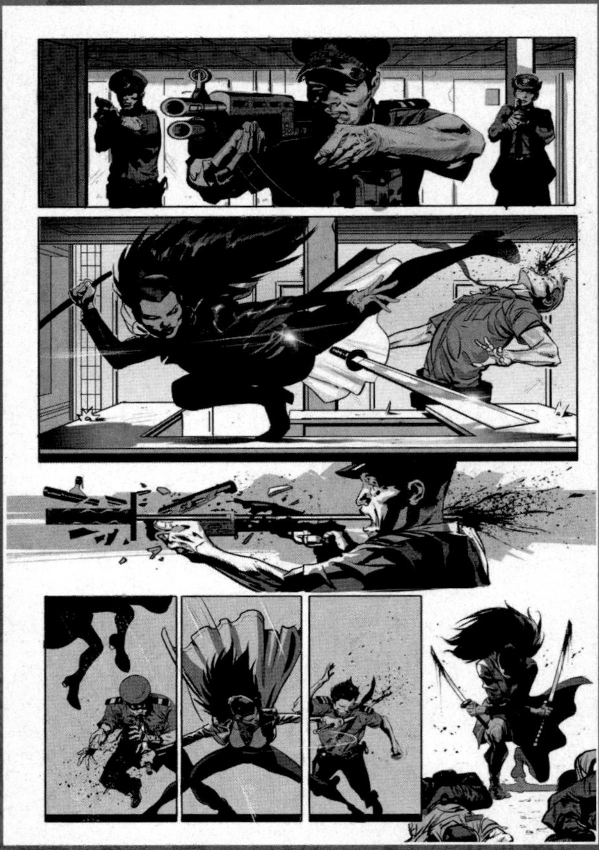

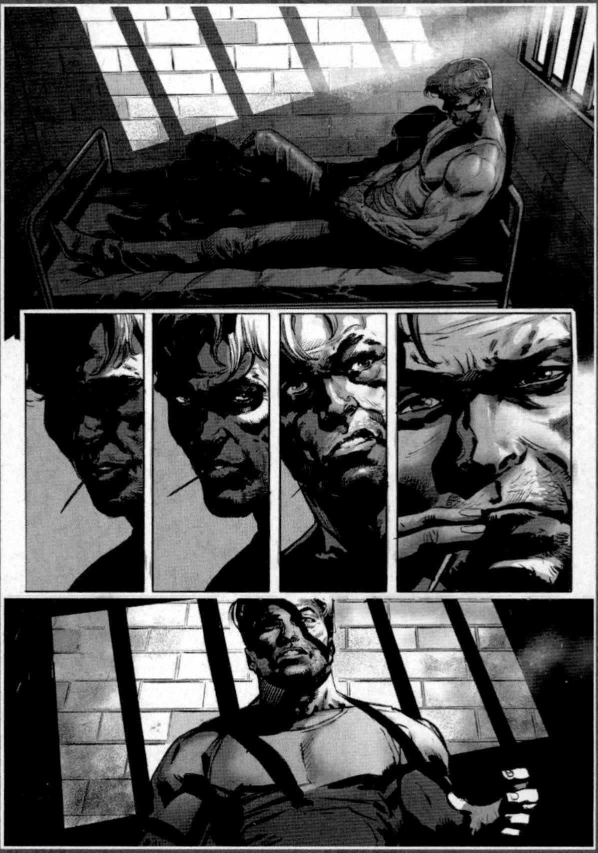

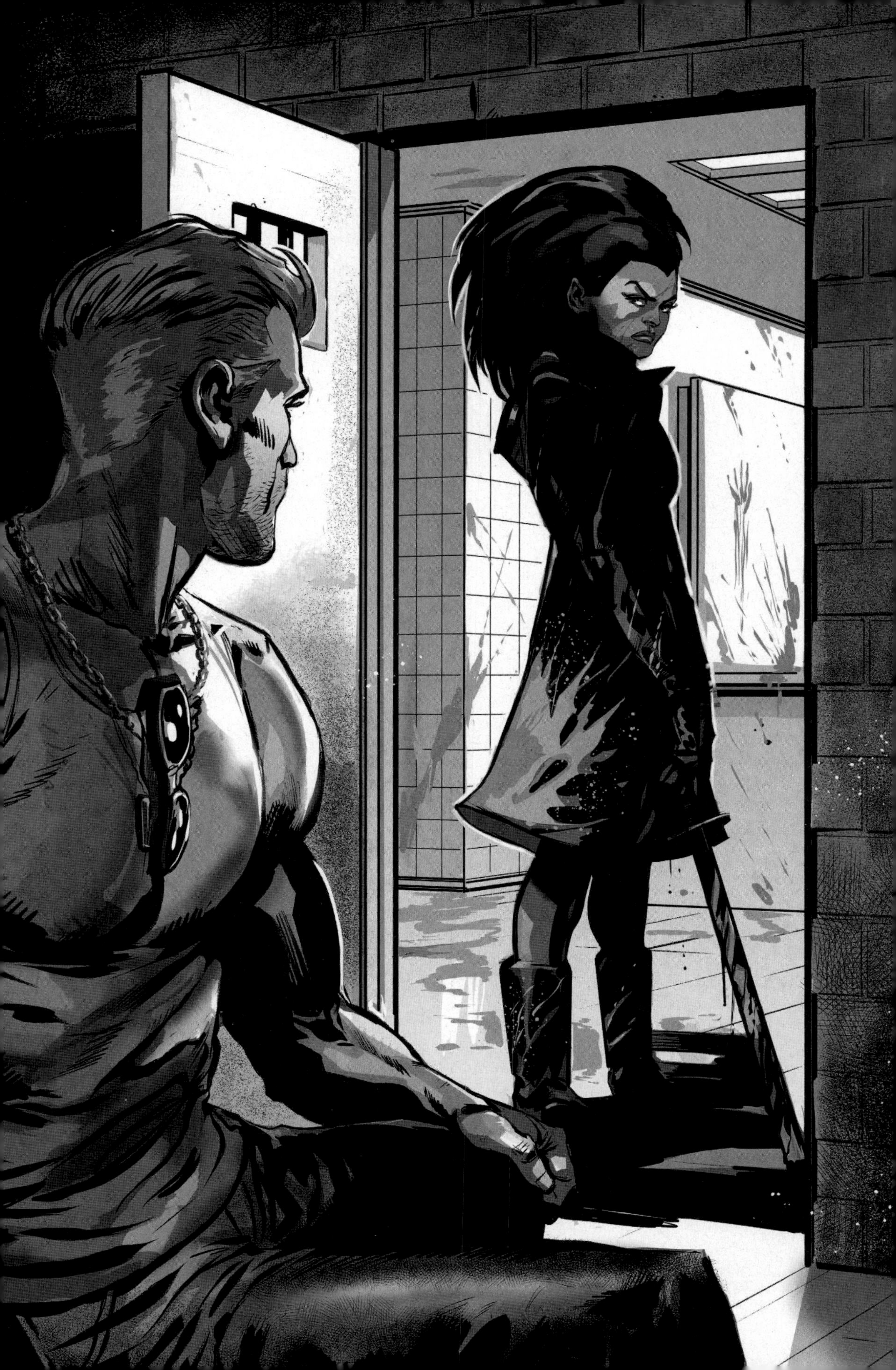

KI-6: KILLERS #5, pages 8, 9, and (facing) 10
Art by FERNANDO DAGNINO

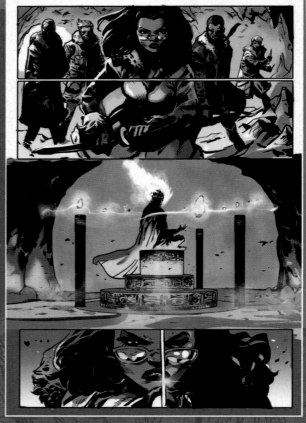

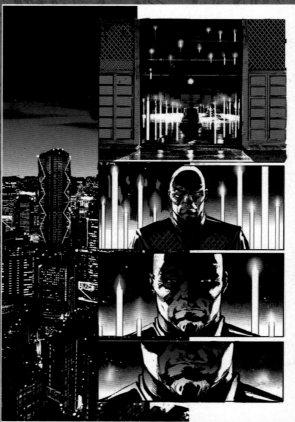

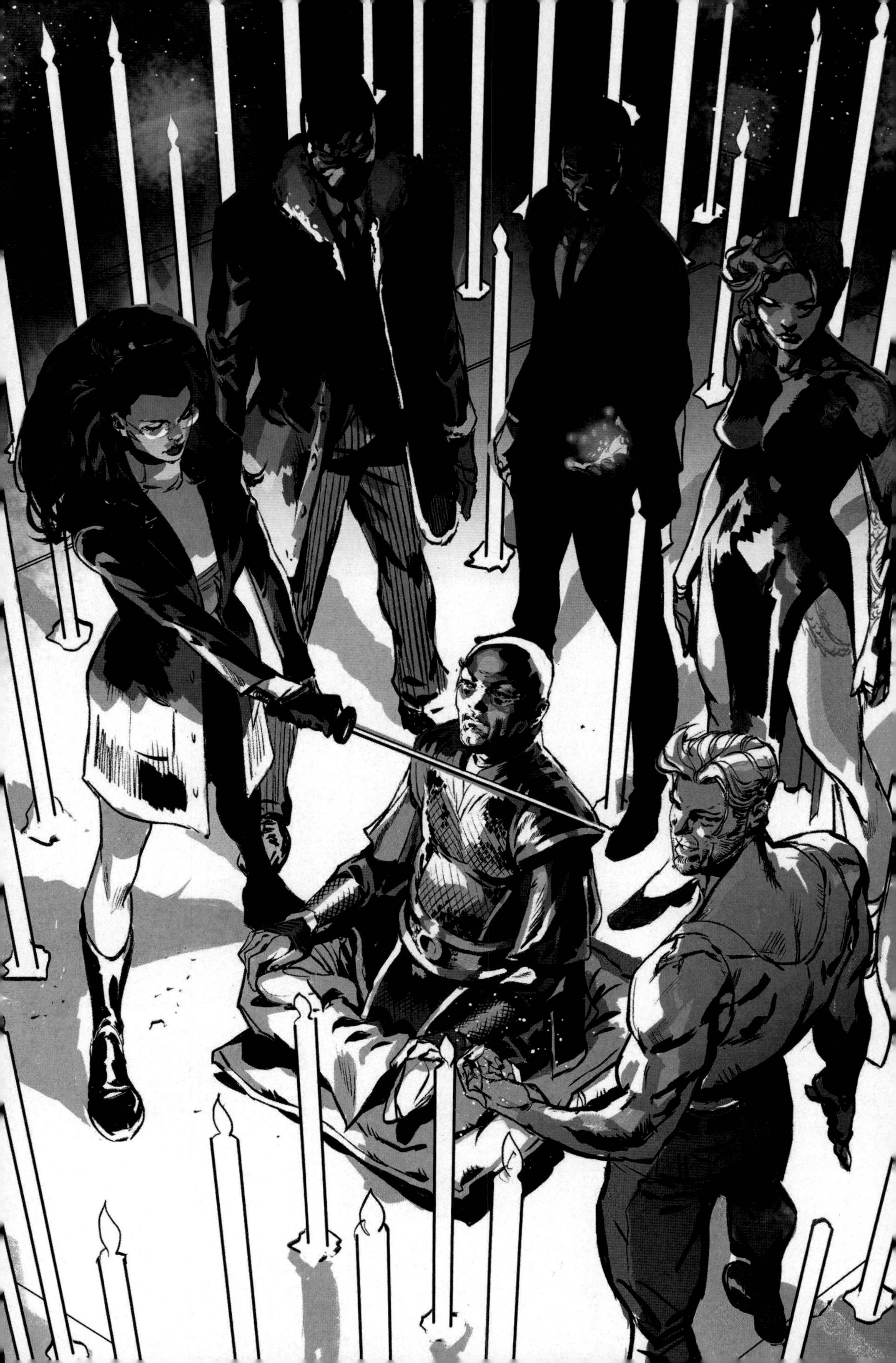

EXPLORE THE VALIANT U

ACTION & ADVENTURE

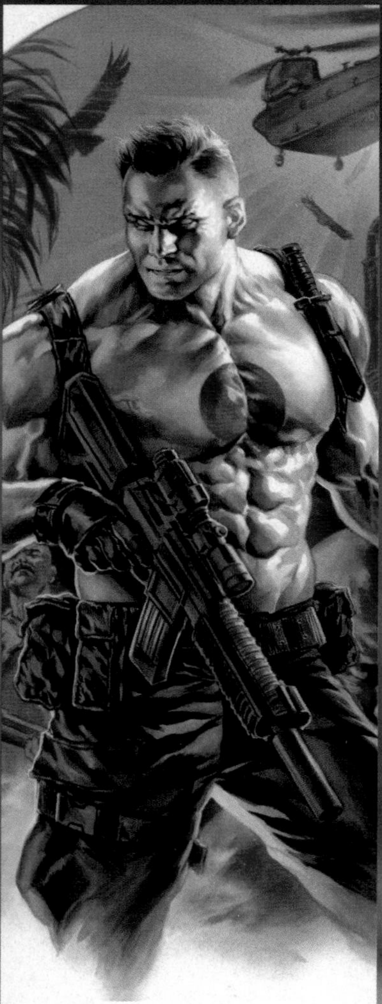

BLOODSHOT BOOK ONE
ISBN: 978-1-68215-255-3
NINJA-K VOL. 1: THE NINJA FILES
ISBN: 978-1-68215-259-1
SAVAGE
ISBN: 978-1-68215-189-1
WRATH OF THE ETERNAL WARRIOR VOL. 1: RISEN
ISBN: 978-1-68215-123-5
X-O MANOWAR (2017) VOL. 1: SOLDIER
ISBN: 978-1-68215-205-8

BLOCKBUSTER ADVENTURE

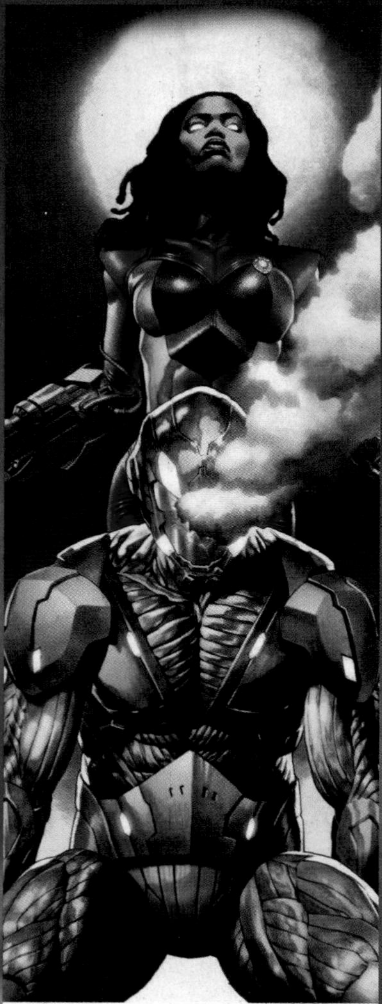

4001 A.D.
ISBN: 978-1-68215-143-3
ARMOR HUNTERS
ISBN: 978-1-939346-45-2
BOOK OF DEATH
ISBN: 978-1-939346-97-1
FALLEN WORLD
ISBN: 978-1-68215-331-4
HARBINGER WARS
ISBN: 978-1-939346-09-4
HARBINGER WARS 2
ISBN: 978-1-68215-289-8
INCURSION
ISBN: 978-1-68215-303-1
THE VALIANT
ISBN: 978-1-939346-60-5

COMEDY

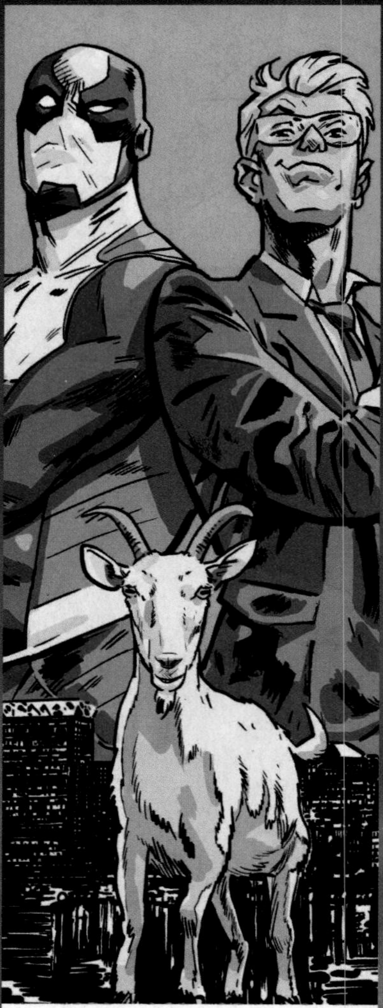

A&A: THE ADVENTURES OF ARCHER & ARMSTRONG VOL. 1: IN THE BAG
ISBN: 978-1-68215-149-5
THE DELINQUENTS
ISBN: 978-1-939346-51-3
QUANTUM AND WOODY! (2017) VOL. 1: KISS KISS, KLANG KLANG
ISBN: 978-1-68215-269-0

IVERSE STARTING AT $9.99

HORROR & MYSTERY

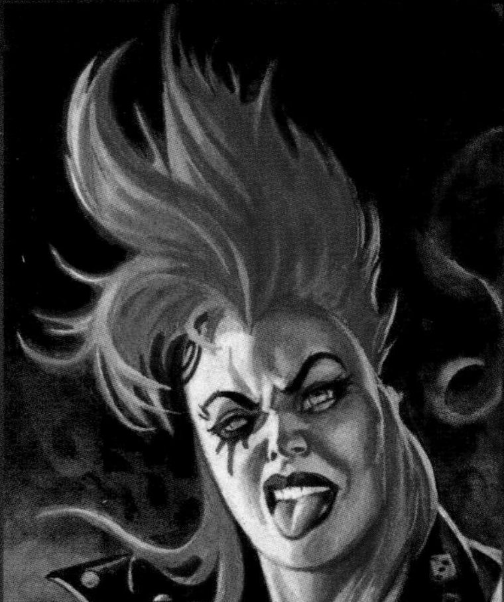
PUNK
MAMBO

BRITANNIA
ISBN: 978-1-68215-185-3
THE DEATH-DEFYING DOCTOR MIRAGE
ISBN: 978-1-939346-49-0
PUNK MAMBO
ISBN: 978-1-68215-330-7
RAPTURE
ISBN: 978-1-68215-225-6
SHADOWMAN (2018) VOL. 1: FEAR OF THE DARK
ISBN: 978-1-68215-239-3

SCIENCE FICTION & FANTASY

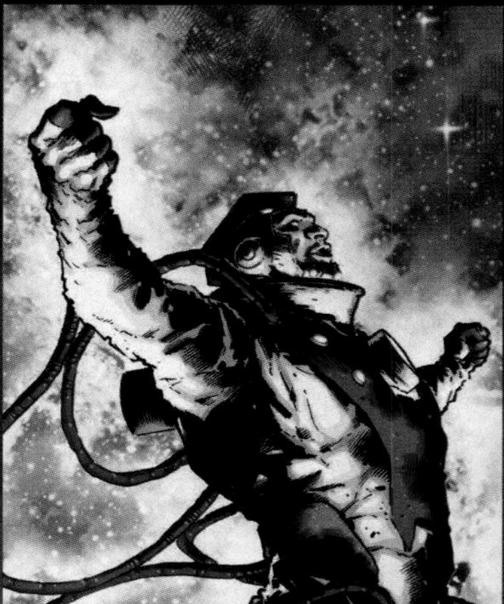

DIVINITY
ISBN: 978-1-939346-76-6
THE FORGOTTEN QUEEN
ISBN: 978-1-68215-324-6
IMPERIUM VOL. 1: COLLECTING MONSTERS
ISBN: 978-1-939346-75-9
IVAR, TIMEWALKER VOL. 1: MAKING HISTORY
ISBN: 978-1-939346-63-6
RAI VOL. 1: WELCOME TO NEW JAPAN
ISBN: 978-1-939346-41-4
WAR MOTHER
ISBN: 978-1-68215-237-9

TEEN ADVENTURE

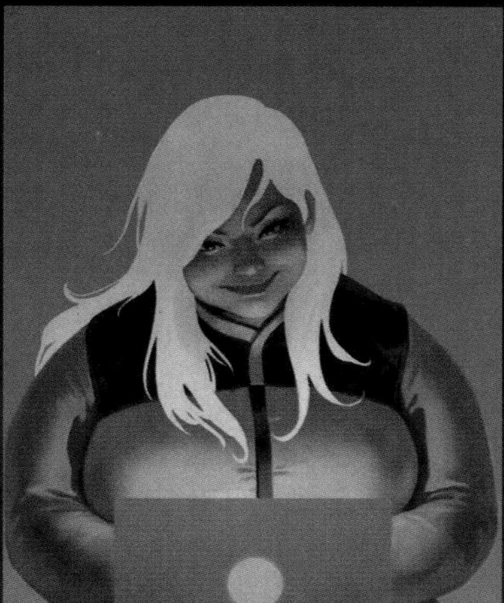

FAITH VOL. 1: HOLLYWOOD AND VINE
ISBN: 978-1-68215-121-1
GENERATION ZERO VOL. 1: WE ARE THE FUTURE
ISBN: 978-1-68215-175-4
HARBINGER RENEGADE VOL. 1: THE JUDGMENT OF SOLOMON
ISBN: 978-1-68215-169-3
LIVEWIRE VOL. 1: FUGITIVE
ISBN: 978-1-68215-301-7
SECRET WEAPONS
ISBN: 978-1-68215-229-4

Discover the entire Valiant Universe of titles at VALIANTENTERTAINMENT.COM/ALL-SERIES/

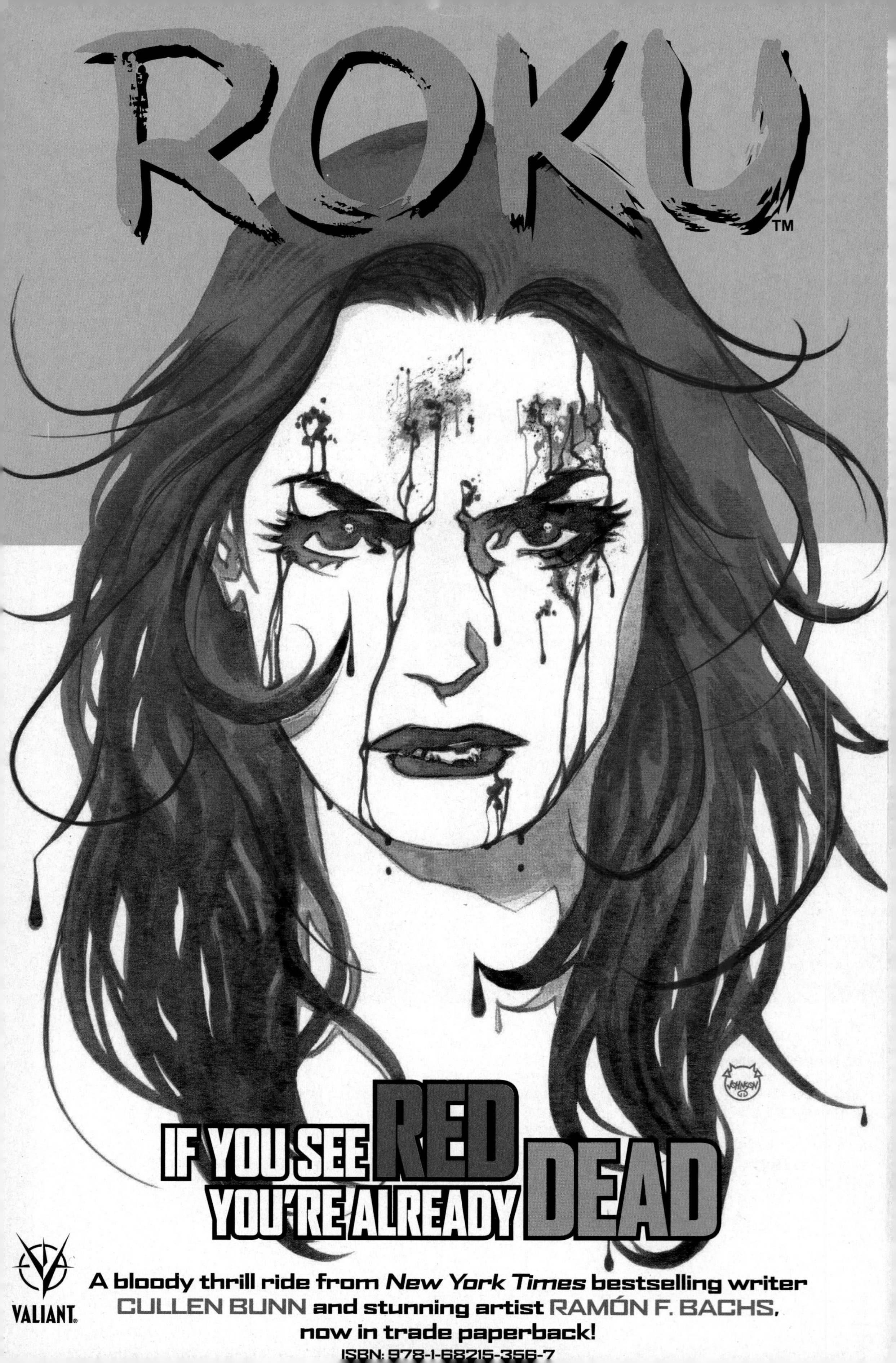
ROKU™
IF YOU SEE RED
YOU'RE ALREADY DEAD
VALIANT
A bloody thrill ride from New York Times bestselling writer
CULLEN BUNN and stunning artist RAMÓN F. BACHS,
now in trade paperback!
ISBN: 978-1-68215-356-7